# COMING OF AGE
# IN THE GREAT DEPRESSION:
## The Civilian Conservation Corps
## Experience in New Mexico, 1933-1942

Richard Melzer

*Yucca Tree Press*

First Printing     April 2000

Melzer, Richard
    COMING OF AGE IN THE GREAT DEPRESSION: The Civilian Conservation Corps Experience in New Mexico

    1. Civilian Conservation Corps, 1933-1942.  2. United States - Great Depression, 1929-1940.  3. New Mexico - Great Depression.  4. Roosevelt, F.D.R. - New Deal.
    I. Richard Melzer.   II. Title.


Library of Congress Catalog Card Number:  99-69919

ISBN: 1-881325-41-5

For My Son, Rick

# TABLE OF CONTENTS

# LIST OF ILLUSTRATIONS

# Illustrations continued

# PREFACE

Over twenty years ago I interviewed a gentleman named Bill Whitley about his life in New Mexico during the darkest days of the Great Depression. Born in 1916, Bill grew up in Dawson, a Phelps-Dodge coal mining camp in northeastern New Mexico. He graduated from Dawson High School in 1934 on what he called the "blackest day of my life." What should have been a joyous occasion turned bleak when Bill suddenly realized that although he had completed his high school education, he and his fellow graduates had little to look forward to in way of employment. There were few new jobs in Dawson for skilled workers, no less for young men without experience. It took Bill two years to land his first job with the Phelps-Dodge Corporation. Meanwhile, young men like Bill had to wait around, frustrated, unproductive, and often a drain on their families' meager resources. Their growth to adulthood had been seriously frustrated.

It was at this moment in our conversation that Bill said something that really caught my attention: rather than wait for jobs to open up in Dawson, "quite a few" of his fellow high school graduates joined the Civilian Conservation Corps (CCC) as an acceptable solution to their distressing problem. As a good young historian, I knew that the CCC was a New Deal program created to help unemployed young men by hiring them to work on conservation projects across the United States, including New Mexico. I also knew that the CCC was among the most popular and effective of all the New Deal programs established by the Franklin D. Roosevelt administration. But I had never heard the CCC described in such human, compelling terms as on that fall day in 1978. I had never thought of the CCC's crucial role in helping to facilitate the transition to adulthood for millions of Americans in general and thousands of New Mexicans in particular. I wanted to learn more about this federal program and, specifically, about its impact on the members of Bill Whitley's generation in their home state of New Mexico.

As I left Bill Whitley's house I never suspected that the seed of curiosity that was planted that day would take over two decades to bear fruit. In fact, it would take over twice as long as the CCC existed (1933-42) for me to convince myself that I had researched in enough archives, read enough sources, and inter-viewed enough former members of the CCC to make fair and accurate conclusions about this valuable program and its impact on New Mexico.

None of my research, reading, and interviewing would have been possible without the unselfish aid of countless friends and associates. They include fellow historians Oswald Baca, Peter Booth, Cheryl Foote, Margaret Espinosa McDonald, F. Kennon Moody, Donald L. Parman, Dorothy Cave, Nelson Van Valen, John P. Wilson, and the many commentators who made solid sug-gestions about the CCC papers I have read at historical confer-ences over the years. Archivists and librarians who never tired of helping to find even the rarest source include Kris Warmoth, Wayne Oakes, Kris White, Judy Marquez, and the entire New Mexico State Records Center and Archives staff in Santa Fe. Preserva-tionists and conservationists Cynthia Buttery Benedict and Judith G. Propper of the National Forest Service, Catherine Colby and Barbara B. Stanislawski of the National Park Service, Kathryn A. Flynn of the New Mexico Secretary of State's Office, Nancy Hanks of the New Mexico Office of Cultural Affairs, and Phil Norton and John Taylor of the Bosque del Apache National Wildlife Reserve were continually kind and helpful. Dr. Richard Madden answered several medical questions, while Cindy Chavez dealt patiently with more technical ones. David Kammer and Roland Rowe read drafts of several chapters, making insightful comments along the way.

Among my many contacts with former members of the CCC, I must thank Roy Lemons (known as 'Mr. CCC' for his undying enthusiasm for the Corps) and Harry Dallas, archivist at the National Association of CCC Alumni Museum in St. Louis,

Missouri. Three presidents of the Albuquerque chapter (#141) of the National Association of CCC Alumni have been most helpful: Cliff Hammond, the late Robert P. Conway, and the late Vince Wathom. Without exception, every former corpsman I have contacted by phone, letter, or in person has been generous with their time, their memories, and their hospitality.

And then there was my family. My sister, Joan, and her husband, Jack, helped track down some obscure facts back East, and I recruited my mother-in-law, Angie Chavez, to help with translations from Spanish into English. My parents have been as supportive of this project as they have been of every project I have attempted in life. My children, Kam and Rick, cheered me on and cheered me up, as needed. And my wife, Rena, offered all the love and encouragement an author could ever want or need to sustain him on the dusty road of history.

Richard Melzer
Belen, New Mexico
July 1999

Location of CCC camps in New Mexico.
*Courtesy: Jill Chapman.*

# CHAPTER 1
# Urgent Need & Urgent Response

Obstacles have hindered the journey from adolescence to adulthood in every period of American history. Youths have faced challenges in assuming adult responsibilities in the best of times. Rites of passage were predictably more difficult to achieve in the worst of times. This was especially true during the Great Depression of the 1930s. Opportunities to receive an education and graduate from grammar school, no less high school, were rare in the thirties when every penny was needed for a family to survive and little could be spared for study. When old enough, few youths could afford to leave their parents' homes and fend for themselves. Of those who did leave, a quarter of a million desperate young men and women took to the road to look for work and reduce the number of mouths to feed at home. Many sought their first jobs, but found only temporary, low-paying employment after frustrating months of searching. Unemployment rates ran as high as thirty percent for those under the age of twenty-five. Lacking adequate training and experience, they lived below the poverty line and were counted among the nation's hard-core unemployed. Unable to achieve traditional rites of passage, dispirited adolescents felt stymied in their efforts to come of age in the Great Depression.[1]

Adults of the Depression era worried about American youths more than one generation normally frets about the destiny of the next. Americans nervously wondered what would become of the young and, indeed, the country, if opportunities for completing school, living independently, and securing regular employment were slim. Many adults shared Eleanor Roosevelt's apprehension when the First Lady lamented, "I have moments of real terror when I think we may be losing this generation."[2] How could youths be expected to shoulder adult responsibilities, learn the American work ethic, and remain loyal citizens in a nation that offered no real hope for the future? How long would it be until more and more of the young turned to lives of crime simply to survive? How much longer would it take until disgruntled youths drew the conclusion that capitalism and democracy had failed them and, in desperation, turned to radical alternatives like Marxism or Fascism? In short, how long could a generation be alienated from society before endangering society itself?

New Mexicans of the 1930s were well aware of the serious problems of poverty and youth during the Great Depression. Already among the poorest states of the Union in the 1920s, New Mexico's economic condition went from bad to worse with the onset of the Depression. Every sector of the economy suffered adversely.

While sixty-one banks had operated in the state in 1927, only forty-one remained open in 1936. Twelve towns, including Hobbs, Ft. Sumner, and Mountainair, lost the only banks they had. Banking resources fell from 52.6 million dollars to 26.2 million dollars in the first few years of the Depression. Deposits plummeted from 45.3 million dollars to 21.5 million in the same short period.[3]

Once the most promising of New Mexico's economic sectors, the oil industry suffered as much, if not more than any other business in the early 1930s. Hobbs, the center of the oil boom in southeastern New Mexico, had grown from a quiet western town to the fastest growing town in the United States, thanks to gigantic oil discoveries in the 1920s. But just as New Mexico became one of the primary oil-producing states in the country, the bottom fell out at the start of the Depression, driving oil prices down to as low as ten cents a barrel. "It was not uncommon to see new wells pumping oil out of the ground directly into earth tanks scoured out of the prairie," wrote historian Paige Christiansen. "There was [simply] no market for the 'black gold.'" And with no market, there would be no jobs for young or old in the oil fields.[4]

Railroads and mining companies, the state's two leading employers, also cut operations as the full impact of the Depression was felt in the Southwest. Even those fortunate enough to retain jobs often faced shortened work weeks and reduced wages. In the coal mining camp of Madrid, New Mexico, everyone listened intently at 5:00 each afternoon to hear how many fire whistles were blown, indicating how many shifts would work the following day. The next generation of miners could hardly expect to join their fathers underground when only two thousand men worked in the state's coal mining industry on an irregular basis in 1934, compared to 3,500 full-time employees in 1929.[5]

Railroads offered no greater hope. Less and less cargo was shipped by rail and tourism "almost disappeared;" by 1933, "sleeper cars coming West were mostly empty." Of the 7,500 workers employed by the Atchison, Topeka and Santa Fe Railroad in 1929, only 3,200 remained on the company payroll four years later. As usual in hard economic times, the young were among the last hired and the first fired.[6]

Even seasonal labor in nearby states was limited for young and old alike. Previously, thousands of New Mexico workers had traveled to the sugar beet fields of Colorado, the sheep fields of Wyoming, and the mineral mines of Utah in annual migrations that had become almost customary in small Hispanic villages. Thousands relied on migrant labor as their families' single largest source of cash from year to year. In Wyoming, a majority of all sheepherders (*borregeros*) were Hispanics from villages like Mora, Valdez, and Arroyo Seco who lived out-of-state for six to ten months each year. Known as excellent workers, New Mexicans were skilled in finding the best pastures and producing the best lambs. Unfortunately, their large families were left behind in New Mexico where "resourceful wives shouldered the responsibility of maintaining the household and raising children a good share of the year." Ironically, families were divided in order to remain united. Much the same could be said of the migrant sugar beet workers in Colorado and the migrant miners who traveled to Utah.[7]

But migrant labor changed in the 1930s with the start of the Great Depression. In the sugar beet industry, for example, production declined so drastically that jobs in the beet fields were jealously reserved for residents of Colorado. Out-of-state workers in general, and Mexican laborers in particular, were often excluded with racial slurs and discriminatory acts. In April 1936 Colorado Governor Edwin C. Johnson went so far as to dispatch National Guard troops to the Colorado-New Mexico border to stop what he called an "invasion" of "aliens and indigent immigrants" from the south. Johnson only recanted ten days later when New Mexico Governor Clyde Tingley threatened "serious trouble," including a New Mexico boycott of Colorado goods, if National Guard troops remained at the northern border.[8]

But armed soldiers were not needed to stem the tide of New Mexican workers to the beet fields, sheep ranches, and underground mines of Colorado, Wyoming, and Utah. A lack of jobs was enough to keep most men home in their native villages. Pojoaque and Chimayo were typical. While about 125 men from Pojoaque had found seasonal work for up to seven months a year prior to 1929, only five were employed out-of-state in 1935. In Chimayo, between 250 and 300 men worked away from home for as much as fifty dollars a month in the 1920s, but only twenty found migrant work by the mid-1930s. Without this essential source of income, many rural New Mexicans could hardly feed their families, no less pay their debts and property taxes. Thousands lost their meager plots of land through foreclosures and tax sales. Sadly, many "remained on the land unaware that, for lack of tax payments, they no longer owned it." Increasing numbers were forced to seek government assistance in these desperate times. By January 1935 a third of New Mexico's population, including eighty percent of all Hispanic farmers in the Rio Grande Valley, received government relief of one kind or another.[9]

A similarly high percentage of farmers and ranchers required help elsewhere in the state. In northeastern New Mexico farmers suffered extreme drought as part of the nation's devastating Dust Bowl. Huge dust storms carried off tons of top soil, leaving farmers and ranchers destitute. With three consecutive crop failures and most of their cattle shipped to distant pastures, Union County residents were described as "literally starving" by mid-1935. Families of six to eight members lived on an average of seven dollars a month; some lived on as little as two dollars in aid. To make matters worse, these same farmers faced annual invasions of grasshoppers who seemed to eat everything the wind had not blown away. Lawmen feared that normally law-abiding citizens might soon be driven to acts of violence in order to survive.[10]

But still the dust storms came. Tomás Brown described the magnitude of one such storm that nearly blinded him as he traveled home from a visit to Maxwell, New Mexico. According to Brown, the wind was so strong and the air was so full of dust that he could see neither the sun nor the nearby mountains. He could hardly see the team of horses that pulled his wagon. The wind blew even stronger on the second day of his journey, reaching sixty to seventy miles per hour, with gusts of up to eighty. Tumbleweeds flew past, landing, he was sure, "somewhere in Oklahoma or Kansas." Stopping at a barely visible ranch house, Brown finally learned his location from a kind rancher who "apologized for [his] place being such a mess, and muttered something about his wife having gone back to her folks. Said she could no longer put up with living in this dust bowl. I noted that there was at least a quarter of an inch of dust over everything in that kitchen." Tomás ever forgot the rancher's droll comment that "it will blow like this sometimes for up to two or three days, and then it will start in and blow like hell."[11]

No longer able to live in these terrible conditions, many New Mexicans joined the rancher's spouse and moved on. Those who stayed were often driven to seek help. New Mexico reportedly had the highest percentage of citizens on relief in the United States. But what was said of nearby states like Texas and Oklahoma was also true of New Mexico: relief programs never met the enormous need of an increasingly desperate population.[12]

XWhile many New Mexicans were frustrated in their efforts to find seasonal labor elsewhere, other Americans crossed New Mexico in search of work further west, especially in the Imperial and San Joaquin valleys of California. An estimated seventy thousand arrived in California in a single month in 1931; approximately eighty percent of the seventy thousand were between eighteen and twenty-five years of age. Traveling by freight cars or on main thoroughfares like Route 66, these homeless nomads were often in desperate straits by the time they reached New Mexico. Penniless, some built a Hooverville (or shantytown) on the outskirts of Albuquerque, using discarded materials collected at the city dump. Alarmed by this crisis, the Bernalillo Board of County Commissioners urged the governor to erect signs on all roads leading into New Mexico stating that "Visitors are welcome but ... there is no employment to be had for any class of labor other than taxpayers of New Mexico." Nothing came of this suggestion, although the state government established transient relief camps for unemployed "visitors" in New Mexico. One such facility, on National Guard property at Camp Luna, Las Vegas, provided room and board, clothing, medical care, and free transportation home for the lucky few who could secure jobs elsewhere. According to one state official, "many of the men had never worked, and some had been so long without work that they had forgotten how."[13]

Despite their own poverty, most New Mexican families were uncommonly generous to homeless strangers. As the novelist Jack London had discovered in his early days as a homeless traveler, the poor were often more generous than the rich. "Charity," wrote London, "is the bone shared with the dog when you are just as hungry as the dog." In New Mexico, where poverty was rampant, transients often knocked on the back door of the humblest homes to ask for a chance to perform odd jobs in exchange for something to eat. The homeless secretly marked the dwellings of consistently generous families. Priscilla Montoya's family home in Albuquerque was undoubtedly marked in this manner. Years after the Depression, a once-homeless man returned to the Montoya home to give Priscilla's father three hundred dollars. When asked why he gave such a gift, the stranger explained that it was for the kindness the family had shown him and countless others during the Depression. In his words, he had since become successful and simply wanted to say "thank you for the people." Other parents were equally generous, often giving half or more of what they earned to displaced families. Located near railroad tracks, William Dishman's childhood home was often visited by homeless travelers. Dishman's mother always shared what little food she had, saying "as long as there's some, there's plenty."[14]

Many businesses were similarly helpful during the nation's prolonged economic crisis. The *Albuquerque Tribune* allowed the unemployed to seek jobs by "advertising" in its classified ad columns, free of charge. The Fred Harvey Company was also known for its acts of mercy. In the summer of 1933 a mother with two small children was traveling through New Mexico to join her husband in California. According to plans, her husband was to wire twenty-five dollars to his family when they arrived in Albuquerque so they could continue their westward trek. But the expected money never arrived. Desperate and hungry, the mother took her children to the Alvarado, Albuquerque's large Harvey House, off Central Avenue. The mother quietly asked the dining room manager if he could spare some sandwiches for her son and daughter and a cup of coffee for herself. Moved by this woman's plight, the manager agreed, but insisted on ordering for the three travelers. He instructed a Harvey Girl to bring each family member a bowl of hot soup as well as beef stew, mashed potatoes, bread and butter, and "cobbler all around." When they were finished eating as "guests of Fred Harvey," the Harvey Girl gave them bags with even more food than they had eaten for dinner. Outside, the boy asked what was in the bags, to which his grateful mother replied, "Loaves and fishes. Loaves and fishes."[15]

But there was just so much that New Mexico families and businesses could do for themselves, no less for others. In scenes reminiscent of John Steinbeck's famous novel, *The Grapes of Wrath*, thousands of hardscrabble families drove through New Mexico in broken-down pickup trucks piled high with mattresses and other meager household possessions. Steinbeck described these vehicles "limping along like wounded things."

> The people in flight streamed out on [Route] 66, some-times in a single car, sometimes [in] a little caravan. All day they rolled slowly along the road, and at night they stopped near water. In the day ancient leaky radia-tors sent up columns of steam, loose connecting rods hammered and pounded. And the men driving the trucks and overloaded cars listened apprehensively. How far between towns? It is a terror between towns.[16]

Years later, Fred Calkins recalled a particularly telling mo-ment when he watched these caravans of run-down cars and trav-elers moving slowly down Albuquerque's Central Avenue.

> I remember that we used to stand around and look at these poor unfortunate people. They were sort of an object of curiosity—you would see [a family's grand-mother] sitting in a rocker up on top of their belongings [and think it rather funny]. I quit finding that amusing when I was standing on the corner one time eating an apple and there was this little boy about my age who was on this truck. There was a red light at Fourth [Street] and Central, and this procession had to stop. This boy was looking at me and I was looking at him. He was seeing me eating this apple, and I knew he was hungry. For the first time I realized the plight of these people.[17]

On another occasion, *Albuquerque Tribune* reporter Larry Bryon spent two weeks hopping freight cars with the "endless stream" of men, women, and children who passed through New

Mexico in search of work. The Southern Pacific Railroad estimated that a thousand of these ticketless passengers journeyed through the state each day by the spring of 1933. Reporter Bryon discovered that the largest single group of travelers were "bewildered" young men with few job skills to offer and fewer job opportunities on the horizon.[18]

Some railroad employees took pity on the homeless in personal acts of kindness. Belen's yardmaster ran a water pipe from his house to the 'hobo jungle' next door so the homeless men living there could have clean water for drinking and bathing. Other railroad employees were not as helpful, at least in their official roles. Railroad police, called 'bulls,' booted many youths off trains in railroad towns like Deming, New Mexico. No more able than other communities to help these homeless youths, Deming reportedly hired a special policeman to deal with transient rail riders. "When the Southern Pacific police ordered the men off the train, [Deming's] special constable ordered them back on again." Thomas C. Donnelly, then a young professor at the State Teachers College in Silver City, remembered waiting in his car at a railroad crossing in Deming, much like Fred Calkins had stood at the corner of Fourth and Central in Albuquerque.

> [A]s we waited at the Southern Pacific railway crossing for a long freight train to pass, we noticed the top of each car was crowded with youths hoboing to California. A short distance out of Deming, we observed through the shimmering summer heat what appeared to be a large, long lake in the miles ahead. As we got closer it turned out to be ... our first mirage. The boys on the Southern Pacific box cars would soon discover California was their [mirage].[19]

Just as the poverty of youth concerned Americans elsewhere, the "social implications" of "wandering youth" concerned New Mexicans. Estimating that the country's "army of vagrants" numbered as high as 300,000 by early 1933, the *Santa Fe New Mexican* worried that life on the roads and rails of America would soon "sap [the boys'] vitality and initiate them into a life of

dependence, shiftlessness and crime ... . The stage is set for a
nation-wide demoralization of youth for which society ... will pay
a heavy penalty." The *New Mexican* concluded that the United
States faced the "serious problem" of assisting an ailing generation, a problem "which today threatens to assume such dimensions as to become a real menace to the established order." The
depth of poverty in the present was only matched by the depth of
anxiety regarding the future.[20]

The human resources of New Mexico, including its youth,
were not the only resources at risk by the early 1930s. Natural
resources were in serious danger as well. Rangelands suffered
from years of overgrazing by sheep, goats, and cattle. Droughts
further reduced vegetative cover, resulting in rapid runoff and
erosion. Droughts of the Dust Bowl era caused particularly low
water levels in lakes and streams which, in turn, "hurt the fisheries
resources terribly." U.S. Forest Ranger and supervisor Elliott S.
Barker recalled that "There were terrific losses of livestock on
the ranges, and big game suffered along with [cattle and sheep]."[21]
Barker realized the many ties between human misery and
environmental crisis. The same farmers and ranchers who struggled
to survive in Dust Bowl conditions often resorted to illegally hunting wildlife to keep their families fed. "To prosecute them was an
exercise in frustration," wrote Barker. "They could not pay a fine
and would have to go to jail; that simply increased the desperation of their families. How could [Game and Fish] wardens do
their duty" when New Mexicans "resorted to killing ... wildlife
for subsistence"?[22]
Financial restraints only compounded the problem. In early
1933 Regional Forester Frank W. Pooler informed Governor
Arthur Seligman that "As matters now stand, in the absence of
emergency relief or other special appropriations, very little construction work [to alleviate the environmental crisis] will be done
on the National Forests." And New Mexico's environmental emergency was not unique; most of the country suffered the same poor
conditions and the same lack of resources through the early, most
trying years of the Great Depression.[23]

\*          \*          \*

What could be done not only to help the environment, but also to help the thousands who struggled to come of age in these hard economic times? Fortunately, Franklin D. Roosevelt offered a bold national solution. Roosevelt referred to his proposed solution as early as March 4, 1933, the day he took office as the nation's thirty-second president and delivered his most famous inaugural address. After reassuring all Americans that "We have nothing to fear but fear itself," the new chief executive declared that the nation "asks for action" in relieving unemployment caused by the Great Depression. FDR asserted that the federal government should take an active role in putting citizens back to work, "treating the task as we would treat the emergency of a war." More specifically, Roosevelt proposed that the government put citizens back to work in "greatly needed projects to stimulate and reorganize the use of our natural resources." With a vast conservation program for poverty-stricken youths in mind, the president declared himself ready to "assume unhesitantly the leadership of this great army of our people dedicated to a disciplined attack upon our common problems."[24]

Despite some doubt within his own Brain Trust of advisors ("just because they're unemployed doesn't mean they're natural-born lumbermen"), FDR vigorously promoted his proposal to put young men to work on long-overdue conservation projects. In the president's words,

> This enterprise ... will conserve our precious natural resources ... . More important, however, than the material gains will be the moral and spiritual value of such work ... . We can take a vast army of these unemployed out into healthy surroundings. We can [largely] eliminate ... the threat that enforced idleness brings to spiritual and moral stability. It is not a panacea for all unemployment but it is an essential step in this emergency.

Using his considerable political skills, FDR therefore responded to the fears of his own generation regarding the fate of the next. Significantly, Roosevelt's original name for his proposed program was the Civilian Corps Reforestation Youth Rehabilitation Movement. Finding this title too cumbersome, its supporters first changed it to the Emergency Conservation Work Corps (or ECW) and finally to the Civilian Conservation Corps (or CCC) with the understanding that its dual goal was to conserve the nation's endangered youth quite as much as it was to conserve the country's endangered natural resources.[25]

Like most legislation proposed by the White House during Roosevelt's active first hundred days in office, the bill to create the CCC was passed by a cooperative Democratic Congress within ten days after it was introduced on Capitol Hill. Elated, the president signed Senate Bill 598 into law on March 31, 1933. Officially established by Executive Order 6108, the CCC represented the federal government's first attempt at mass unemployment relief in American history.[26]

The concept of a civilian conservation corps was not entirely new in 1933. Its intellectual origins date to at least the early years of the twentieth century. In 1910 William James had envisioned a "moral equivalent of war" in which young men would serve in conservation projects to "greatly benefit the country, while forming a habit of citizen service without a warlike spirit." Later, in the wake of World War I, others suggested conservation programs with a more militant focus. One such proposal came from New Mexico in "A Report on Flood Control of the Gila River" by Frank H. Olmstead. Written in 1919, Olmstead's report envisioned "a great army of the youth of the nation encamped in the glorious mountains of the upper Gila ... for, say, one year under competent instructors and subjected to drill and obedience not alone in the use of [military] arms but of [conservation] tools." Olmstead believed that the country could greatly benefit from such "a pronounced conservation achievement" in a "spirit of true national defense."[27]

Similar proposals followed. F.A. Anderson of the Mississippi Forestry Association outlined a "Plan for Relieving Unemployment and Perpetuating Forest Growth." According to Anderson's plan, thousands of unemployed men could enlist in the U.S. Army for six-month periods, during which they would be paid a dollar a day (plus room and board) in exchange for conservation work in Southern forests. Senators and members of the House of Representatives took such ideas to the halls of Congress even before Franklin Roosevelt entered the White House. Just weeks before FDR's inauguration in 1933, Congressman Scott Leavitt of Montana and Senator Robert F. Wagner of New York worked on bills that would have given short-term employment in National Forests to as many as 269,000 needy citizens.[28]

Reflecting these current ideas, several states and whole countries had experimented with their own versions of what later became the CCC. In California, thousands of men were put to work building highways and fire trails in exchange for food and shelter. In Idaho, hundreds lived in scattered camps while working to eliminate blister-rust on trees in 1932. In Colorado, the city of Denver established two rustic camps in the Pike National Forest. Unemployed urban workers received room and board in return for performing various reforestation tasks under the supervision of U.S. Forest Service personnel. Denver's program met with such success that cities in Michigan, Minnesota, Wisconsin, and North Carolina considered similar action by the fall of 1932.[29]

At least eight European nations, including Germany, France, Switzerland, and Austria, had also established work camps by the 1930s. Of these, Germany's *Arbeitsdeinst*, or Work Service, was the most famous—and infamous. Although originally voluntary, the *Arbeitsdeinst* became practically mandatory for all German males between the ages of eighteen and twenty-five, regardless of social class. For a small daily wage, plus meals and lodging, young Germans worked on a variety of public projects, while living in quasi-military surroundings. With Adolf Hitler's violent rise to power, many observers recognized and feared the *Arbeitsdeinst* as a dangerous arm of authoritarian Fascist rule.[30]

If only to distance his creation from such suspect foreign organizations as the German *Arbeitsdeinst*, President Roosevelt claimed that earlier efforts had little impact on his support for a Civilian Conservation Corps in the United States. When asked what had inspired the CCC, FDR replied that "the idea ... was not taken from any one source," be it an essay by William James (the president's former Harvard professor) or the example of similar programs at home or abroad. It was rather, he insisted, the "obvious conflux" of needs involving human and natural resources at the height of the Great Depression.[31]

Franklin Roosevelt might have added that the CCC was also the obvious conflux of experiences in his own life. In many ways he was as devoted to the conservation movement as was his familial predecessor in the White House, Theodore Roosevelt. FDR had earnestly implemented conservation measures at his huge family estate in Hyde Park, New York, reportedly planting as many as fifty thousand trees a year. As a young New York state senator from 1911 to 1913, Roosevelt "threw himself" into the passage of conservation measures "without reserve." Later, as governor of New York from 1928 to 1932, he continued to champion conservation causes in his home state. In fact, much of what he did in conservation and work relief as governor was said to be "but a miniature" of what he attempted on a national scale as president. Most significantly, Governor Roosevelt led the way in putting 10,345 unemployed men to work in New York's state forests, resulting in the reforestation of 27,000 acres in 1932 alone. In the words of one of Roosevelt's closest advisors, "We took the gas house gang, the bad boys who were loafing on the street and getting into trouble, and put them on the 4 a.m. train that ran [to] Bear Mountain [state park] ... where they worked all day" in honest, productive labor. Based on the record of this successful state project, a similar national project seemed the logical next step when Franklin Roosevelt assumed power in March 1933.[32]

Realizing the urgency of the task at hand, President Roosevelt insisted that camps be created, young men be enrolled, and conservation work be started as soon as possible. As the nation's commander-in-chief, he ordered the U.S. Army to enroll a quarter of a million young men and build no less than 1,330 camps by July 1933. Army officers, led by chief of staff General Douglas MacArthur, realized the magnitude of this assignment. While it had taken three months to mobilize 181,000 soldiers at the start of World War I, the Army was now directed to mobilize 275,000 young men in no less a period of time. General Omar Bradley later admitted that the Army "was not happy at being saddled with the CCC" because it was so contrary to the military's traditional mission. Reduced in strength from 838,000 officers and men in 1919 to only 134,000 in 1933, the Army seemed understaffed for such an assignment, especially if it was suddenly needed in a military emergency. Even privates resented the Army's extra duty with the CCC, if only because CCC enrollees were promised thirty dollars a month in wages when privates earned $252 a year, or twenty-one dollars a month, in 1933.[33]

But General Bradley and his fellow officers soon admitted that the Army's "magnificent performance" in 1933 was a "good drill" and "one of the highlights" of the military's work between the world wars. Compared to the high cost, delay, and frequent inefficiency of mobilization in World War I, the Army met and exceeded expectations in its mobilization of the CCC in 1933. In the process, the Army helped improve its stained public image in the aftermath of the military's role in the suppression of the Bonus Army in 1932. As General MacArthur told his fellow officers about the CCC, "Only high morale, [a] spirit of cooperation, pride of service and devotion to duty could have accomplished such fine results. It was well done, Army." Generals Bradley and MacArthur may well have remembered the lessons of this improved mobilization when even greater numbers of men were processed and encamped by the Army in World War II. In the words of a contemporary observer, the Army's assistance in the CCC was its "greatest peace-time achievement."[34]

The CCC's first enrollee entered the program on April 7, 1933, just thirty-seven days after President Roosevelt's inauguration. The first CCC camp, appropriately named Camp Roosevelt, opened ten days later in the George Washington National Forest near Luray, Virginia. Hundreds of camps mushroomed across the country. By June 1933 New Mexico had opened sixteen camps of its own. The country—and New Mexico—had responded to an urgent social and economic need with an equally urgent, well planned response.[35]

## Endnotes - Chapter 1

[1]    Michael Uys and Lexy Lovell, *Riding the Rails* (Boston: WGBH video production for the American Experience, 1997); John A. Salmond, *The Civilian Conservation Corps, 1933-42: A New Deal Case Study* (Durham: Duke University Press, 1967): 3-4; George R. Leighton and Richard Hellman, "Half Slave, Half Free: Unemployment, the Depression, and American Young People," *Harper's Monthly*, 169 (August 1935): 342-53; Robert A. Margo, "The Microeconomics of Depression Unemployment," *Journal of Economic History*, 51 (June 1991): 334-36. On rites of passage to manhood, see Ray Raphael, *The Men From the Boys: Rites of Passage in Male America* (Lincoln: University of Nebraska Press, 1988); Nancy Geyer Christopher, *Rites of Passage: The Heroic Journey to Adulthood* (Washington, D.C.: Cornell Press, 1996).

[2]    Quoted in James R. Kearney, *Anna Eleanor Roosevelt: The Evolution of A Reformer* (Boston: Houghton Mifflin, 1968): 23.

[3]    Lucinda Lucero Sachs, "Clyde Tingley's Little New Deal for New Mexico, 1935-38" (Unpublished M.A. thesis, University of New Mexico, 1989): 193.

[4]    Paige W. Christiansen, *The Story of Oil in New Mexico* (Socorro: New Mexico Bureau of Mines and Mineral Resources, 1989): 29-30; H.J. Hagerman, "How the Depression Is Affecting New Mexico, *New Mexico Tax Bulletin,* 10 (November-December 1931): 125-6.

[5]    Richard Melzer, *Madrid Revisited: Life and Labor in a New Mexican Mining Camp in the Years of the Great Depression* (Santa Fe: Lightning Tree Press, 1976): 15; Toby Smith, *Coal Town: The Life and Times of Dawson, New Mexico* (Santa Fe: Ancient City Press, 1993): 121.

[6]    Sachs, "Little New Deal," 192; Hagerman, "Affecting New Mexico," 122-24; Charles D. Biebel, *Making the Most of It: Public*

*Works in Albuquerque during the Great Depression, 1929-1942* (Albuquerque: Albuquerque Museum, 1986): 21.

⁷ Richard L. Nostrand, *The Hispano Homeland* (Norman: University of Oklahoma Press, 1992): 139-50; Marta Weigle, *Hispanic Villages of Northern New Mexico* (Santa Fe: Lightning Tree Press, 1975: 35-6, 159, 204; Peg Arnold, "Wyoming's Hispanic Sheepherders," *Annals of Wyoming*, 69 (Winter 1997): 29-34.

⁸ James F. Wickens, *Colorado In the Great Depression* (New York: Garland, 1979): 104-6.

⁹ Weigle, *Hispanic Villages*, 38-212.

¹⁰ *Santa Fe New Mexican*, August 10, 1935.

¹¹ Tomás Wesley Brown, *Heritage of the New Mexico Frontier* (New York: Vantage Press, 1995): 169-70.

¹² Brown, *Heritage*, 105; James N. Gregory, *American Exodus: The Dust Bowl Migration and Okie Culture in California* (New York: Oxford University Press, 1989): 14.

¹³ Alison T. Otis, W.D. Honey, T.C. Hogg, and K.K. Lakin, *The Forest Service and the Civilian Conservation Corps, 1933-42* (Washington, D.C.: U.S. Forest Service, 1986): 5; Biebel, *Making the Most of It*, 23-4; Glen O. Ream, *Out of New Mexico's Past* (Santa Fe: Sundial Books, 1980): 148; *Santa Fe New Mexican*, January 5, 1934.

¹⁴ Richard Wormser, *Hoboes: Wandering in America* (New York: Walker and Company, 1994): 37; Irving L. Stevens, *Fish Bones: Hoboing in the 1930s* (Milo, Maine: Milo Printing Company, 1982): 16-17; Kathryn Sargeant and Mary Davis, *Shining River, Precious Land: An Oral History of Albuquerque's North Valley* (Albuquerque: Albuquerque Museum, 1986): 123; Rita Kasch Chegin, *Survivors: Women of the Southwest* (Las Cruces: Yucca Tree Press, 1991): 31; *The History of Luna County* (Deming: Luna County Historical Society, 1978): 151; William Dishman interview, December 30, 1997.

¹⁵ Biebel, *Making the Most of It*, 21; Lesley Poling-Kempes, *The Harvey Girls: Women Who Opened the West* (New York: Paragon House, 1989): 186-7.

¹⁶ John Steinbeck, *The Grapes of Wrath* (New York: Penguin Books, 1976): 129.

¹⁷ Sargeant and Davis, *Shining River*, 123.

¹⁸ *Albuquerque Tribune*, May 26, 1933.

¹⁹ James R. Chiles, "Hallelujah, I'm a Bum," *Smithsonian*, 29 (August 1998): 74; Thomas C. Donnelly, *I Came Down From the Hills* (Portales: Bishop, 1979): 62. Also see the *Santa Fe New Mexican*, January 30, 1934.

[20]  *Santa Fe New Mexican*, February 8, 1933.

[21]  Dan Scurlock, *From the Rio to the Sierra: An Environmental History of the Middle Rio Grande Basin* (Ft. Collins, Colorado: U.S. Department of Agriculture, 1998): 390-1; Weigle, *Hispanic Villages*, 26-7; Elliott S. Barker, *Ramblings In the Field of Conservation* (Santa Fe: Sunstone Press, 1976): 58.

[22]  *Ibid.*, 59.

[23]  Frank W. Pooler to Arthur Seligman, Albuquerque, February 25, 1933, Governor Arthur Seligman Papers, New Mexico State Records Center and Archives, Santa Fe, New Mexico (hereafter cited as NMSRCA); Irving Bernstein, *A Caring Society: The New Deal, the Worker, and the Great Depression* (Boston: Houghton Mifflin, 1985): 157. Also see Joseph M. Petulla, *An Environmental History* (Columbus, Ohio: Merrill, 1988).

[24]  Davis Newton Lott, ed., *The Presidents Speak: The Inaugural Addresses of the American Presidents from Washington to Clinton* (New York: Henry Holt and Company, 1994): 278-81.

[25]  Rexford G. Tugwell, *The Democratic Roosevelt: A Biography of Franklin D. Roosevelt* (Garden City: Doubleday, 1957): 278; Edgar B. Nixon, ed., *Franklin D. Roosevelt and Conservation, 1911-45* (Hyde Park, New York: Franklin D. Roosevelt Library, 1957): I, 138-51; Ted Morgan, *FDR: A Biography* (New York: Simon and Shuster, 1985): 379; *Congressional Record,* 73rd Congress, 1rst session (Washington, D.C.: U.S. Government Printing Office, 1933): 650; T.H. Watkins, *The Great Depression: America in the 1930s* (Boston: Little, Brown and Company, 1993): 130.

[26]  Salmond, *CCC*, 20-3.

[27]  William James, *Essays on Faith and Morals* (Cleveland: World, 1962): 311-28; *Forest Pioneer*, 4th quarter, 1938. Fittingly, a CCC camp in Vermont was eventually named after William James. Unfortunately, as an experimental camp with many unique features, it failed, closing within three months. Calvin W. Gower, "Camp William James: A New Deal Blunder?" *New England Quarterly*, 38 (December 1965): 475-93.

[28]  Kenneth W. Baldridge, "Nine Years of Achievement: The Civilian Conservation Corps in Utah" (Unpublished Ph.D. dissertation, University of Utah, 1971): 5; Frank Pooler to Arthur Seligman, Albuquerque, February 25, 1933, Governor Seligman Papers, NMSRCA.

[29]  Otis *et al.*, *Forest Service and the CCC*, 5; R.L. Deering, "Camps for the Unemployed in the Forests of California,: *Journal of Forestry*, 30 (May 1932): 554-57; Baldridge, "Nine Years," 5-6; Salmond, *CCC*, 5.

[30] Henri Fuss, "Unemployment Among Young People," *International Labour Review*, 31 (May 1935): 660; Edward Robb Ellis, *A Nation in Torment: The Great American Depression, 1929-39* (New York: G.P. Putnam's Sons, 1970): 299. For a comparison of German youth camps and the CCC, see John N. Garraty, "The New Deal, National Socialism, and the Great Depression," *American Historical Review,* 78 (October 1973): 910-11.

[31] Nixon, *Roosevelt and Conservation,* 354; Henry Clepper, "The Birth of the CCC," *American Forests*, 79 (March 1973): 8-11.

[32] F. Kennon Moody, "F.D.R. and His Neighbors: A Study of the Relationship Between Franklin D. Roosevelt and the Residents of Dutchess County (Unpublished Ph.D. dissertation, State University of New York at Albany, 1981): 287-90; Whitney R. Cross, "Ideas in Politics: The Conservation Policies of the Two Roosevelts," *Journal of the History of Ideas*, 14 (June 1953): 421-38; Anna Lou Riesch, "Conservation Under Franklin D. Roosevelt" (Unpublished Ph.D. dissertation, University of Wisconsin, 1952): 21, 44, 47, 49; Kenneth S. Davis, *FDR: The New York Years, 1928-33* (New York: Random House, 1985): 31-2; Olen Cole, Jr., *The African-American Experience in the Civilian Conservation Corps* (Gainesville: University Press of Florida, 1999): 2; Thomas W. Patton, "Forestry and Politics: Franklin D. Roosevelt as Governor of New York," *New York History*, 75 (October 1994): 416; Salmond, *CCC*, 6-8.

[33] Charles W. Johnson, "The Army and the Civilian Conservation Corps, 1933-42," *Prologue*, 4 (February 1972): 147; Kathy Mays Smith, "The Role of the Army in the CCC," *NACCA Journal*, 21 (February 1998): 1, 5; Omar N. Bradley, *A General's Life: An Autobiography* (New York: Simon and Schuster, 1983): 72; Captain X, "A Civilian Army in the Woods," *Harper's Monthly,* 168 (March 1934): 487-97.

[34] Bradley, *General's Life*, 72; Smith, "Role of the Army," 7; Enoch Graf, "The Army's Greatest Peace-Time Achievement," *Quartermaster Review*, 15 (July-August 1935): 7-13.

[35] Leo Donovan, "The Establishment of the First Civilian Conservation Camp," *Infantry Journal*, 40 (July-August 1933): 245-49; Otis *et al., Forest Service and the CCC*, 84-6.

# CHAPTER 2

## Early Reaction

News of the Civilian Conservation Corps's creation was generally well received across the United States, including in New Mexico. As early as March 1933, the *Santa Fe New Mexican* praised the new program, editorializing that while the CCC would only be a "drop in the bucket" in curing nationwide unemployment, it represented a "substantial start," especially because it promised to be of great help in conserving many endangered resources of the Southwest, The *Albuquerque Journal* also admired plans for the CCC in a favorable editorial within two weeks of the program's creation. The *Gallup Independent* liked the concept of the CCC and hoped that young enrollees would soon be available to help in local emergencies, such as floods and forest fires. Enthusiastically, the *Raton Range* declared that the CCC's "purpose ... is splendid and should be acclaimed by all ... who want to see human suffering ... wiped out as far as possible." By September 1933 the *Clovis News-Journal* had already called the CCC "one of the most completely successful of all the items in the 'new deal' program." The *News-Journal's* editor in fact wondered if the CCC shouldn't become a permanent government institution because "this forest army is too good an outfit to be discarded." Such favorable press coverage, including front page photos of young men entering the first CCC camps, added to the program's early support. Projections on the number of camps and enrollees planned for New Mexico peaked the interest of many who hoped to benefit from the CCC, either directly or indirectly.[1]

The CCC enjoyed early popularity because, unlike other programs of its day, this one appealed to nearly every segment of American society. For many Americans, the CCC represented a return to the country's romantic agrarian roots, idealized by leaders like Thomas Jefferson, historians like Frederick Jackson Turner, and novelists like James Fenimore Cooper. Conservationists saw the CCC and its ready supply of labor as a golden opportunity to tackle conservation projects on a scale never equaled before or since. Political conservatives liked the prospect of enforcing law and order by taking potential delinquents off the streets and allowing the Army to instill discipline and respect for authority in them. Other Americans saw the CCC as an opportunity to build character in young working class males, much as Boy Scout and YMCA camps had previously helped build character in young middle class males. With strong character, CCC enrollees would become good citizens. According to a CCC official in Santa Fe, the CCC would help "boys, turned adrift by the depression, to find themselves ... [and get] on the road to good citizenship." Outdoor work promised to help build healthy bodies as well as healthy minds, In the admiring words of the *Raton Range*, CCC enrollees would have "health actually forced into their bodies, jump and ginger developed in their spines, respect for law drilled into their intelligence, and courage and ambition planted into their hearts."[2]

Employers recognized the CCC as a training ground for future employees who would learn important work values, including punctuality, corporate loyalty, safety, and pride in a job well done. Nearly all Americans agreed that wages earned in the CCC, however small, were far better than the "evils of the dole" with its demoralizing effect on all recipients. In short, the CCC offered something for nearly everyone; it was seen as a cure for various ills, depending on one's greatest fears, as well as a positive force for national progress, depending on one's favored cause.[3]

\*    \*    \*

Despite much praise, the CCC had its share of detractors, especially in its early, unproven days. When criticism came, it often originated on the extreme right or left of the political spectrum. The left frequently feared the CCC's organizational ties to the military. John Nevin Sayrem, the chairman of a national peace organization, argued that the Army's influence in the CCC would be so prevalent that the program should be renamed the MDC, or Military Destruction Corps. Some observers went so far as to accuse Franklin Roosevelt of creating the CCC as a quasi-military force to increase his political power, much as Hitler had used the German *Arbeitsdeinst* to increase his. Others feared that CCC enrollees might soon don black or brown shirts like right-wing groups in Europe, taking the U.S. one step closer to Fascism. A leftist newspaper, the *Champion of Youth*, branded the CCC as Fascist and referred to it as "Black Legionism." John Dewey's Committee on Unemployment shared similar concerns, as did a play entitled *The Young Go First*, performed in New York in the spring of 1935. Even Eleanor Roosevelt complained to her husband that the CCC was "too militaristic," a charge that FDR emphatically denied.[4]

In sharp contrast, critics on the right feared that Franklin Roosevelt's New Deal, including the CCC, was part of a plot to take the United States "down the same road as Communism." Rather than rescuing capitalism with government programs like the CCC, Roosevelt was accused of sabotaging the free enterprise system in hopes of assuming so many additional powers that he would soon become a Socialist or Communist dictator. The CCC was considered a key element in FDR's nefarious plans. After traveling from coast to coast in 1935, a leading conservative declared that "CCC camps are becoming hotbeds of radicalism." He warned that if the youths in these camps were not released and absorbed into private industry immediately they would soon "become a revolutionary army." Short of this extreme, other conservatives feared that CCC camps would serve as "ideal forums for communist propaganda." Leftist organizers had, in fact, infiltrated Canada's version of the CCC with disastrous results by 1934.[5]

Although less extreme in its reaction, mainstream labor also found fault with the CCC in its early days. Testifying at Congressional hearings that led to the creation of the CCC in March 1933, American Federation of Labor (AF of L) president William Green expressed his "grave" concern that low wages in the CCC would drive wages down in private industry. Other union leaders feared that the CCC might be used as a strike-breaking tool by management. A number feared that CCC enrollees would take jobs that might otherwise go to unemployed local workers. When a CCC camp was planned for Albuquerque in mid-1934, the Common Labor Union met and asked the Albuquerque city commission "how the unskilled labor of the city and county are going to make a living for the period ... that a CCC camp will be established?" With enrollees performing unskilled labor, workers feared that "the home man will be forced to declare a 'holiday'" and turn to charity in order to survive.[6]

Elsewhere in New Mexico, some also worried that out-of-state workers would be recruited to build CCC camps and, later, to work in the camps as enrollees. The *Santa Fe New Mexican* posed this concern as early as April 1933: "The CCC camps are ... largely employing people from outside .... What is being done for the needy native people of New Mexico?" Two years later a woman from Hillsboro, New Mexico, called this problem "the greatest injustice that I have ever ... personally experienced." Edith D. Capt reported to Governor Clyde Tingley that her husband and other local men had been hired as carpenters to help build a nearby CCC camp, but had been let go when no-more-qualified workers from El Paso "began coming in ... driving cars with Texas license plates, [and] even bring[ing] part of their groceries up from El Paso with them." Capt complained that the rejection of local men and the "influx of outside labor" was "a dirty deal from start to finish." State unions agreed, writing their own letters of protest to political leaders, including Governor Tingley and New Mexico's two U.S. senators, Dennis Chavez and Carl Hatch.[7]

\*     \*     \*

Franklin Roosevelt addressed early concerns about the CCC with decisive words and action. In response to those who thought the CCC was too militaristic, the Roosevelt administration took steps to make sure that it did not become "just another military unit," in FDR's terms. Yes, each camp would be administered by an Army or Navy officer, but regular officers were soon replaced by reserve officers and, by the late 1930s when reserve officers were needed for war preparedness, by civilian supervisors. Also, while the military would run each camp, it would do so in conjunction with other non-military government agencies, like the U.S. Forest Service and the Soil Conservation Service, that would supervise daily work projects.[8]

Even military jargon and procedures were scrupulously avoided. Young men who "enrolled" in the CCC, rather than "enlisted," were called "enrollees" rather than soldiers. Officers were politely referred to as "sirs," but enrollees were never required to formally salute their military superiors. Bugles (or whistles) were blown to awaken enrollees, but only to teach punctuality for the work place rather than for the battlefield. Calisthenics were performed each morning, but there were no military drills or combat training. Flag raising ceremonies were considered acts of patriotism and good citizenship rather than daily military rituals. Uniforms were required, but the CCC soon developed its own style of dress after first using Army surplus goods. To further avoid even the appearance of a military focus. Army recruiters were banned from entering camps until the start of World War II. Although some critics still feared excessive militarism, most Americans soon realized that early concerns and comparisons with Hitler's *Arbeitsdeinst* were groundless. In the words of one historian, "If the Army was making a secret attempt to convince the enrollees of the virtues of military life, it was ... astonishingly unsuccessful."[9]

The government also responded to conservative concerns that CCC camps were potential "hotbeds of radicalism." Enrollees identified as agitators were dealt with quickly, leading to dishonorable discharges from the CCC in the worst cases. And, despite cries of censorship, certain books and magazines were banned from camp libraries when they were deemed too radical for enrollee consumption. William Ogburn's *You and Machines* was the most famous example of this form of censorship. Although written as part of a special series for the CCC under the direction of the American Council on Education, Ogburn's small book was considered objectionable because it identified the modern machine as the root of all modern evils. According to Ogburn, a University of Chicago Sociology professor, the machine had produced the American factory system based on an upper class of factory owners and a lower class of factory workers. Ogburn asserted that this factory system was unfair because "wealth was distributed unequally between these [upper and lower] classes." Distressed by these conclusions, CCC officials in Washington declared that *You and Machines* could produce a "philosophy of despair" that might well "induce a desire to destroy our present economic and political structures." Such ideas could not be tolerated. Ogburn's book was banned from all CCC camp libraries in November 1934.[10]

Magazines like *Spark* and the *Champion of Youth* were similarly banned when they called for such "radical" action as enrollee pay increases, the right of enrollees to organize unions, and the outlawing of racial discrimination against blacks in the CCC. Camp inspectors were ordered to carefully watch for these publications in their travels from camp to camp; *Spark* was considered so potentially dangerous that camp inspection forms included a specific question regarding its presence in camp libraries. CCC reaction to suspected communist publications may appear paranoid in retrospect, but can only be understood in light of the public's fear of communist agitation, as had occurred in Canada's equivalent of the CCC. The Roosevelt administration hoped to avoid similar turmoil in the United States, especially when protests in British Columbian camps helped cause the downfall of at least one Canadian government of the 1930s.[11]

The Roosevelt administration felt equally compelled to respond to mainstream labor's early criticism of the CCC.

Organized labor was important to the administration for many reasons, including the fact that labor had played a key role in FDR's winning coalition in 1932; its support was considered essential to his reelection hopes in 1936. Roosevelt mollified labor by appointing a labor leader as the first national director of the CCC. Robert W. Fechner had started his career as a railroad machinist apprentice, had worked as a journeyman in railroad shops across the country, and had entered labor politics before the First World War. By the early 1930s he had risen to the rank of General Vice President of the International Association of Machinists in the American Federation of Labor. FDR knew and admired this union leader, especially after Fechner had worked long and hard in Roosevelt's presidential campaign of 1932. Trusted by labor and government, Fechner proved to be a fine choice for director of the CCC from 1933 till his death in 1939.[12]

Labor's greatest concerns were resolved with time. Wages in private industry were not adversely effected by the CCC in most parts of the country, including New Mexico. Moreover, the removal of thousands of CCC enrollees from local job markets improved job opportunities for others and helped drive down unemployment figures in many states. Also, in a politically wise move, the CCC offered employment to many local workers, especially during each camp's building phase, using union labor whenever possible. Once built, CCC camps employed Local Experienced Men (LEMs) to serve as foremen and skilled workers who helped insure the quality of enrollee labor, while improving camp relations with surrounding communities. By July 1933, 35,000 LEMs had added their maturity and skills to the early success of the CCC nationwide.[13]

But what of local complaints that out-of-state workers displaced local men on CCC projects? Although CCC regulations eventually specified that LEMs must "usually [be] chosen from the community in which the project is to operate," the use of out-of-state workers in camp construction proved harder to control. Constant vigilance by labor unions, individuals, and state politicians was required. Governor Tingley and U.S. Senators Chavez and Hatch were especially vigilant. Tingley, for example, responded immediately to protests by the New Mexico Building Trades Association in July 1935. The union reported the use of "imported" labor from San Antonio, Texas, in the building of CCC camps in southern New Mexico. It was, of course, ironic that while Tingley and other state leaders were eager to guard New Mexico's borders against intruding labor from Texas in 1935, they had strenuously objected when the shoe was on the other foot and Colorado attempted to block New Mexican labor from crossing its southern border only a few months later.[14]

Early apprehension regarding the CCC was clearly alleviated in New Mexico and across the nation. A public opinion poll in 1936 showed that eighty percent of all Americans favored continuing the CCC, with the strongest support coming from Rocky Mountain and Pacific Coast states. While no separate polling was done in New Mexico, editorial comments clearly reflected on-going enthusiasm and diminished misgivings. By the late summer of 1933 highly favorable editorials were the norm in newspapers like the *Silver City Enterprise*, the *Gallup Independent*, the *Clovis News-Journal*, and the *Albuquerque Journal*. A 1935 *Journal* editorial entitled "The Value of the CCC" asserted that the CCC was "one of the few New Deal agencies which has won almost unanimous public approval ... . Pride ... in the CCC is a vital factor which must be encouraged." Editors across the country agreed. With such praise and support, it is no wonder that the AF of L's William Green eventually called the CCC a "great movement" for American youth. Franklin Roosevelt praised his pet New Deal project in his fireside chats and in a special radio address broadcast to CCC camps in the summer of 1933. Reflecting FDR's affection for the CCC, the president's longtime aide Louis Howe added that "we have turned 300,000 boys of an average age of nineteen, from despairing down and outers, to cheerful, optimistic young men full of determination to win the battle of life." The administration was convinced that it had helped thousands come of age in the CCC, despite the enormous odds against young Americans in the darkest days of the Great Depression.[15]

## Endnotes - Chapter 2

[1]  *Santa Fe New Mexican*, March 25, 1933; *Albuquerque Journal*, April 8, 1933; *Gallup Independent*, August 9, 1933; *Raton Range*, March 28, 1933; *Clovis Evening News-Journal,* September 16, 1933. For examples of front page photos of the CCC, see the *Santa Fe New Mexican*, April 15, 19, 20, 1933.

[2]  David I. Macleod, *Building Character in the American Boy: The Boy Scouts, the YMCA and Their Forerunners, 1870-1920* (Madison: University of Wisconsin Press, 1983); *Santa Fe New Mexican*, October 11, 1933; *Raton Range*, July 23, 1935.

[3]  *Clovis Evening News-Journal*, September 16, 1933.

[4]  Salmond, *CCC*, 85, 114-16; *New York Times*, February 9, 1935; Johnson, "Army and the CCC," 149; Franklin Folsom, *Impatient Armies of the Poor: The Story of Collective Action of the Unemployed, 1808-1942* (Boulder: University Press of Colorado, 1991): 375; Arthur J. Todd, "Social Implications of the CCC," *The Clearing House*, 10 (November 1935): 157; Joseph P. Lash, *Eleanor and Franklin* (New York: W.W. Norton, 1971): 539-40, Eleanor Roosevelt also objected to the all-male composition of the CCC, arguing that unemployed young women should have camps and work of their own, Bernstein, *Caring Society*, 291.

[5]  George Wolfskill and John A. Hudson, *All But the People: Franklin D. Roosevelt and His Critics, 1933-39* (London: Macmillan, 1969): 154-55; Elmo R. Richardson, "Was There Politics in the Civilian Conservation Corps?" *Forest History,* 16 (July 1972): 13; Richard A. Reiman, *The New Deal and American Youth* (Athens: University of Georgia Press, 1992): 191; Glen Makahonuk, "The Saskatoon Relief Camp Workers' Riot of May 8, 1933: An Expression of Class Conflict," *Saskatchewan History,* 37 (Spring 1984): 55-72.

[6]  Salmond, *CCC*, 17-19; Richardson, "Politics," 13; *Albuquerque Journal*, June 29, 1934.

[7]  *Santa Fe New Mexican*, April 8, 1933, and August 30, 1933; Edith D. Capt to Clyde Tingley, Hillsboro, June 23, 1935, and Charles LeFeber to Clyde Tingley, Albuquerque, July 12, 1935, Governor Clyde Tingley Papers, NMSRCA.

[8]  *New York Times*, February 9, 1935; Smith, "Role of the Army," 7; Secretary of War to the Editor, *Silver City Enterprise*, March 30, 1934.

[9]  Salmond, *CCC*, 86; Stephen H. Roberts, *The House that Hitler Built* (London: Methuen, 1937): 213-15; Frank E. Hill, *The School in*

*the Camps: The Educational Program of the Civilian Conservation Corps* (New York: American Association for Adult Education, 1935): 66; Charles W. Johnson, "The Civilian Conservation Corps: The Role of the Army" (Unpublished Ph.D. dissertation, University of Michigan, 1968): 228.

[10] Calvin W. Gower, "Conservatism, Censorship, and Controversy in the CCC, 1930s," *Journalism Quarterly*, 52 (Summer 1975): 279-82; *New York Times*, April 12, 1937; Jonathan Mitchell, "Roosevelt's Tree Army," *New Republic*, 83 (June 12, 1935): 127; William F. Ogburn, *You and Machines* (Chicago: University of Chicago Press, 1934).

[11] Gower, "Censorship," 282; Martin Glaberman and George P. Rawick, "*The Champion of Youth*: An Introduction and Appraisal," *Labor History*, 11 (Summer 1970): 351-4; Pierre Berton, *The Great Depression, 1929-39* (Toronto: McClelland and Stewart, 1990): 266-338. For an example of a camp inspection form with questions regarding communist propaganda, see Camp Inspection Report, Jemez, June 30, 1934, Civilian Conservation Corps Records, Record Group 35, National Archives, Washington, D.C. (hereafter cited as CCC, NA).

[12] Salmond, *CCC*, 27-9, 77-9.

[13] Ellis, Torment, 298; John C. Paige, *The Civilian Conservation Corps and the National Park Service, 1933-42* (Washington, D.C.: National Park Service, 1985): 77; Salmond, *CCC*, 34; Chegin, *Survivors*, 32, 34-5; Frank W. Pooler and eight fellow Regional Foresters to Major Stuart, n.p., April 4, 1933, CCC File, Franklin D. Roosevelt Library, Hyde Park, New York (hereafter cited as FDRL).

[14] New Mexico Relief and Security Authority, Manual of Instructions, Selection of Men for the Civilian Conservation Corps, Civilian Conservation Corps Papers, NMSRCA; Dennis Chavez to Clyde Tingley, Washington, D.C., July 13 & 22, 1935, Governor Tingley Papers, NMSRCA.

[15] *Silver City Enterprise*, September 29, 1933; *Gallup Independent*, September 29, 1933; *Clovis Evening News-Journal*, September 16, 1933; *Albuquerque Journal*, May 29, 1935; Salmond, *CCC*, 106-7, 201-2; Russell D. Buhite and David W. Levy, eds., *FDR's Fireside Chats* (Norman: University of Oklahoma Press, 1992): 21; *Forestry News Digest* (August 1933): 9; Alfred B. Rollins, Jr., *Roosevelt and Howe* (New York: Alfred A. Knopf, 1962): 424.

# CHAPTER 3
## Signing Up

A large group of eager young men crowded into the Clovis city hall on the morning of April 26, 1933. After completing government applications for enrollment in the new Civilian Conservation Corps, the youths waited anxiously for word of who had been selected and assigned to one of New Mexico's first nine CCC camps. By noon, one young man had been chosen. Ten more were identified by the following day, filling Curry County's initial quota of eleven enrollees. By nightfall on April 27, all eleven young men had left, transported by train for orientation and training at Ft. Bliss, Texas. The CCC had come to New Mexico.[1]

Similar recruitment scenes were played out in towns across the state in late April and May 1933. Fifteen youths were sent from Santa Fe County. Thirty-five departed from Raton. Dozens left from other county seats, including Albuquerque, Alamogordo, Silver City, Deming, Taos, and Gallup, until New Mexico's initial quota of 750 enrollees was met. Most of these 750 young men had never left home before; others had never ventured more than twenty miles from where they had been born.[2]

Excitement mixed with trepidation filled the enrollees and the families they left behind. Some family members understandably still confused the CCC with the Army. At least one Santa Fe mother "wept and pleaded that her boy not [be] taken" because she had a "peculiar horror" of the military, undoubtedly as a result of losing loved ones in World War I. Early recruitment on the Zuni Reservation went slowly because many youths "feared that they were being drafted for 'another World War.' Once their leader explained the real purpose of the CCC, they readily volunteered."[3]

What was required of New Mexicans—and all Americans— who hoped to join the CCC? First, each interested young man had to complete a one-page application that asked for such general information as his age, level of education, and previous employment. Based on this data and a personal interview, state relief workers determined whether applicants were not married, not employed, not in school, not felons, and not "mentally deranged." More positively, an applicant had to be between the ages of eighteen and twenty-five, be a male citizen of the United States, and be considered of "good character." Although judges in some parts of the country had at first "seized the chance to rid [their communities] of undesirables" by "sentencing" them to CCC camps, this practice was soon abandoned. The CCC was never meant to be a Boy Scout camp, but it was also never meant to serve as a reformatory school or boot camp for delinquent juveniles.[4]

In addition, all applicants had to agree to serve at least six months ("unless he secures other employment that will better his condition") and send twenty-five of the thirty dollars they would earn each month to designated dependents in their families. The latter requirement was especially important because enrollees "must in every case represent families on public relief rolls." Their wages were meant to assist their financially strapped families as well as themselves.[5]

Finally, each applicant had to pass a physical exam to show that he was at least five feet tall (but no taller than six feet, six inches), weighed more than 107 pounds, possessed at least three "serviceable natural masticating teeth" (top and bottom), and was "free from contagious or communicable disease" that might "menace the health" of fellow members of the CCC. Most youths passed their physicals without difficulty. Of 134 boys from Bernalillo,

Valencia, and Sandoval counties, only thirteen (or less than ten percent) did not qualify for physical reasons in July 1934.[6]

If a young man met these criteria and there was room available in New Mexico's quota (based on New Mexico's population in proportion to other states), an applicant could confidently expect acceptance into the CCC. Entry was official when each qualified youth raised his right hand and swore an oath of enrollment. By this oath, an enrollee affirmed that all the information he had previously provided was true and that he was ready to serve for at least six months. He also gave up any right to sue the government for "any injury received or disease contracted" while in the CCC. On the other hand, he agreed that he was financially and legally responsible for the "willful destruction, loss, sale, or disposal" of all government property issued to him while serving in the CCC. Moreover, he agreed to follow the rules and regulations of the Corps or face "expulsion therefrom." The lengthy oath concluded with the words, "So help me God." Each enrollee then signed the oath he had just made, although, given their generally low level of education, a "startling number" simply signed with an 'X,' followed by the signature of a CCC official who served as a witness.[7]

Such were the official requirements to join the CCC. While most New Mexican applicants easily cleared these initial hurdles, others did not. Age was the most frequent obstacle. With an average eighth grade education and few local job opportunities, a large percentage of males between the ages of fourteen and eighteen were eager to enroll, but too young to legally qualify. In desperation, a good many simply exaggerated their true age. Tony Sanchez of southwest Albuquerque thus enrolled at age sixteen, as did Juan Herrera and George 'Midge' Green from their homes in northern and southern New Mexico, respectively. José Chacon was only fifteen when he graduated from high school and left home in Peñasco. As the oldest male child in a family of five on a ten-acre farm in Texas, Roy Huffman also misrepresented his age in order to enter the CCC and serve in New Mexico.[8]

Other enrollee hopefuls were too small to meet the 107 pound weight requirement. Amadeo Quintana and Alex Salazar of Española shared this problem, but overcame it by eating several pounds of bananas and drinking plenty of water just prior to their physicals. Nabor Rael and a friend each ate three pounds of bananas for the same purpose; ironically Rael eventual rose to the rank of head cook in the CCC. Fred Poorbaugh, a camp commander from 1937 to 1942, remembers a youth from San Antonio, New Mexico, who was so eager to enroll in the CCC that he altered the weight on his application when his examining physician left the room. Once enrolled in the CCC, this rookie insisted that his mess sergeant feed him five to six times a day until the figure on his application was in fact correct. Tragically, for all his efforts to enter the CCC, the young enrollee was soon struck by lightning and electrocuted so badly that even the nails in his shoes were melted.[9]

Potential enrollees solved other enrollment problems with innovative solutions. Salo Maestas's father worked for the Santa Fe Railroad in Belen and, while hardly rich, made too much money for his son to enter the CCC. Salo nevertheless enrolled in 1938 by listing his grandmother as the dependent who officially received his twenty-five dollar monthly allotment and unofficially channelled it back to the Maestas family. Leonard 'Si' Porter had no trouble proving his family's poverty. 'Si''s father owned a bean farm near Corona, New Mexico, but "couldn't make a living on it anymore" in the 1930s; 'Si' facetiously explained that his dad was so poor that when a doctor told him to take as much medicine as would fit on a dime, his father had to use a nickel twice because he lacked a dime. More soberly, this proud farmer refused to sign a pauper's oath that would have allowed 'Si' to enter the CCC. Determined to enroll, 'Si' was able to join the CCC as a Local Experienced Man, although he was the first to admit that he really "had no experience with anything except dry land farming and trapping skunks." R.L. Coker faced other problems. While not poverty-stricken, Coker's family could not afford the expense of an appendix operation that R.L. needed in 1939. When his condition worsened, Coker enrolled in the CCC to receive free medical attention. He somehow passed his physical, joined the CCC company at Elephant Butte, and was successfully operated on at Beaumont Hospital in El Paso at the government's expense.[10]

Some New Mexicans suffered the mistaken impression that additional entry requirements existed. Youths with several brothers in large families often thought that only one male could join the CCC from each family unit. To circumvent this illusionary problem, some brothers claimed to be cousins with the same last names. Others went so far as to travel out-of-state to enroll in Arizona or California. Political connections were also thought necessary, although this too was an erroneous impression. Tony S. Baca of San Jose wrote a sincere letter to Democratic Senator Dennis Chavez asking for assistance in joining the CCC so that Baca could earn a decent wage and would no longer have to "look like a beggar [sic]." Playing the political card, Baca ended his plea with the words, *"Viva El Partido Democratica."*[11]

Less blatantly, Mrs. J.M. Espinosa of Belen and Procopio Martinez of Albuquerque wrote to Democratic Governor Tingley for assistance. Mrs. Espinosa, writing in behalf of her son, received a simple letter in response. Tingley promised to "take this up with the proper department and do what I can to assist you." Procopio Martinez recalled a more positive response. The governor "wrote me back almost immediately and said to report to a certain woman at the CCC office. And, sure enough, she had heard from [the governor] and allowed me to join." It is likely that Tingley didn't need to pull any political strings in referring Procopio to the proper bureaucratic office. But, as a consummate politician, Tinley did nothing to discourage the impression that he had come to the rescue. According to Martinez, "Governor Tingley understood there was financial need. It hadn't been for him ... ."[12]

But few could accuse the New Mexico Democratic Party as a whole of exploiting CCC enrollment for its political advantage. Indeed, as early as the summer of 1933 party leaders complained about the number of non-Democratic enrollees in New Mexico's camps.[13] A survey of 333 enrollees conducted by the Democratic

State Central Committee showed that while forty-five percent of those polled considered themselves Democrats, twenty-six percent were Republicans, eight percent were independents or affiliated with lesser-known parties, and twenty-one percent had unknown political ties. This meant that non-Democrats outnumbered Democrats by ten percent.[14] A year and a half later, members of the local Democratic committee of Truchas, New Mexico, vehemently protested to Governor Tingley that Republican enrollees from their village had outnumbered Democrats twenty-one to one since 1933. The committee submitted its data as "proof of political discrimination that has been done against the democrats [sic] in this precinct and the complete control that the republicans [sic] have taken." Tingley was asked to "do all in his power to bring about a more equal distribution of [these] benefits ... and take it out of the hands of those who unscrupulously use it to inrich [sic] themselves at the expense of the needy."[15] With no real power to disburse patronage in CCC enrollment, the governor could only respond that he was glad that the committee had written him, but that the group should contact the New Mexico relief administrator, a bureaucratic rather than political office.[16] Better able to use political favoritism in distributing jobs to camp foremen and LEMs, Democratic hands were tied regarding enrollee positions, much to their leaders' chagrin.[17]

Who were these New Mexican youths who went to such great lengths to join the CCC? In many ways they were like their fellow enrollees across the United States. First, they were similar to most enrollees in terms of age. While some New Mexicans altered their dates of birth in order to enroll, most did not, entering the Corps at the minimum legal age. The largest age group at time of enrollment thus equaled eighteen in both New Mexico and the country as a whole. Most enrollees also came from large families of six or more children. Moreover, the largest percentage of enrollees in the state and the nation had completed at least an eighth grade education. And most youths had never been employed prior to CCC enrollment. As late as 1941 over two-thirds of all new enrollees in New Mexico had never held a job because so few jobs were available.[18]

José Chacon's village of Peñasco, New Mexico, was typical. When José graduated from high school in 1941, only three men had regular, full-time jobs in his village: the postmaster, the letter carrier, and the forest ranger. Unfortunately for young men like José, none of the three government workers planned to ask for transfers or take early retirements. As the oldest son, José saw the CCC as his only alternative. Faced with similar circumstances, Tony Sanchez did odd jobs, like yardwork, but eventually resorted to running away with a friend to find work. Hopping a freight train, they traveled as far as Dodge City, Kansas. But employment was no better in Kansas. They survived by helping clean a Dodge City saloon and finding "small change that cowboys would lose when drunk." Discouraged, the boys returned home. Similarly tragic conditions existed for young men in poor communities across New Mexico and the United States.[19]

Despite some similarities, large differences separated New Mexican enrollees from those in other states in the nation. While the largest group of New Mexico's enrollees had completed at least the eighth grade, the percentage of illiterate enrollees in the state (6.9) equaled more than twice the percentage of illiterate enrollees nationwide. Such a dismal record could be expected in a state that ranked behind only two others (Louisiana and South Carolina) in the number of illiterate residents per capita. With its high rate of illiteracy, New Mexico's percentage of high school graduates was predictably worse than the country's average as a whole. While twelve percent of all enrollees in the nation had completed four years of high school, only five percent had received high school diplomas in New Mexico.[20]

New Mexico enrollees also had different ethnic origins. As many as eighty-one percent of all New Mexico enrollees had Spanish surnames. This high percentage of Hispanic enrollees surpassed neighboring Colorado's enrollment of Hispanic youths by forty percent and next-door Arizona's by sixty percent. New Mexico's percentage of Hispanic enrollees even surpassed the total

percentage of Hispanics in the state, an estimated forty-nine percent according to the census of 1930. Rural Hispanics in particular were among those hit hardest by the depression. Two-thirds of
New Mexico's CCC enrollees came from the predominantly Spanish-speaking towns and villages of the Rio Arriba (or upper Rio
Grande valley), where a 1935 survey found at least one member
of the CCC in every twenty families.[21]

In short, a typical member of the CCC in New Mexico was
an eighteen-year-old Hispanic male from a large family living in a
poor rural community where Spanish was the primary language.
The typical enrollee enjoyed at least a grammar school education,
but was more likely to be illiterate than his CCC colleagues elsewhere in the country. With few jobs available back home, he had
seldom held a regular job prior to joining the CCC. His main
motivation in enrolling in the CCC was to secure employment,
help his poverty-stricken family, and begin to assume the responsibilities of adulthood. The CCC offered these opportunities when
few other forms of relief, short of the dole, existed for the young.
No wonder most youths were grateful for the opportunity to serve.
With no stigma attached to participating in the CCC, new enrollees were, in fact, often "envied by their fellows" in most communities of New Mexico. Like their fathers and uncles who left to
labor for long periods of time in seasonal jobs, these young men
left home with a strong sense of obligation and determination.
And, like their fathers and uncles before them, they would be
missed, but much appreciated by their loved ones left behind.[22]

Once approved for entry in the CCC, New Mexico enrollees
were ready to leave home and begin their new experience in often
distant camps. According to CCC regulations, each enrollee could
carry only one package or suit case, although those who played
small musical instruments were encouraged to bring them as well.
Remembering this time fondly, Vidal Sedillo went so far as to
compose a *corrido*, or traditional New Mexico ballad. Translated,
the first verses told of his signing up for the CCC and optimisti-
cally departing by train:

1934
We should not forget.
It is the year we came
To the forest to work.

July 16
We started walking
For Los Lunas
To enlist.

Five friends
From my neighborhood
Left after registering
In Albuquerque.

To the Federal Building
We were called.
There were many of us gathered
For the physical exams.

About twelve at night
The train arrived.
In it we all left.
All felt fine.

We found mostly
Young people on the train.
As youth they were not afraid
And all went well.

Some played music
And sang well.
And as we traveled by their houses
They gave a little yell.[23]

Tomás Brown told of a similarly joyful departure far to the
northeast in Maxwell, New Mexico. Finding "absolutely no work

available" and eager to help his large family, Tomás completed a CCC application in Raton and passed his physical, despite a medical history of rheumatic fever. Accepted after several anxious weeks of waiting, Tomás headed for the bus that took him on the first leg of his journey to his assigned camp in Santa Fe. In one hand he carried a "cheaply made cardboard suitcase" tied with binding twine and filled with clothes, a Bible, and some paper on which to write letters home. Under his other arm Tomás carried the guitar his father had acquired for him in exchange for a steer. He wore his regular clothes, including an old Stetson hat, although he worried that the Army would confiscate this prized possession. Years later, Tomás wrote in his memoirs that

> I had mixed feelings as I got on that bus. Somehow I was aware that things would never be the same again. It was my first break away from the entire family. There was a mixture of joy over the freedom I felt as an adult, and yet one of sadness over the end of the family life I had known.[24]

Tomás was premature in declaring himself an adult as he rode off to Santa Fe, but by joining the CCC he had taken a large step toward that previously illusive goal. Like so many of his generation, the CCC gave Tomás a golden opportunity to leave home, assist loved ones, and secure worthwhile employment. Pleased but anxious, young enrollees sensed that other rites of passage lay ahead in their CCC experience.

## Endnotes — Chapter 3

[1]   *Clovis Evening News-Journal*, April 25-27, 1933; *Albuquerque Tribune*, May 31, 1933.

[2]   *Santa Fe New Mexican*, April 20 and May 15, 1933; *Raton Range*, April 25 and May 9, and 16, 1933; *Albuquerque Tribune*, April 19, 1933; *Alamogordo News*, May 18, 1933; *Deming Headlight*, April 28, 1933. New Mexico's quota eventually rose to as high as three thousand.

[3] *Santa Fe New Mexican*, April 28, 1933; Elmo R. Richardson, "The Civilian Conservation Corps and the Origins of the New Mexico State Park System," *Natural Resources Journal*, 6 (April 1966): 257n. A separate unit of the CCC was created for Native Americans; 4,470 Native Americans served in New Mexico. See Donald L. Parman, "The Indian and the Civilian Conservation Corps," *Pacific Historical Review*, 40 (February 1971): 39-56; Donald L. Parman, "The Indian Civilian Conservation Corps" (Unpublished Ph.D. dissertation, University of Oklahoma, 1967). Perry H. Merrill, *Roosevelt's Forest Army: A History of the Civilian Conservation Corps* (Monpelier, Vermont: Perry H. Merrill, 1981): 154. Another special CCC unit served unemployed veterans of World War I. An estimated ten percent of all CCC enrollees were veterans. A single camp for veterans (BR-3-N) was established in New Mexico, at Carlsbad. David Kammer, *The Historic and Architectural Resources of the New Deal in New Mexico* (Santa Fe: New Mexico Historic Preservation Division, 1994): 68; Salmond, *CCC*, 35-7; James J. McEntee, *Final Report of the Director of the Civilian Conservation Corps, April 1933 to June 30, 1942* (Washington, D.C.: Federal Security Agency, 1942): 16-7, 108.

[4] David D. Draves, *Builder of Men: Life in C.C.C. Camps of New Hampshire* (Portsmouth: Peter E. Randall, 1992): 368; Manual of Instructions, Selection of Men for the CCC, CCC Papers, NMSRCA; *New York Times,* January 5, 1936; *Santa Fe New Mexican,* April 19 and June 28, 1933; Roy Colbert interview, February 22, 1980; *Carson Pine Cone*, May 5, 1939. Age qualifications changed slightly over the years; by 1937 enrollees were required to be between the ages of seventeen and twenty-three. Gower, "Camp William James," 476n.

[5] M.P. Bryant, "Education in the CCC Camps of New Mexico" (Unpublished M.Ed. thesis, Texas Tech University, 1940): 51; Manual of Instructions, Selection of Men for the CCC, CCC Papers, NMSRCA. The amount required to be sent home was later lowered to twenty-two dollars a month, while the total kept by enrollees increased to eight dollars a month.

[6] Manual of Instruction, Selection of Men for the CCC, CCC Papers, NMSRCA; Watkins, *Depression*, 130; *Albuquerque Journal*, July 17, 1934. The CCC's physical exam was identical to the Army's, although CCC doctors were known to be far more lenient than Army medical doctors. *New York Times*, August 11, 1940.

[7] Paige, *CCC and the Park Service*, 74-5; Robert Allen Ermentrout, *Forgotten Men: The CCC* (Smithtown, New York: Exposition Press, 1982): 82.

⁸  Tony Sanchez interview, March 11, 1991; Arnold Vigil, "Blood, Sweat and Mud," *New Mexico Magazine*, 67 (July 1989): 81; George 'Midge' Green interview, March 25, 1997; José Chacon interview, July 25, 1984; Roy Huffman interview, May 25, 1992.

⁹  Amadeo Quintana and Alex Salazar interviews in María E. Montoya, Oral History Project, Bandelier National Monument, Los Alamos, New Mexico (hereafter cited as OHPB); Nabor Rael interview by Corine Romero, May 9, 1999; Fred Poorbaugh interview, June 21, 1991.

¹⁰  Salo Maestas interview, June 7, 1991; Leonard 'Si' W. Porter, Unpublished Memoirs of Company 3855, Camp F-41-N, 5, 12 (in author's possession; hereafter cited as Porter Memoirs); R.L. Coker interview, April 12, 1994.

¹¹  Doug Hall interview, May 15, 1991; Bennie Casaus interview, April 19, 1991; Sanchez interview; Tony S. Baca to Dennis Chavez, San Jose, New Mexico, November 18, 1940, Dennis Chavez Papers, Center for Southwest Research, University of New Mexico, Albuquerque, New Mexico (hereafter cited as CSWR).

¹²  Mrs. J.M. Espinosa to Clyde Tingley, Belen, January 7, 1935, Governor Tingley Papers, NMSRCA; Paul Logan, "CCC: A Golden Memory," *Impact*, 6 (April 5, 1983): 6.

¹³  E.B. Swope, New Mexico Democratic State Chairman, to James A. Farley, Democratic National Committee Chairman, n.p., July 20, 1933, Governor Tingley Papers, NMSRCA.

¹⁴  E.B. Swope to Arthur Seligman, Santa Fe, August 14 and 19, 1933, Governor Seligman Papers, NMSRCA.

¹⁵  A.L. Romero, J.A. Lucero, and Nestor Rael to Clyde Tingley, Truchas, January 30, 1935, Governor Tingley Papers, NMSRCA.

¹⁶  Clyde Tingley to A.L. Romero, Santa Fe, January 31, 1935, Governor Tingley Papers, NMSRCA.

¹⁷  Sachs, "Little New Deal," 11; Dennis Chavez to Paul A. Roach, n.p., December 23, 1940, Senator Chavez Papers, CSWR.

¹⁸  Bryant, "Education," 55-7, 63; Michael W. Sherraden, "The Civilian Conservation Corps: Effectiveness of the Camps" (Unpublished Ph.D. dissertation, University of Michigan, 1979): 4; Harold K. Steen, *The U.S. Forest Service: A History* (Seattle: University of Washington Press, 1991): 215; Salmond, *CCC*, 135; McEntee, *Final Report*, 17, 50-1,   112; Casaus interview; Hall interview; Maestas interview.

¹⁹  Chacon interview; Tony Sanchez interview in the *NACCCA Journal*, 16 (November 1997).

²⁰  Bryant, "Education," 66-7, 69; *Albuquerque Journal*, June 10,

1934; George I. Sanchez, *Forgotten People: A Study of New Mexicans* (Albuquerque: Calvin Horn, 1967): 29; Richard A. Bruce, "School Enrollment in New Mexico" (Unpublished M.A. thesis, University of New Mexico, 1935).

[21] Calculated from CCC Enrollment Cards, CCC Papers, NMSRCA; Parham, "CCC in Colorado," 41n; Peter M. Booth, "The Civilian Conservation Corps in Arizona, 1933-42" (Unpublished M.A. thesis, University of Arizona, 1991): 32; Sigurd Johansen, *The Population of New Mexico: Its Composition and Changes* (State College: New Mexico College of Agriculture and Mechanic Arts, 1940): 22; Weigle, *Hispanic Villages*, 41-212.

[22] Charles P. and Nellie H. Loomis, "Skilled Spanish-American War-Industry Workers From New Mexico," *Applied Anthropology*, 2 (October-November-December 1942): 33.

[23] Manual of Instructions, Selection of Men for the CCC, CCC Papers, NMSRCA; Vidal Sedillo, "En el CC Camp," in author's possession.

[24] Brown, *Heritage*, 106, 173, 175.

CCC tents at Redrock camp. Early camps often included surplus
Army tents from World War I. *Courtesy of the Stewart Henry
Robeson Papers, Rio Grande Historical Collection, New Mexico State
University, Las Cruces, New Mexico.*

# CHAPTER 4

## Arrival in Camp

X The same young men who had enrolled in the CCC from communities across New Mexico now traveled to their assigned camps across the state. Most traveled by train or by bus to towns near their camp destinations. From there, Army trucks took them over rough roads to isolated camps where conservation work was needed, but access was difficult. After hours of travel, the new enrollees often arrived at their destinations late at night with hardly enough energy to eat a meal and crawl into bed. For most, they had just completed the longest, hardest journey of their young lives.[1]

Enrollees had their first real opportunity to inspect their new surroundings the following morning. If they arrived in the spring or summer of 1933, or when new camps were created thereafter, they usually found only temporary facilities, including surplus tents left over from World War I. Tents were soon replaced by slightly more permanent Army structures, numbering twelve in the average 200-man camp. Camps normally included four barracks, a latrine, a bathhouse, a mess hall, an infirmary, a recreation hall, a supply building, garages, and administrative headquarters. Buildings were neatly arranged with connecting walkways and a central yard, complete with flagpole and American flag. Some camps went to great lengths to obtain wood for their patriotic poles. Enrollees in Mirage, New Mexico, traveled sixty miles to the

*above*: CCC Camp at Bandelier National Monument. *Courtesy of Jim Johnson.   below*: CCC camp at Glenwood, New Mexico. *Courtesy of Levi Baca.*

nearest timbered region to cut down, transport, and erect their camp's honored flagpole in 1936.[2]

The longer a CCC company stayed in one location, the more finished and even elaborate its camp became. Many boasted lawns, flowers, signs, stone walks, and playing fields. While two enrollees from Farmington, New Mexico, found only nine large and twelve small tents when they arrived at their Sacramento Valley camp in June 1933, they proudly reported that the place resembled a small town by August. The camp at Mirage was similarly described as "a veritable little city in the midst of the wide open spaces." Enrollees worked hard to improve their camps and living conditions in the wilderness.[3]

But as well as most camps were kept, their facilities were generally spartan and not to be confused with a country club atmosphere. Most buildings were portable prefabs, designed to allow whole camps to be moved once conservation work in an area was complete. Each barracks, measuring twenty feet by 130 feet, housed fifty enrollees. Corpsmen were assigned steel-framed Army beds and simple shelves; footlockers were optional and had to be purchased at the enrollees' expense. Wood-burning Army stoves kept enrollees nominally warm on cold winter nights, a difficult task with poorly insulated barracks walls. In some places, like at the Bandelier National Monument, power generators were so small and weak that they had to be shut down by nine o'clock each evening. Latrines were described as primitive, "dispiriting" places, although any indoor plumbing was a luxury to many enrollees who had never had such amenities at home. Warm water was usually limited, meaning that only early risers enjoyed the luxury of hot showers on many mornings. At a camp near the legendary Ghost Ranch, water was so scarce that camp personnel remained "among the great unwashed" for most of the camp's first winter. Once washed and dressed, enrollees ate at military-style mess halls, sitting on benches and eating at long wooden tables. Conditions at temporary 'side' or 'fly' camps in remote districts were even more basic. With such functional facilities, the CCC could never be accused of pampering enrollees at the federal government's and taxpayers' expense.[4]

New enrollees were issued a standard set of clothes and supplies soon after they arrived in camp. When forty-two rookies arrived at the High Rolls, New Mexico, camp in early 1935, they each received clothes and supplies totaling about forty-eight pounds, including

| | |
|---|---|
| 2 face towels | 1 belt |
| 1 bath towel | 1 overseas cap |
| 1 overcoat | 2 pairs of gloves |
| 3 pairs of long underwear | 1 neck tie |
| 1 wool olive drab (O.D.) coat | 4 pairs of socks |
| 2 flannel (O.D.) shirts | 2 pairs of shoes |
| 1 pair of (O.D.) pants | 1 barracks bag |
| 1 pair of work pants | 1 pair of overshoes |
| 1 lumber jacket | |

Additional light-weight clothing was issued in the summer. Combined, the cost of clothing each enrollee equaled as low as $78.47 in 1935 and as high as $102.51 two years later when Army surplus goods had worn out and new goods had to be procured. A coincidence at New Mexico's Bandelier camp proved how old Army surplus goods were when they were inherited by the CCC. According to Gordon L. Brown, when a fellow enrollee at Bandelier was issued an army canteen in 1934, "he found his father's name, rank, and serial number inscribed on it. The same canteen had been used by his father as a soldier in World War I."[5]

Although conditions improved with time, early enrollees often faced problems with the surplus Army goods they received. Old tents were known to fall apart in bad weather, just when their shelter was needed most. Old woolen uniforms were understandably uncomfortable in New Mexico's summer heat. Over-sized clothing was uncomfortable regardless of the season. Inventory at the Hot Springs camp in 1935 revealed 155 pairs of pants with waist sizes of thirty-six inches or more, although only three of the camp's two hundred enrollees required pants this large. Shirt sizes were no better: fifty-four shirts in stock had neck sizes of seventeen inches or more, but only one fellow in the two hundred needed this large a size.[6]

Of course, ordering the correct number of sizes was nearly impossible for supply clerks who had little information about enrollee dimensions prior to their arrival in camp. The Glenwood camp's clerk faced a range of enrollees from 4'11" to 6'6" in height and from 109 to 285 pounds in weight. Adding to the problem, an officer noted that "some of the trouble could be attributed to the large gain in weight of enrollees since their enrollment." A well-fitted enrollee might soon outgrow his uniform after eating consistently well for the first time in his young life.[7]

Faced with these circumstances, enrollees were forced to make do or attempt to alter their uniforms themselves. Some simply complained. On a list of improvements that would have made the camp near Deming a better place to serve in 1937, better fitting O.D. trousers was rated near the top. In a spurious tale, a rookie enrollee was reportedly issued a size forty-four pants when he wore a size thirty. When he complained, a less-than-sympathetic officer just laughed and told the young man that his pants would shrink, given time. Displaying the best attitude under the circumstances, enrollees like Lee Roy Jones and Roy Huffman realized that while some government-issued clothes did not fit well, they often fit better than the clothes enrollees had signed up in or, in fact, ever owned prior to their lives in the CCC.[8]

Enrollee orientation to camp life continued with a series of vaccination and inoculation shots administered by camp medical personnel. The threat of smallpox and typhoid was thereby reduced, albeit with some short-range costs. Weak from poor diets and a lack of exercise before joining the CCC, some rookies fainted when getting their shots. Most also suffered from fever, nausea, and muscle soreness, making them poor candidates for normal work details. As a result, they were kept in and around camp for their first few weeks of duty. But they were hardly idle. When Jim Johnson arrived at Bandelier in 1934, he and his fellow new enrollees cleared brush and logs from nearby trails during

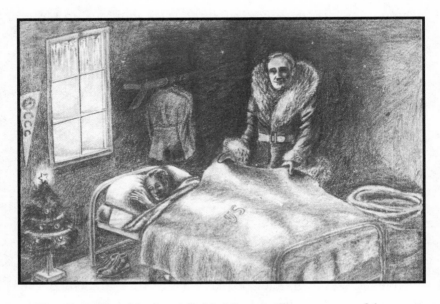

"Our Santa Claus" by Loye Smith. Most enrollees were grateful to President Roosevelt for the clothes, food, and shelter they received in exchange for their hard labor in the CCC. This cartoon appeared in *Life Magazine*.

their initial period of adjustment. Others were assigned light duty with rakes, brooms, or mops in camp. The goal, according to one camp leader, was to get enrollees used to the idea of work, while keeping them "endlessly on the go" until they were so tired they "could barely eat ... supper and fall into bed." Exhausted, they had "little or no time to think about [themselves], succumb to homesickness, and [be tempted to] go absent without leave."[9]

Despite this treatment, homesickness was the rookie enrollees' worst enemy. A small percentage of every new group could simply not adjust to CCC life. Some never even made it to camp. When fifteen enrollees from out of state stopped by train en route to Las Cruces in July 1937, one was said to have failed to resist the temptation "to see what was on the other side" of a nearby hill. He never returned from his unauthorized exploration. Other deserters seemed to compete in setting records for the shortest stay in camp. Of eleven deserters from a Carlsbad camp in September 1937, seven hadn't slept a single night in camp. The remaining four left as soon as they were issued clothing and supplies. Demicio Perea remembers several of his fellow rookies jumping a fence and heading up the highway on their first day in camp in Rodeo. Some Easterners were accused of joining the CCC for the sole purpose of securing free transportation out West. As many as two out of every five desertions occurred during the first few months in New Mexico's camps.[10]

This persistent ailment was treated with appeals to both pride and shame. Camp officers and chaplains lectured enrollees that curing homesickness by returning home and being absent without leave (AWOL) could lead to a dishonorable discharge, the CCC's ultimate punishment. Camp newspapers also reminded rookies of this fate and the black mark it would leave not only on one's reputation, but also on future job opportunities; those with dishonorable discharges could never hope for government employment again. Editorials referred to those who went AWOL by such derogatory names as the "couldn't take it boys," compared to the "real men" who remained in camp and successfully fought the "germ of indecision." Camp newspapers in Mayhill and Deming went so far as to shame deserters by listing their names in print. Cartoons depicted deserters as too dumb or foolish to even find a hill to go over. Poems with titles like "Over the Hill" and "Can't Take It" sent similar messages. Amateur poet "T.J.H." offered his thoughts on the matter in "Green Pastures":

> The ... green pastures just over the hill,
> ... attract our fancy, and ... always will.
> We can see them there so bright and so gay,
> And long for them more ... each passing day.
>
> "If we could but reach them," we sadly sigh,
> "We would be content, as the days go by."
> So we pack our grips with a very firm will;
> Say good-bye to friends, and go over the hill.
>
> But our fancy has fooled us -- true it be
> A lovely mirage is what we did see.
> That 'twas all in fancy is easily seen;
> The skies are no bluer, the grass no more green.
>
> So let us not wander and roam at will,
> Nor be forever looking "just over the hill."
> But remember that no matter where you be,
> The grass is still green in the C.C.C.

Turning from verse to drama, at least one camp produced and performed a play to discourage desertions. Meanwhile, parents were asked to write encouraging, up-beat letters to their sons, especially during their first few weeks away from home. In response, enrollees were asked to remember their parents and siblings who relied on their wages from the CCC. Going AWOL meant deserting one's family as well as deserting a worthwhile government program.[11]

New enrollees who stayed learned other lessons as they grew accustomed to life in the CCC. With sixty-five percent having never seen a doctor and eighty percent having never visited a dentist, health issues were stressed from the outset. Camp doctors taught personal hygiene at camp meetings, in camp newspaper columns, and by personal counseling. The danger of venereal disease was emphasized in a state where the incidence of VD was high, but medical treatment was rare; only five percent of all New Mexicans who suffered from syphilis received proper medical care. In addition to hearing lectures on VD from their first days in camp, enrollees were regularly checked for the disease and warned that contracting it could likely lead to a dishonorable discharge. These efforts met with mixed results in Southwestern camps. While it did not rank highest in incidence of VD in the CCC nationwide (a dubious distinction held by Southern camps), the Southwest (including New Mexico) was said to be "very susceptible" to this serious illness. Nationally, CCC enrollees could at least claim a better record than the men drafted in 1941, with only a third as many reported cases of VD in the CCC as in the Army.[12]

Next, new enrollees were told about educational opportunities in the Civilian Conservation Corps. By 1934 an educational advisor was assigned to each camp to offer instruction in subjects ranging from literacy to vocational skills. After providing general advice and some teaching materials, national CCC administrators left it up to each advisor to create educational programs to meet the particular needs of enrollees in his camp. This was no easy job, given the limited time enrollees had to study and the wide range of abilities and interests in each two-hundred-man camp. Conscientious advisors interviewed new enrollees and, in some cases, administered standardized tests to measure academic skills and intelligence. Seventeen new enrollees from Wagon Mound were tested in this manner when they arrived at their Abiquiu camp in early 1937. Rookies in Deming took Stanford Achievement Tests (SATs) normally required for college entry. Fifty-seven newcomers at Bandelier underwent seven and a half "grueling" hours of testing administered by Dean H.L. Ballinger of the New Mexico Normal School at Las Vegas. When the appropriateness and length of these exams were questioned, a simplified achievement test was developed and given to new enrollees in various

New Mexican camps. But while the use of long standardized tests may have been criticized as too demanding, locally designed tests could be criticized as far too simple. Sample questions from one such exam asked what the initials CCC stood for and who the first U.S. president was, with Franklin Roosevelt as one of five possible answers.[13]

New enrollees also learned about the CCC's organizational structure. They learned that there were nine CCC Corps areas, or administrative units, in the country. New Mexico was in the 8th Corps Area, along with the nearby states of Arizona, Colorado, Oklahoma, Texas, and most of Wyoming. Corps areas were further divided into districts; most New Mexico camps were included in the Albuquerque, Colorado, or El Paso districts. CCC companies reported directly to district headquarters in this chain of command. Individual camps were designated by a systematic nomenclature of letters and numbers. Letters and numbers were assigned based on the government agency that supervised a camp's work, the number of camps supervised by that agency, and the state in which the camp was located. F-1-N, for example, stood for the first U.S. Forest Service (F) camp established in New Mexico (N), while SCS-24-A stood for the twenty-fourth Soil Conservation Service (SCS) camp created in Arizona (A).[14]

CCC camps had not always been named in this exacting manner. In 1933 camps had been named to honor "soldiers, explorers, frontiersmen, settlers, statesmen, civil officials, or plain citizens" who had played "leading parts in the history or life of particular camp localities." An August 1933 letter explained the value of this early practice. According to Major H.C. Holdridge, naming camps after "outstanding individuals who had participated in significant historical developments in each locality" was meant to "stimulate local pride" and help establish amicable camp ties to nearby communities. As with military forts named after military heroes, using famous names would hopefully create an esprit de corps within the camps as well. Several New Mexico camps were therefore named after Spanish explorers and conquerors, such as Francisco Coronado, Juan de Oñate, and Don Diego de Vargas.

Other camps were named after heroes of the U.S. territorial period, including Kit Carson, General Stephen W. Kearny, and Governor Lew Wallace of Lincoln County War fame. Even Republican leaders were honored in an agency run by a Democratic administration: Camp Stephen B. Elkins was named after the territory's Republican Congressional Delegate of the 1870s, while Camp Solomon Luna was named after the Republican kingpin at New Mexico's constitutional convention of 1910. Although Major Holdridge reported that the purpose for naming camps after heroes "appear[ed] to have been achieved" by mid-1933, the use of these names soon declined in favor of letters and numbers. A preference for letters and numbers may well have resulted from either the New Deal's affinity for abbreviations or the CCC's aversion to camp names that sounded too much like the names of military forts.[15]

New enrollees quickly learned the names and ranks of their camp commander and his staff. In addition to the camp commander (usually a captain), each camp was assigned a second in command (usually a lieutenant) plus an educational advisor, a chaplain, and a doctor (usually civilians). Enrollees with good leadership skills were designated as Leaders, roughly equivalent to noncommissioned officers in more military settings. Civilian LEMs and work supervisors topped the chain of command at daily work sites.[16]

While all officers were important to the operation of an efficient camp, enrollees agreed that having a well-respected camp commander was most essential. A military publication of 1935 summarized the camp commander's duties:

> The [CCC] company commander will exercise the normal functions of the company commander in the Army, omitting only that of military training, and will temper all his actions to conform to the civilian status of the enrollee. He will command the work camp, and in all matters relating to health sanitation, discipline, company administration, supply, education, and welfare will have final decisions within the camp.

These duties were large and difficult, especially given the "civilian status of the enrollee." Rather than command respect based on rank alone, as in the regular military, officers had to individually win the respect and obedience of their civilian charges. As captains like Charles W. Miller knew, the best way to earn such respect was to "make fair decisions, set a good example, and demonstrate understanding by relating to [your] men and their problems." With few exceptions, commanders learned these critical leadership skills, often applying them not only in the CCC, but also in the world war that followed.[17]

Hard hit by the Depression themselves, many camp officers were glad to secure work in the CCC. Stewart Henry Robeson, for example, had graduated from New Mexico A&M in 1925 with a degree in Civil Engineering, while also serving in the Reserve Officer Training Corps (ROTC). Securing a job with the Southern Pacific Railroad after his graduation from college, he worked until the Depression began and many men were laid off. Robeson's co-worker and friend, Rockwell 'Rocks' Davis was one of those who lost his railroad job, despite the fact that he was married and had twin infant sons. Still single, Robeson offered to change places with Davis so Davis could continue to support his growing family. Now unemployed, Robeson entered the Army as a second lieutenant and was assigned to duty in several CCC camps of the Southwest, including in New Mexico. Robeson's unselfish act helped save a family, while leading him to a productive career in conservation that lasted long after his days in the CCC were through.[18]

With good officers to guide them, enrollees soon learned CCC rules and regulations. Reflecting military rules and regulations, the CCC expected enrollees to obey orders, pass inspections, appear at reveille, work hard, and be in bed by curfew. More negatively, enrollees were not allowed to miss work trucks, switch work crews, confiscate supplies, go AWOL, drink hard liquor, gamble, or entertain "unauthorized female companions" in camp. Penalties for breaking these and other infractions were spelled out, although company commanders enjoyed a great deal of latitude in enforcing camp rules and meting out appropriate punishments.[19]

Most punishments were bothersome, but mild. Depending on the nature of one's crime, an enrollee could face extra duty (usually in the camp kitchen or latrine), pay small fines (not to exceed three dollars a month), or be sentenced to confinement in camp (normally on weekends). K.P. (kitchen police) duty was so dreaded that it became the subject of several poems and songs, including "The Call of the K.P."

> I used to like the old CC,
> But now they have me on K.P.
> and every time I turn around
> I'm sure to hear that doleful sound --
> K.P.! K.P.! K.P.![20]

Punishment was more strenuous in some camps than in others. Bennie Casaus remembers a large pile of coal that had to be moved from one site to another as a form of punishment at his camp near Mountainair. Other commanders required the guilty to dig a four- foot by four-foot by four-foot hole and, once dug, fill it in again. Without military-style brigs in camp, CCC officers were known to let troublemakers roost in local jails overnight when arrested for minor offenses in town; commanders or their designated assistants typically bailed out offenders the following morning. A commander's greatest form of punishment was, of course, a dishonorable discharge, reserved for the most serious grievances, including desertions and refusal to work. The mere threat of such a discharge, with all the stigma that accompanied it, was usually enough to keep order in most camps. But with little more than the threat of a discharge to rely on, there was little discipline "except what you made enrollees *think* you had," according to former commander Leon Ullrich. Civil authorities had no such problem when enrollees were charged with breaking laws away from camp. In the few cases involving more serious crimes committed by enrollees in nearby towns, local judges imposed penalties ranging from exile from New Mexico in one instance to forced enlistment in the Army in another.[21]

This, then, was the official side of orientation in the CCC. Unofficially, enrollees indulged in an orientation of their own in the form of hazing. But the extent of hazing was surprisingly limited and usually harmless. Initiation rites like running the gauntlet or painting private parts may have been typical in other states, but not in New Mexico where tamer pranks prevailed. Here rookies were routinely assigned benign tasks like watering the flag pole or retrieving mythical items like reveille oil, sky hooks, and pie stretchers. Newcomers were also susceptible to mess hall tricks; sugar cups filled with salt ruined many a rookie's morning cup of coffee.[22]

Wild and domestic animals were sometimes used to help break-in new enrollees. At the Jornada camp (F-27-N), a green enrollee was assigned an innocent looking horse, although this steed "had the reputation of being able to 'unload his pack' if things were not just right." When the naive enrollee mounted the horse and hit its ribs with his heels, "immediate action followed." The wild beast snorted and "soared to dizzy[ing] heights." After three "such gyrations," the boy grabbed for the saddle horn, but was unceremoniously thrown to "mother earth."[23]

Their first few weeks behind them, most enrollees settled into camp life successfully. Everett Higgins and Leslie Clark, at Camp Stephen B. Elkins (F-16-N) in the Sacramento River Valley, were typical. Reporting on their early experience in the CCC for their hometown newspaper in Farmington, Higgins and Clark described their long journey from home to camp via Gallup, Albuquerque, El Paso, and Alamogordo. The last leg of the trip, a "beautiful ride" through the mountains in an Army truck, brought them into camp about 7:00 p.m. Exhausted after two nights without sleep, they ate dinner from a mess kit and went to bed. The next day, they were issued uniforms and supplies. "Our clothing is good," the enrollees noted, "altho [sic] some of it is large." Higgins and Clark seemed far more impressed by their natural surroundings ("the deer come right into camp") than with camp food, which was rated only "fair."[24]

Some fellows had a harder time adjusting to the CCC than others, according to the *Farmington Times-Hustler's* novice reporters, because "they are not used to [the] hardships of camp life." Even Higgins and Clark showed a tinge of homesickness, admitting that "we look forward [to] the news from home every week." Otherwise, the pair seemed well oriented and prepared for the six months to come. Their attitude clearly reflected the Corps's apt slogan: "we can take it." With few exceptions, most did.[25]

## Endnotes - Chapter 4

[1]  Across the U.S., 211 special trains transported enrollees to camps during the first three months of the CCC's history. Smith, "Role of the Army," 6; *Santa Fe New Mexican*, January 9, 1934. Early enrollees were often sent to nearby military forts for orientation before being assigned to their first CCC camps. Youths from New Mexico usually went to Ft. Bliss, Texas. Leon Blake interview by Cheryl Foote, September 29, 1988, included in Cheryl Foote to the author, Albuquerque, n.d.; Otis *et al.*, *Forest Service and the CCC*, 29. A small percentage of New Mexicans were sent to out-of-state camps, including in Arizona. Later stories of rookie travel to distant camps were much the same as in 1933. See, for example, Demicio Perea interview, August 20, 1998; *Ft. Sumner Bugler*, January 1941.

[2]  Salmond, *CCC*, 135-6; Draves, *Builder*, 59; Kenneth Holland and Frank E. Hill, *Youth in the CCC* (Washington, D.C.: American Council on Education, 1942): 36-7; Robert H. True to the author, n.p., June 13, 1991; *The History of Luna County, New Mexico*, Supplement #1 (Deming: Luna County Historical Society, 1981): 100; Otis *et al.*, *Forest Service and the CCC*, 71-3.

[3]  *Farmington Times-Hustler,* June 30 and August 11, 1933; *Luna County History*, 100.

[4]  Harry Kemp interview, March 13, 1991; Ray Dawson interview, May 14, 1991; Lee F. Sanders Memoirs included in Lee F. Sanders to the author, Bloomfield, New Mexico, October 3, 1996 (hereafter

cited as Sanders Memoirs); James R. Johnson interview, OHPB; *Happy Days*, September 16, 1933; Octavia R. Bassett, "Health and Culture in the CCC Camps" (Unpublished M.A. thesis, George Washington University, 1938): 32; Laura Soulliere Harrison, Randall Copeland, and Roger Buck, *Historic Structure Report: Bandelier National Monument, New Mexico* (Denver: National Park Service, 1988): 15; Otis *et al.*, *Forest Service and the CCC*, 8, 29-31, 75-80; Arthur Newton Pack, *We Called It Ghost Ranch* (Abiquiu: Ghost Ranch Conference Center, 1966): 34.

[5]  *Fresnal Ranger*, January 11, 1935; Carl O. Walker interview, January 25, 1997; *Forest Pioneer*, October 1938; Gordon L. Brown interview, OHPB; *Santa Fe New Mexican*, June 7, 1933. New uniforms designed for the CCC were introduced and distributed in 1938. Salmond, *CCC,* 137-38.

[6]  Richardson, "State Park System," 255; Camp Inspection Report, Redrock, September 1935, CCC, NA.

[7]  Newsclipping, October 13, 1934, CCC, NA; Camp Inspection Report, Sandia Peak, July 30, 1937, CCC, NA.

[8]  *Mirager*, January 1937; *Mal Pais*, April 1937; Lee Roy Jones interview, May 14, 1991; Huffman interview.

[9]  *Kangarowl*, May 4, 1935; Jim Johnson interview, October 31, 1992; Ermentrout, *Forgotten Men*, 84.

[10]  *Organ Echoes*, July 31, 1937; Camp Inspection Report, Carlsbad, September 21, 1937, CCC, NA; Perea interview; *Civilian Conservation Corps: Official Annual, 1936, Albuquerque District, 8th Corps Area* (n.p.: Direct Advertising Company, 1936): 51; Otis *et al.*, *Forest Service and the CCC,* 171.

[11]  Johnson and Platt L. Welker interviews, OHPB; *Gila Monster*, July 1936; *Dark Canyon Avalanche*, February 15, 1937; *Camp Chatter*, April 1937; *Pink Pebble Periodical*, October 4, 1935, and January 15, 1938; *Mayhill Lookout*, February 22, 1937; *Mirager,* July 1936 and June 1937; *Lonely Pennsylvanian*, March 1940.

[12]  Lyle Saunders, *A Guide to Materials Bearing on Cultural Relations in New Mexico* (Albuquerque: University of New Mexico Press, 1944): 37-8; *Albuquerque Journal*, July 19, 1934; *Organ Echoes*, May 31, 1937; Camp Inspection Report, Mountainair, October 8, 1935, CCC, NA; Fernando Reta interview, October 18, 1991; Eric Gorham, "The Ambiguous Practices of the Civilian Conservation Corps," *Social History*, 17 (May 1992): 242.

[13]  Bryant, "Education," 62, 102; *Ghost Talks*, January 1937; *Mirager*, April 1937; *Los Frijoles,* April 1937; Rio Arriba

Sub-District Educational Advisors Association, Minutes of Meeting, Española, New Mexico, August 25, 1936, Alfred M. Bergere Papers, NMSRCA (hereafter cited as Educational Advisors Association Minutes).

[14] Leslie Alexander Lacy, *The Soil Soldiers: The Civilian Conservation Corps in the Great Depression* (Radnor, Pennsylvania: Chilton Book Company, 1976): 27; Booth, "CCC in Arizona," 24n. See Appendix A for camp designations and locations in New Mexico.

[15] Col. A.B. Cox, General Orders #8, Civilian Conservation Corps Headquarters, Arizona-New Mexico District, Ft. Bliss, August 14, 1933; Col. A.B. Cox, Memorandum #115, CCC Headquarters, Arizona-New Mexico District, Ft. Bliss, August 16, 1933; Major H.C. Holdridge to Arthur Seligman, Ft. Bliss, August 18, 1933, Governor Seligman Papers, NMSRCA.

[16] Leon Ullrich interview, July 25, 1984; Julian Shish interview, July 2, 1999; Perea interview; Graf, "Peace-Time Achievement," 12. Regular Army officers commanded camps until February 1934, reserve officers to December 1939, and civilians to July 1942. Smith, "Role of the Army," 7. Enrollee leaders received from six to fifteen dollars in additional pay per month.

[17] Graf, "Peace-Time Achievement," 10; John D. Guthrie, "The CCC and American Conservation," *Scientific Monthly*, 57 (November 1943): 412; Huffman interview.

[18] Eva Jane Matson, "A CCC Romance" included in Eva Jane Matson to the author, Las Cruces, August 5, 1998.

[19] Ermentrout, *Forgotten Men*, 87; *Organ Echoes*, April 1937.

[20] Perea interview; *Animas Announcer,* February 20, 1936.

[21] Casaus interview; Dawson interview; Ullrich interview; W.W. Westwood interview, May 28, 1996; *Albuquerque Journal*, August 16, 1936.

[22] Draves, *Builder*, 29-30; Baldridge, "Nine Years," 248, 318; *Lonely Pennsylvanian*, October 1939; David Gonzalez interview, May 23, 1996; Green interview; Hernandez interview; Jones interview; Hilario Baca interview, June 5, 1993; *Camp Cactus Carrier*, October 1939.

[23] Fred N. Ares, *The Jornada Experimental Range: An Epoch in the Era of Southwestern Range Management* (Denver: Society for Range Management, 1974): 44-5.

[24] *Farmington Times-Hustler*, June 30, 1933.

[25] *Farmington Times-Hustler*, August 11, 1933.

CCC enrollees departing for work in the forest.
*Courtesy:  U.S. Forest Service, Regional Office, Albuquerque, New Mexico.*

# CHAPTER 5

## Work Days

Civilian Conservation Corps leaders filled enrollee schedules with activities from dawn to dusk. Each activity was designed to teach young men important lessons for their future roles as productive workers and responsible adults. Enrollees learned throughout the day, but especially during their hours at work.

Punctuality was taught from the first moments of an enrollee's day. Bugles (or, more often, whistles) woke enrollees at 6:00 a.m. sharp. Enrollees had little time to wash, dress, and make their beds in neat military style. At 6:30 a.m. they fell in for roll call, flag raising ceremonies, and calisthenics. Breakfast followed in the mess hall. The morning meal usually included a variety of foods, from hot or cold cereal to fruits and drinks, especially coffee. Hardly gourmet fare, camp food was at least well-balanced and nourishing, according to dietary standards of the 1930s. Meals, wrote CCC director Robert Fechner, were meant to be "wholesome, palatable and of the variety that sticks to your ribs."[1]

With breakfast completed, it was time to fall in and prepare to leave for work. Following sick call, most enrollees boarded Army trucks for departure to work sites by 7:45 a.m. By 8:00 a.m. the majority were dispatched for the day, leaving only enrollees assigned to camp jobs, such as company clerks and cooks, behind. Punctuality was therefore observed from the start of each

Enrollees assisting in a soil composition study on the Jornada
Experimental Range, April 21, 1936. *Courtesy of the Photo Archives,
College of Agriculture, New Mexico State University.*

day in order to synchronize enrollees to industrial time. As one observer put it, if enrollees were to be trained as modern workers, their schedules in the wood and in camp would have to mimic factory time as closely as possible.[2]

Once delivered to their work sites, enrollees learned to follow directions and work cooperatively. Supervised by foremen from one of several state or federal agencies (depending on the nature of each project), corpsmen worked at over a hundred labor-intensive tasks in New Mexico. These tasks can be divided into six major categories:

- the conservation of threatened resources;
- the development or restoration of natural resources;
- the construction of rural infrastructure;
- the building of recreational areas;
- the preservation of Southwest history and culture;
- the control of certain animals and the preservation of others.[3]

CCC enrollees worked to conserve natural resources by protecting existing resources, including valuable trees and soil. Under the leadership of U.S. Forest Service supervisors, they attempted to save trees threatened by disease. At Bandelier enrollees sprayed, cut down, or burned ponderosa pines infected with pine bark beetles. To conserve soil, enrollees labored to stop soil erosion by building 799,646 check dams in New Mexico. Constructed with rocks and brush, check dams varied in size from as small as two cubic yards to as large as fifteen cubic yards in the Gila Wilderness. More permanent dams were built as well. The Spring Canyon dam in southern New Mexico was said to be the largest Soil Conservation Service structure of its kind in the United States. Not many miles distant, enrollees on the Jornada Experimental Range assisted scientists in the analysis of chemical and organic soil composition from 1933 to 1936.[4]

Enrollees also worked to either develop or replace natural resources. Reforestation headed the list of these important projects. Nationally, the CCC planted approximately two billion trees, or

*above*: Enrollees building concrete picnic table, April 20, 1934.
*Courtesy: Photo Archives, College of Agriculture, New Mexico
State University.    below:* Enrollee-built stone water tower at
Bottomless Lakes State Park east of Roswell, New Mexico. *Courtesy: The Author.*

twelve for every American citizen. Of these two billion, 5,968,200 were planted in New Mexico, for an average of fourteen trees for every citizen of the state. Andres Hernandez recalls the careful, but tedious method used in planting trees. Working in three-men teams, one enrollee dug a small hole in the ground, while another planted a small tree, taken from a sack he carried. A third enrollee finished the job by filling in dirt around the new growth. Employing this method, enrollee teams planted hundreds of trees per day.[5]

Next, CCC labor vastly improved access to remote regions of New Mexico. By September 1941, the CCC had constructed just less than five thousand miles of truck trails and roads in the state, mostly in isolated, formerly unaccessible locations. In the Lincoln National Forest, for example, "old-timers ... always declared that a road would never be built off the West Rim of the Sacramento [Mountains] down into Rincon." But after three months of intensive labor by enrollees from camp F-16-N, a road was completed; even automobiles could now pass "easily over ... country formerly considered 'hell on a horse.'"[6]

Far to the north, access to Frijoles Canyon had been limited to a steep trail until the 1930s. "One look at the trail turned away many who peered over the edge of the canyon and decided that the climb was too difficult. Neither the beauty of the canyon nor the small hotel at its base could draw the less hardy visitor." Those who ventured below had to call from a phone at the canyon's rim so a wrangler could ride up the trail, load their belongings on a tram, and bring the visitors down by horseback. The only motorized vehicle in the canyon was a truck that had been taken apart, lowered piece by piece with a pulley, and reconstructed on the canyon floor. Despite considerable opposition by those who feared an invasion of tourists and damage to natural surroundings, the CCC constructed a twelve-foot wide road into the canyon soon after a CCC camp was established in the fall of 1933. The first car was driven down the long-awaited road on December 9, 1933.[7]

In another canyon project, CCC enrollees built the famous Catwalk along Whitewater Canyon southwest of Mogollon. Originally a water pipeline leading to a mining camp below, the

*above*: A period postcard showing the improved walkways to the entrance of Carlsbad Caverns which were built with the help of CCC enrollees. *Courtesy: Jay Leck, Carlsbad, New Mexico.*    *below*: Kiwanis Cabin on Sandia Crest, Cibola National Forest overlooking Albuquerque was another enrollee-built project. *Courtesy: Fred Lechman.*

CCC converted the Catwalk into a narrow wooden walk anchored with cables to high rock walls. Impressed by the CCC's work, a long-time resident of the region wrote that it was thrilling for hikers and fishermen to "make a trip over that walk on a warm summer day with the gin-clear water murmuring among the rocks [some twenty-five feet] below."[8]

CCC projects opened recreational areas in other parts of New Mexico as well. At White Sands, 103 enrollees worked on early access roads and facilities, leading to the national monument's opening in April 1934. Enrollees also helped build some of the first ski runs in the state, including those in the Sandia Mountains, at El Rito, and at Hyde Memorial State Park; once in operation, a seven hundred foot long tow rope pulled skiers up the slope at Hyde Park for a towing charge of fifty cents a day. Picnic areas were developed throughout the Sandias for summer recreation. By 1936 a visitor to the Sandias counted twenty CCC-built cement tables and benches in Juan Tabo Canyon alone. "One is built atop a huge boulder; another around the trunk of a tree; still another hangs by chains from a rocky wall ... . Each table is built at some point which affords a bit of scenery or shade." In 1935 and 1936, thirty drinking fountains, thirty-seven latrines (or 'comfort stations'), and 260 signs were built for the added convenience of visitors to the Sandias.[9]

New Mexico's state park system owes its creation to the CCC. In August 1933, Governor Arthur Seligman organized the first New Mexico State Park Commission specifically "to take advantage of federal relief funds and Civilian Conservation Corps labor." Responding to Seligman's public appeal, land and money were donated for the construction of New Mexico's first four state parks. In Santa Fe, the state acquired and the CCC built recreational sites along the Santa Fe River in the downtown section of town. At Bottomless Lakes near Roswell, the CCC constructed a stone tower and shoreline facilities from 1934 to 1935. At Hyde Memorial State Park (on land donated by the widow of well-known Santa Fe naturalist Benjamin Babbitt Hyde), the CCC not only finished a ski run, but also built recreational areas and a

*above*: This is one of seventeen CCC-built cabins at the Elephant Butte marina. Courtesy: *The Author.*    *below*: 1935 New Deal painting by Odon Hullendremer featuring CCC enrollees at work. The painting is located at the Carrie Tingley Hospital, Albuquerque, New Mexico. *Photo courtesy: Kris White.*

large stone structure called The Lodge. At Portales, Eastern New Mexico State Park was created with water wells, adobe buildings, and a large bathhouse adjoining a small lake. Only a forty-one inch rainfall (several times the seasonal average) caused the roofs to cave in and the adobe walls to melt on CCC park structures in 1941.[10]

On another front, enrollees improved facilities at Carlsbad Caverns. Among other projects, the CCC constructed a five-hundred space parking lot and flagstone walks leading to the caverns' entrance. Inside the caverns, James Rivers recalls helping to build concrete steps in the cold, damp interior. After pouring wet concrete for hours, Rivers and his fellow enrollees had to be lifted out of the caverns in large guano buckets so they would not disturb the drying cement. In addition, electrical wiring was installed for electric lamps because old gas lamps had begun to discolor cavern walls. Amadeo Quintana remembers helping to build new trails as well as the first elevator down into the caverns. Working on a swing shift after tourists had left each day, Quintana also helped build the caverns' large, much-appreciated underground lunchroom.[11]

CCC building skills were employed in the construction of whole buildings, especially for recreational purposes. In the Sandia Mountains, enrollees based at F-8-N hauled blocks of local limestone to the highest point in the mountain range to build a 384-square-foot structure. Finished in 1936, the Kiwanis Cabin still provides hikers a breathtaking view of Albuquerque and its western horizon from Sandia Crest, elevation 10,400 feet. The Mt. Withington Observatory, Lookout Cabin at Grassy Mountain, and the high stone tower overlooking Bottomless Lakes State Park were built in a similar fashion. In Tucumcari, workers from SP-7-N built a bathhouse and pool at the western edge of town. Charles Clugston remembers that flagstone for the bathhouse was carried down from Tucumcari Mountain in seemingly endless truck loads. Enrollees dug the pool with picks and shovels, mixing cement in a mixer no larger than a washing machine.[12]

*above*:  The National Park Service's Southwest Regional Headquarters under construction in Santa Fe, New Mexico.  *Courtesy: Nat'l Park Service, Southwest Reg. Office, Santa Fe, New Mexico.*     *below*:  The Headquarters as it looks today.  *Courtesy:  The Author.*

At Elephant Butte, enrollees built various facilities along the shoreline, including a bathhouse, a concession stand, and at least sixteen small cabins unpretentiously marked with the letters 'CCC' on their exterior walls. Access roads were widened and the shoreline was stabilized for the launching of recreational boats. Elephant Butte soon became known as a "mecca for fishermen and campers," according to a 1935 headline in the *El Paso Times*.[13]

At Bandelier, enrollees built no fewer than thirty-one structures, ranging from an impressive visitors center to an administrative headquarters. Enrollees used the road they had earlier constructed into Frijoles Canyon to transport equipment, material, and supplies for the building of a new lodge to replace a far humbler one operated by George and Evelyn Frey since 1925. The new lodge included guest rooms, cabins, a hotel lobby, a curio shop, a dining room and kitchen, a manager's home, and an employees dormitory. Walls were built with volcano-formed rocks blasted from a local rock quarry, painstakingly chiseled to the correct sizes and shapes, and transported to the construction site down the canyon road. Over seven thousand cubic yards of stone and 51,150 lineal feet of aspen (for ceiling construction alone) were used in this extensive project. With the use of traditional architecture and the planting of native vegetation, the Park Service achieved one of its most important goals at Bandelier: to simply "make the development look as if it belonged there."[14]

In Santa Fe, the National Park Service's massive Southwest Regional Headquarters Building was built with mostly CCC labor from March 1937 to June 1939. Enrollees from SP-1-N, including Benito Montoya and Rupert Lopez, used no less than 280,000 adobe bricks to finish this 24,000-square-foot structure, said to be the largest adobe office building in the United States. Ponderosa pine for its *vigas* (beams) came from the mountains northeast of Santa Fe; flagstone was trucked in from a site near Pecos. Hundreds attended the building's grand opening on August 4, 1939. Corpsmen not only helped visitors park their cars, but also showcased their handiwork by leading tours throughout the

*above*: Southwestern style furniture built by enrollees under the supervision of local experts. This durable furniture remained in service for many years at the Bandelier National Monument's visitors center headquarters. *Courtesy: Nat'l Park Service, Southwest Regional Office, Santa Fe, New Mexico.*    *below*: CCC-built bench still in use at the Southwest Regional Headquarters in Santa Fe. *Courtesy: The Author.*

building and its surrounding land in the foothills of the Sangre de Cristo Mountains.[15]

Regardless of their locations in New Mexico, CCC buildings were known for their quality workmanship and Pueblo Revival Style of architecture. Designed with the consultation of artists like Carlos Vierra of Santa Fe, most buildings boasted indigenous features, including thick adobe walls, high ceilings, *vigas*, lintels, *nichos* (wall recesses), *bancos* (wall benches), kiva fireplaces, deep window sills, long *portals*, and central courtyards. Adding to the beauty of each structure, enrollees built highly decorative Spanish-style wooden cabinets, furniture, and tin fixtures under the watchful eyes of craftsmen hired as Local Experienced Men. According to George Collins of the Park Service, "We'd train boys through having journeymen bricklayers, carpenters, and mechanics ... on the payroll;" most LEMs "liked working with the young boys," complementing them as "very good to have as workers." At Bandelier, former enrollee Jim Fulton learned the fine art of cabinetmaking by building Spanish-style cabinets. At the National Park Service's regional headquarters in Santa Fe, enrollees built furniture and assembled light fixtures crafted by local tinsmith Eddie Delgado. No detail was too small. Enrollees even used small cones from sequoia trees in California's Sequoia National Park as models for the iron doorknobs at the National Park Service headquarters. Building with meticulous care, it is no wonder that enrollees took great satisfaction in their finished products. Their work reflected not only years of hard labor, but pride in Southwestern culture and style. Most CCC buildings remain standing today. A dozen CCC buildings and work projects are listed on the National Register of Historic Places and the New Mexico State Register of Cultural Properties as crowning proof of their lasting value to New Mexico and the nation.[16]

Enrollee pride in Southwestern culture was reflected in CCC projects throughout New Mexico. Many enrollees, for example, helped in the excavation and restoration of at least three Franciscan missions from New Mexico's Spanish colonial past: Quarai, Abo, and Jemez.

Starting in 1934 under the supervision of archaeologists A.G. Ely and Wesly Hunt of the University of New Mexico and the School of American Research, enrollees spent several summers at the Quarai mission ruins northwest of Mountainair. Leon Blake remembers that the ruins were almost totally buried when he and his fellow enrollees began work at the site. Digging six feet down through dirt and rubble, they uncovered many interesting finds, including two of a highly mysterious nature. The first was a sub-terranean square pit in the middle of the mission's courtyard. Experts have since debated whether this unusual pit was once an Indian kiva, or religious center. If so, what was it doing in the middle of a Catholic mission? And why was this kiva square when most others in New Mexico were round?[17]

A second mysterious discovery followed on the heels of the first. Digging below the church floor, enrollees unearthed forty-one burial sites, including the skeleton of an adult buried with a child's skeleton wrapped in its arms. Awed by this scene, but lacking the skills of modern forensic scientists, enrollees and their super-visors could only speculate about the tragedy that had caused an adult and child to die together and share a common grave. Did the pair succumb to natural causes, such as disease, or did they die violently in a nomadic Indian raid or pueblo revolt?[18]

When not speculating about such intriguing discoveries, enrollees helped to fence the perimeter, install a cattle guard, and build recreational facilities for visitors to Quarai. But their most valuable work was in restoration, as acknowledged by archeolo-gist Ely when he asserted that "had the repair been delayed for many more years, the massive walls of the church would have collapsed." The same essential work was completed by CCC crews at nearby Abo.[19]

Further north, enrollees assisted archaeologists from the University of New Mexico at the Franciscan mission ruins in Jemez. Their hours of hard labor were occasionally rewarded with finds that matched those at Quarai for interest and intrigue. At Jemez, these discoveries included a mysterious underground shaft with an eight-foot vertical opening. Their curiosity aroused, enrollees attacked this excavation with "wild enthusiasm." Only the fear of a disastrous cave-in caused the work to be halted. Observers speculated that the shaft "may have been used as a mode of escape [for Spanish priests] during [Indian] attack or siege."[20]

Other important work was accomplished at prehistoric Indian ruins. At Bandelier, enrollees helped stabilize Indian ruins dating back hundreds of years. In a unique form of labor, workers carefully sanded wood samples to help calculate the age of cut trees by studying their ring growth. A few corpsmen also served as tour guides through the ruins, and some, including George Schneider, posed as models (representing Pueblo Indians) for a sculptor who visited Bandelier in the mid-1930s.[21]

At Chaco Canyon, enrollees worked with National Park Service personnel to prevent natural forces, like soil erosion, from harming fragile ruins. One such natural force appeared especially ominous by the late 1930s. Threatening Rock, a hundred-foot high, 150-foot long boulder, had rested precariously on a rise about ancient Pueblo Bonito for centuries. Fearing that the rock might fall on the abandoned pueblo below, Chaco Canyon's monument custodian had installed two gauges to measure possible movement. CCC enrollees checked the gauges daily.[22]

Suddenly observers noted an ominous change. The huge mass was slowly moving. Something had to be done to keep it from falling. Various options were considered. With time running out, it was decided that the enrollees would remove as much debris as possible from behind the rock in hopes of quickly stabilizing it. As their foreman recalled years later, "It was a dangerous job but the men liked the challenge and worked hard." Enrollees removed countless wheelbarrows of debris, but their progress was too slow. Not even the use of a primitive donkey engine (hastily converted from an old truck engine) could move the debris fast enough. Frequent rain storms slowed work further in December 1940. Foreman Claire J. Mueller and his enrollee workers

> watched the situation grow steadily worse. The gauges
> were indicating the [deteriorating] condition ... . And

the rain continued ... . [W]ork was [finally] stopped ...
and all  equipment removed. The fall of Threatening Rock was inevitable.[23]

Cameras set on tripods were positioned to capture the tragic
event on film. Enrollees watched and waited through the morning
of January 22, 1941. They were off at lunch when they heard a
loud noise and looked towards the rock, only to see a large cloud
of dust. When the dust finally settled, they inspected the damage
and "found that Pueblo Bonito had survived better than had been
anticipated." Navajo residents soon learned of the fall. By the
following morning, Mueller discovered that every "exposed break
of the rock had been sprinkled with corn pollen and turquoise
dust" to ward off evil spirits that might have caused additional
disaster.[24]

CCC enrollees were usually more successful in preserving
historic places and memories in New Mexico. Enrollees at the
CCC camp north of Santa Fe helped make the distinctive roadside markers that still inform travelers of historic points of interest from one end of the state to the other. The first of these rustic
markers were built by the CCC in conjunction with the New
Mexico Tourist Bureau. Thirty-five markers were erected in 1937;
another hundred were in place by 1940.

Two historical makers were eventually placed in or near Lincoln, New Mexico, center of the turbulent Lincoln County War of
1878 to 1881. Enrollees also helped convert the Lincoln County
courthouse into a museum commemorating Billy the Kid's daring
jail break and flight. One enrollee recalls that his overly enthusiastic foreman shot holes in the courthouse's interior walls to make
the scene of Billy's escape appear even more dramatic than it
actually was on April 28, 1881.[25]

Animal and insect control consumed many additional hours
of CCC labor. Porcupines, accused of destroying trees by gnaw-
ing off bark, were attacked by six-men crews; eighteen of the
culprits could be killed in a single day. Rodents were accused of

similar mischief. Kangaroo rats and gophers ate valuable range forage and dug deep burrows that became "perfect traps" for off-road vehicles and unsuspecting riders. As one range scientist said, kangaroo rats represented a serious hazard for human "life, limb, and disposition." Enrollees helped control this menace by spreading poisoned grain in the entry of rodent dens. Corpsmen walked as many as nine miles a day, distributing their fatal grain in all directions. Others set traps, capturing 738 gophers in one three-month period alone, from November 1936 to January 1937.[26]

There were, however, unexpected consequences to this labor. CCC headquarters in Washington, D.C., received regular complaints about the poisoning of animals, resulting in "very unfavorable" publicity for the CCC as a whole. On a more personal level, at least one enrollee engaged in this work wrote of a horrible dream in which he appeared in a 'Ratland' court to face charges for the "wholesale slaughter" of helpless rats near Redrock, New Mexico. Andrew Candelaria found himself surrounded by rats shouting their "ideas as to how to punish me." Their sadistic ideas differed, but "some even wanted me ... kept for food." The "little fellows" were so agitated that the presiding judge rat could not maintain order in his courtroom. Only the sound of 6:00 a.m. revelry awakened Candelaria, saving him from a terrible fate in the hands (or claws) of his small captors. Understandably, the author of "The Rat Killer's Nightmare" soon left the CCC and his lethal work on the range for a less frightening career as a college student at the School of Mines in El Paso.[27]

The human public may well have reacted more indignantly had they known how the CCC disposed of wild rabbits who were also accused of devouring valuable forage on ranches in southern New Mexico. According to experts, three wild rabbits ate as much forage as one head of cattle. Given this rate of destruction, New Mexican ranchers were happy to have the Corps' assistance in seemingly cruel roundups on the open range. Former enrollee Henry Arellanes recalls one such roundup. According to Arellanes, enrollees formed a wide circle and, moving gradually forward, drove their unsuspecting prey closer and closer to the center. Once trapped in a small space, the rabbits were unceremoniously clubbed to death. So many animals were disposed of in this manner that piles of their remains reached three feet high. While some participants, including Arellanes, were repulsed by these methods, others were not. Writing in his camp's newspaper, one enrollee described a "rabbit drive" near Deming as the "most enjoyable day" in recent memory. "Hunting" on private ranch land, the author helped force hundreds of rabbits into a confined area where they met with "plenty of opposition in the shape of rocks, pick handles and clubs of various sizes." Close to three hundred rabbits were killed in a single day's work. The ranch's grateful owner rewarded the entire CCC crew with "all the barbecue [beef we] could eat." Enrollees looked forward to another drive scheduled for the following week.[28]

Cattle ranchers in Catron County appreciated a CCC project to facilitate animal drives of a different nature, although ultimately of the same results. Work by enrollees from camp DG-42-N began in January 1936. By early 1939, enrollees had fenced off a sixty-five mile stretch of land, creating a broad passageway through which ranchers could drive their cattle to the stockyards and railhead at Magdelena. Varying in width from one to four miles, the Magdelena Stock Drive encompassed eighty thousand acres of land on the San Augustin Plains. The CCC dug wells at ten-mile intervals to provide water for trail herds traversing this dusty trail.[29]

Farmers welcomed CCC help in dealing with far smaller animals than kangaroo rats, jack rabbits, or cattle in what became known as the Grasshopper Wars of the Depression era. Already plagued by drought and terrible wind storms, the Dust Bowl region of the Great Plains faced an invasion of immeasurably destructive grasshoppers in the mid- and late 1930s. Northeastern New Mexico was among the worst hit areas. By July 1937 more than a half million acres of land in Union County alone were covered with grasshoppers, with an estimated twenty to thirty of the insects on each square foot of earth. The following year the invading insects advanced at the rate of half a mile a day along an eighty-mile battle-line in Colfax and Union Counties. Grasshoppers were so thick that they temporarily blinded drivers on rural roads. They also devoured every plant in their path; in one case 25,000 acres of grassland were destroyed in just three days. In South Dakota, grasshoppers ate clothes hanging out to dry. In Wyoming, their path of destruction made range land look "as though it had been gone over with a safety razor." But grasshoppers were hard to kill; a Dust Bowl farmer told journalist Ernie Pyle that "For every one that dies, a thousand come to his funeral." Pyle concluded that trying to control grasshoppers was "like trying to bore a hole in water."[30]

Determined to save farms and ranches in the northeast corner of his state, Governor Clyde Tingley declared war on these insect invaders. Taking command in the ensuing campaign, the governor met with hundreds of farmers and personally inspected the front line of battle. Tingley also wrote to Senator Dennis Chavez, appealing for federal aid by describing hoards of grasshoppers covering areas forty miles wide and forty miles long. The governor and the effected northeastern counties "threw all available manpower into the fray," including members of the National Guard, employees of the Works Progress Administration (WPA), and dozens of CCC enrollees. One-hundred-and-sixty enrollees were assigned to this duty in 1938. Working in two shifts, the youths shoveled tons of sawdust into trucks, hauled the sawdust to thirty-four poison mixing stations, and shoveled their heavy cargo out again. WPA workers then mixed an "efficient poison" of sawdust, bran, and arsenic. Ranchers and farmers dutifully spread the concocted poison on their fields. A reporter described the morbid scene that followed:

> The mash, when eaten by a 'hopper, kills the insect. The dead insect is eaten by his fellows, who likewise perish. This process [goes on] until the arsenic in the first grasshopper's fatal meal is so diluted as to be harmless.

The killing cycle continued until the crisis was contained. Hundreds of enrollees helped in similar campaigns each spring and summer from 1937 to 1940.[31]

This untitled sketch by an anonymous artist appeared in the *Narrative Report*, Bosque del Apache Camp, October-November-December 1940. Bosque del Apache is now home to 295 species of birds.

But it would be wrong to think that the CCC only worked to destroy animals and insects in New Mexico. As many, if not more, hours of labor were devoted to the conservation of fish and wildlife in the Southwest. Enrollees like Fred Beck helped build fish hatcheries, including one at Elephant Butte. Others stocked New Mexico's streams with fish raised in local hatcheries. Birds were also preserved in both large and small efforts. On a small scale, an enrollee wrote home about his work driving heavy road building equipment. Frank explained that one day

> there was a mother bird with her nest in a tree which had to  be cut ... for it was right in the middle of the road [we were building]. The road couldn't even be curved to go around [the tree and nest], as there was a deep ravine on the lower side. When the boys talked to [their foreman] about it, he ordered the work stopped [at] that spot. The tree was not cut, and not until the eggs were hatched and the little ones able to fly was that section of the road worked on [again].

Learning of this simple act of kindness, at least one of Frank's neighbors back home was convincingly moved by "the rightness of the CCC."[32]

Wild birds were assisted on a far more ambitious scale at La Joya and at Bosque del Apache. At La Joya, CCC crews built dikes along the Rio Grande, helped create a game reserve, and constructed an attractive stone lodge, featuring a building-long porch from which visitors could observe the ponds and wildlife below. At Bosque del Apache, a timely Congressional appropriation funded the creation of a badly needed refuge and breeding ground for migrating birds and other wildlife. Until the CCC arrived in September 1939, the area was largely swampland where only beavers, muskrats, Canada geese, and swans survived. According to Burt Long, a member of the first CCC company on the scene, "we did everything," from draining the swamp to leveling the land for the carefully planned refuge. When not occupied with these tasks, enrollees made adobe bricks for the refuge's first

Supervisors at Camp F-27-N, April 23, 1935. *l. to r. seated*: Frank Goodin, Fred Carr, Joe Wofford, W.H. Ramsey. *l. to r. standing*: C.K. Parker, ? Caron, Hal R. Cox, Gordon J. Gray, John R.J. Bradshaw, Ellis Mayfield. *Courtesy: Photo Archives, College of Agriculture, New Mexico State University.*

headquarters and built dikes to hold off floods on the Rio Grande. Largely thanks to the CCC, Bosque del Apache is now home to fifty-eight species of mammals and 295 species of birds, including its most famous seasonal residents, whooping and sandhill cranes.[33]

Enrollees labored long and hard in most circumstances. But, as with most employees, they worked particularly well under good, well-respected leadership. A supervisor's attitude about a project, and work in general, usually made the difference in enrollee work habits and eagerness to complete assigned tasks thoroughly and with pride. One case speaks volumes. While 'Si' Porter had nothing but praise for supervisors like Charles Scott Wood of the U.S. Forest Service, he thought much less of a new foreman assigned to his fence building crew at camp F-41-N. The new foreman neglected to visit his crew's work site "and never even came back to tell us it was lunchtime ... . Pretty quick the men decided that if he didn't care about what they were doing, they didn't either. They just quit trying to do the job right." Enrollees responsible for digging fence post holes stopped digging deep enough. Those responsible for setting posts could not do so in the shallow holes; as a result, wire stretched between the posts sagged terribly. The whole project had become a fiasco. The situation only improved when better supervision was provided. And what was true of a single fence building crew was also true of whole projects: CCC inspectors believed that the consistently high quality of work at Bandelier was largely due "to the enthusiasm displayed by the superintendent and his foremen, who would roll up their sleeves, 'don overalls and perform both skilled and unskilled labor along with the enrollees.'" Young men learned much about pride in work and supervisory skills from the pride in work and attention to detail displayed by their leaders.[34]

Regardless of the work assigned, enrollees were normally vigilant about safety on the job. This was not always easy, especially when handling dangerous tools like axes and sledge hammers, and dangerous materials, especially explosives. Enrollee

Jesus Cobos was, for example, seriously injured when he was hit by a flying piece of steel from a drillbar he was operating near Carlsbad. The steel struck Cobos on his left arm, severing an artery and causing the loss of much blood. Rushed to the Army hospital at Ft. Bliss, Cobos was fortunate to survive this ordeal. Twenty-two-year-old Blaine Porter was not as lucky. Working with dynamite near Los Alamos, Porter was killed in an accidental explosion on August 25, 1933, making him probably the first CCC fatality in New Mexico.[35]

Even experts were not immune to accidents. Former enrollee Gordon Brown recalls a Local Experienced Man who set a fuse in a canyon wall during the construction of the narrow road into Frijoles Canyon. When his dynamite did not explode in the expected time, the LEM went to examine the troublesome fuse. In Brown's words, "Just as he got to it, it blew up." The man died instantly. Orvil Hamlin, a forty-four-year-old LEM, was also killed when a box of one hundred dynamite caps accidently exploded in southwestern New Mexico in October 1933.[36]

Natural forces took their toll as well. Hilario Baca remembers a fellow enrollee who was spreading poison in gopher holes when a terrible hail storm blew in. Unable to find safe shelter, the enrollee from San Antonio, Texas, was struck and killed by a bolt of lightning. Falling objects, from rocks to trees, made work sites additionally hazardous and potentially fatal.[37]

While the CCC did much to preserve wildlife in New Mexico, animals sometimes turned on enrollees with potentially disastrous results. Working near his Española camp in 1936, enrollee Adam Garcia came face to face with a large bull. Garcia ran as fast as he could and reportedly jumped over an eight-foot fence "without touching it," easily qualifying him for the next Olympics, according to the editor of his camp's newspaper. Other confrontations with dangerous animals were usually not as comical, especially when they involved poisonous snakes and insects. While native New Mexicans normally displayed a healthy respect for such creatures, leaders cautioned all enrollees to wear work gloves to protect them against rattlesnakes and black widow spider bites in particular.[38]

Despite such warnings, Tomás Brown had stripped to his waist while working in the hot summer sun when he discovered a centipede crawling up his exposed arm. Brown's fellow enrollees looked on in horror, convinced that a centipede's poison was fatal. Most believed that only the amputation of an infected limb could save a victim before the centipede's poison spread to the rest of his body. With no medical help available, Brown's fatalistic colleagues made bets on how quickly he would die. His survival helped dispel erroneous notions about centipedes, but disappointed those who had hoped to profit from Brown's expected demise.[39]

David Gonzalez also lived to tell of his encounter with potentially dangerous animals at a CCC work site. Gonzalez and his fellow workers were laying poison for kangaroo rats near Engle, New Mexico, when they came across between twenty and thirty rattlesnakes. Nonplused, the enrollees killed the dangerous reptiles, piled them in a small area, and lit a fire with dry wood and cacti thrown over their remains. Some sixty years later, Gonzalez still remembers the eery sound of burning snakes, wood, and cacti in a most unusual funeral pyre.[40]

But of all the dangers faced by enrollees, accidents involving cars, trucks, and heavy equipment were the most often fatal, accounting for almost fifty percent of all deaths in the CCC nationwide. In fact, with young, often inexperienced drivers transporting truck loads of enrollees over rough country roads, the trip to and from work sites was one of the most hazardous parts of an enrollee's day. Fortunately, most drivers drove thousands of miles without incident. This was certainly true of Woodrow 'Buffalo' Adams of the Corona camp who drove 135,000 miles in a two-year period without a single mishap.[41]

'Buffalo' Adams proved to be as brave as he was competent. In May 1937, while working on a water channel project in Devil's Canyon, Adams rescued a fellow enrollee whose legs were caught in the tread of a moving bulldozer that had gone out of control. The Clayton, New Mexico, native saved Carl Sander's life, while risking his own, by jumping onto the bulldozer's driver's

*above*:  Redrock camp enrollees with a tractor. Woodrow 'Buffalo' Adams brought a similar tractor under control, saving a fellow enrollee's life in May 1937. *Courtesy:  Stewart Henry Robeson Papers, Rio Grande Historical Collection, New Mexico State University Las Cruces, NM.    below*:  Enrollee working on a CCC truck, March 8, 1937. *Courtesy:  Photo Archives, College of Agriculture, New Mexico State University.*

seat and bringing the moving machine to a stop. Though injured, Adams refused medical attention for himself until he made sure that Sanders was safely en route to the hospital. Sanders lost his left leg, but survived the ordeal. Adams's bravery was recognized nationally when he was awarded the CCC's Certificate of Valor, given "for acts of heroism beyond the regular call of duty." Adams was one of only five winners of this CCC equivalent to the Medal of Honor in 1937.[42]

The CCC inspired enthusiasm for safe practices in a number of ways. As a new crop of enrollees was told when they arrived at their Carlsbad camp in April 1937, CCC work was meant to be pleasant and productive, but it was to be completed "with every possible precaution taken to insure safety." Mandatory safety and first aid training meetings were held as often as once a week in some camps. One camp leader went so far as to film his enrollees at work to demonstrate "the right and wrong way of doing things" like lifting heavy rocks and loading trucks. Enrollees were said to be more safety conscious after seeing themselves on film, if only because "Mr. Lindsay may be hiding nearby with his camera." At F-52-N safety tips were broadcast over the camp's public address system, followed by music and other entertainment. Safety lessons were also taught at work sites where demonstrations were easier to perform and comprehend. According to superintendent Oliver C. Payne at the Bosque del Apache camp, on-site demonstrations were particularly effective "since our Company is mainly composed of youths of Spanish origin, many of whom do not understand much English." Safety was similarly encouraged in the columns and editorials of camp newspapers. The *Lincoln Lookout* included a series of safety poems, with accompanying cartoons, in mid-1937. Other newspapers printed safety sayings; the "ABC of the CCC" was said to be "Always Be Careful."[43]

Given the danger they presented, cars and trucks received special attention in safety campaigns. Safety tips often focused on this hazard in terms that young males could readily understand. Tips in the *Dark Canyon Avalanche* reminded enrollees at a Carlsbad camp that it was "Better to shove on the brakes and be

*above*:  Safety sign at Camp F-39-N, March 8, 1937. *Courtesy:*
*Photo Archives, College of Agriculture, New Mexico State University.*
*below:*  Eduardo Chavez, *(r).*, and fellow enrollee at the Elephant
Butte CCC camp. Former enrollees aften assert that the number
one work-related lesson they learned in the CCC was how to work
side-by-side with others. *Courtesy:  Angie Chavez.*

laughed at than step on the gas and be cried over." The *Avalanche* also proposed that there should have been a hall of fame for drivers with no hits, just like there is a hall of fame for pitchers who threw no-hitters. Other safety slogans appeared on posters in camp garages and on dashboards in CCC vehicles.[44]

X Only the most trusted, responsible enrollees were selected to be drivers. Driving tests were, therefore, demanding. In some states, driver candidates had an egg placed behind a tire of their trucks while parked on a slope. The challenge was to put the trucks in gear and move them forward without first rolling backward and crushing the eggs. Once selected as drivers, enrollees were often monitored by foremen who rode in the passenger seat to make sure that no chances were taken and all rules were obeyed. When not accompanied by a foremen, drivers were restricted to speeds of no more than thirty or thirty-five miles per hour; governors were installed to enforce this safety precaution. Although governors could be removed from vehicles once out of sight of camp, most drivers took great pride in their safety records. Harry Newbury, who spent much of his time in the CCC as a driver, recalls that red discs were displayed on the hoods of vehicles driven by enrollees with few accidents; a silver disc was displayed when a number of red discs were accumulated. Drivers who navigated 25,000 miles without an accident were rewarded with certificates of proficiency. CCC drivers even served as models for other motorists. According to the *Silver City Enterprise*,

> CCC enrollee drivers have set an example which proves that individual care in observing highway laws and careful attention to driving will decrease materially the accident rate now prevalent on [our] highways.

To help insure road safety, every vehicle in camp had to be inspected (with appropriate forms completed) every day, every week, and at the conclusion of every sixty-day period.[45]

Camps, like the factories they were meant to emulate, took pride in their safety records. No-accident flags flew over camps for as long as their workers remained injury-free. One such flag flew over the Mountainair camp for over a year, or until an enrollee sprained his ankle when trying to stretch a single into a double at a baseball game. The Mayhill camp proudly flew its banner for more than fifty days, while the Gila camp avoided lost working hours due to injuries for at least five months. A safety record board at the Bosque del Apache camp served as a daily reminder of the need for caution; the board showed 278 consecutive accident-free days as of January 15, 1942. The camp at San Ysidro received a safety certificate for its impressive record. Only one other Soil Conservation Service camp in the region and seventy-seven in the nation were so honored in 1941.[46]

CCC enrollees at work sometimes served as subjects in paintings and other art forms funded by the federal government during the Great Depression. Employed in New Deal programs like the Public Works of Art Project (PWAP) and the Treasury Relief Art Project (TRAP), artists often celebrated American labor and its accomplishments in their creations. Enrollees at work were a natural choice as subjects for at least two painters in New Mexico. W. Stuart Walker of Albuquerque painted as many as ten twenty-two inch by twenty-eight inch watercolors showing enrollees at Forest Service jobs. Walker gave his work-related paintings such appropriate titles as "Fencing" and "Five O'Clock."[47]

Odon Hullendremer, the second government-sponsored painter to paint CCC subjects, was a Dutch artist who had traveled the world in search of interesting subjects; he finally settled in Santa Fe where he discovered countless new subjects, including CCC enrollees. Three of his most famous works include a canvas depicting a distressed older couple (representing the past), a picture of CCC enrollees at work (representing the present), and an oil of happy young children (representing the future). As one art critic has said of these paintings, "If there were no other record left of the depression than this, it would be enough to tell the story in New Mexico."[48]

\*          \*          \*

Enrollees labored through their work days with up to an hour off for lunch plus periodic breaks for rest, water, and a quick cigarette. Only inclement weather or an emergency could shorten work days once they had begun. Barring such events, corpsmen completed their tasks and departed in Army trucks for their return trip to camp at four o'clock each weekday afternoon.[49]

Consciously or subconsciously, enrollees learned (or reenforced) several work values in the course of their labors. They clearly learned the importance of punctuality, a respect for authority, the need for safety, and the satisfaction of seeing a job through to completion; they could be proud of what they produced with the sweat of their brows and the skill of their hands. But that was not all. Enrollees also grew to value and admire those who led well, worked hard, and did their share and more. Social approval went to those who "knuckl[ed] down to hard work and lik[ed] it" rather than to 'goldbrickers' who sought only easy, unfulfilling jobs. Hard workers could expect promotions to more responsible positions, becoming Assistant Leaders and Leaders in camp or truck drivers, head cooks, and chief clerks at work. CCC promotions were long remembered with justifiable pride that helped build self-esteem and self-reliance. The assignment of new duties or responsibilities was the turning point in many a young man's working career.[50]

Perhaps most importantly, enrollees learned to work side-by-side with others, regardless of differences in background or culture. Of all the lessons learned in the CCC, this was the work-related value most often mentioned and appreciated by former New Mexico enrollees fifty to sixty years later. Getting along with others prepared enrollees for jobs and responsibilities long after their few months or years in the Civilian Conservation Corps were done. Yes, they sometimes learned job skills that served them well in later life, but it was their attitude toward work in general—their work ethic—that proved most valuable to them as individuals and future workers in the nation's larger economy. Thousands of enrollees came of age as working adults by internalizing what they had seen, heard, and learned in New Mexico's distant work sites and camps.[51]

**Endnotes - Chapter 5**

¹   Robert B. Bennett, Gordon L. Brown, and Austiano Gallegos interviews, OHPB; Camp Inspection Report, Silver City, April 5, 1934, CCC, NA; Salmond, *CCC*, 137-8; Holland and Hill, *Youth*, 38.
²   Ullrich interview; Salmond, *CCC,* 137-8; Gorham, "Ambiguous Practices," 236.
³   Supervising state and federal departments in New Mexico included the New Mexico State Parks, the U.S. Department of Labor, the U.S. Department of Agriculture (with its Forest Service and Soil Conservation Service), and the U.S. Department of the Interior (with its National Park Service, Division of Grazing, and Bureau of Reclamation). Remarkably, most of these departments cooperated effectively and efficiently in their dealings with the CCC. The following discussion is hardly meant to be a complete listing of all CCC work accomplished in New Mexico. For a partial list of the main CCC projects in the state, see Appendix C. For a list of project types throughout the United States, see McEntee, *Final Report*, 104-7.
⁴   Brown and Johnson interviews, OHPB; Thomas R. Cox *et al.*, *This Well-Wooded Land: Americans and Their Forests from Colonial Times to the Present* (Lincoln: University of Nebraska Press, 1985): 219; A Brief Survey of Certain Phases of the CCC Program in New Mexico, April 1933-September 30,1941, Governor Miles Papers, NMSRCA; Kenneth E. Hendrickson, Jr., "The Civilian Conservation Corps in the Southwestern States" in Donald W. Whisenhunt, ed., *The Depression in the Southwest* (Port Washington, New York: Kennikat Press, 1980): 14; Ares, *Jornada*, 42-5; H.C. Stewart, "The Soil Conservation Service Activities in the Southwest," *New Mexico Business Review,* 7 (1938): 179; Perea interview. Enrollees also worked to reenforce dams at Lake McMillan and Lake Avalon near Carlsbad. *Carlsbad Current-Argus*, January 11, 1998. For other valuable work accomplished at the Jornada Experimental Range, see Margaret Page Hood, "Conservationists Help the Cowman," *New Mexico Magazine*, 12 (June 1934): 19-20, 38.
⁵   Ellis, *Torment*, 305; Cox *et al.*, *Well-Wooded Land*, 220; David Townsend, *You Take the Sundials and Give Me the Sun* (Alamogordo: Alamogordo Daily News, 1984): 30-1; Phoebe Cutler, *The Public Landscape of the New Deal* (New Haven: Yale University Press, 1985): 95; A Brief Survey of Certain Phases of the CCC Program in New Mexico, April 1933-September 30, 1941, Governor Miles Papers, NMSRCA;

Hernandez interview. Also see H.R. Kylie et al., *CCC Forestry* (Washington, D.C.: U.S. Government Printing Office, 1937); JohnT. Cassady and George E. Glendening, *Revegetating Semidesert Range Lands in the Southwest* (Washington, D.C.: U.S. Government Printing Office, 1940).

⁶ A Brief Survey of Certain Phases of the CCC Program in New Mexico, April 1933-September 30, 1941, Governor Miles Papers, NMSRCA; *Forest Pioneer,* October 1933.

⁷ Harrison *et al.*, *Bandelier*, 7, 9-10, 14; Hal K. Rothman, *On Rims and Ridges: The Los Alamos Area Since 1880* (Lincoln: University of Nebraska Press, 1992): 190-3; Evelyn Frey interview, OHPB.

⁸ *Albuquerque Journal,* March 12, 1989; H.A. Hoover, *Tales From the Bloated Goat: Early Days in Mogollon* (El Paso: Texas Western Press, 1958): 35; Edwin A. Tucker and George Fitzpatrick, *Men Who Matched the Mountains: The Forest Service in the Southwest* (Washington, D.C.: U.S. Department of Agriculture, 1972): 166-7.

⁹ Dietmar Schneider-Hector, *White Sands: The History of a National Monument* (Albuquerque: University of New Mexico Press, 1993): 101-2, 208n; CCC Press Release on State Parks, Washington, D.C., February 4, 1935, CCC File, FDRL; Alice Bullock, *Mountain Villages* (Santa Fe: Sunstone Press, 1981): 27; *El Cibollero*, December 23, 1939; Robert S. Maxwell *et al.*, "Timeless Heritage," Unpublished ms., U.S. Forest Service Papers, CSWR, UNM; Kammer, *Historic and Architectural Resources*, 72, 74; Stan Cohen, *The Tree Army* (Missoula, Montana: Pictoral Histories Publishing Company, 1980): 112; A.B. Barela interview, March 12, 1991; *Albuquerque Journal*, March 21 and August 6, 1941; *Health City Sun*, April 24, 1936; Richardson, "State Park System," 256; Kathryn A. Flynn, ed., *Treasures on New Mexico Trails: Discover New Deal Art and Architecture* (Santa Fe: Sunstone Press, 1995): 293; F.A. Koch to Dennis Chavez, Santa Fe, March 14, 1940, F.A. Koch Papers, NMSRCA. A side camp of F-35-N in Manzano helped in various landscaping projects at the University of New Mexico, including the installation of a sprinkler system, the creation of walks, and the building of a parking lot. Van Dorn Hooker to the author, Alameda, September 1, 1998; *Civilian Conservation Corps: Official Annual, 1936, Albuquerque District, 8th Corps* (n.p.: Direct Advertising Company, 1936): 69; John Churches, "History of the CCC [in the] Cibola National Forest," (Unpublished U.S. Forest Service report, n.d.): 14, 18, 48.

¹⁰ John V. Young, *The State Parks of New Mexico* (Albuquerque: University of New Mexico Press, 1984): 1, 7, 60-1, 93.

¹¹ *Carlsbad Current-Argus*, October 9, 1987; Chacon interview;

James Rivers interview, October 31, 1992; Flynn, *Treasures*, 293; Quintana interview, OHPB.

¹² Development Sites in the Public Sector: Kiwanis Point Observation File and Kiwanis Cabin Plans, Cibola National Forest Headquarters, Albuquerque, New Mexico; Kammer, *Historic and Architectural Resources*, 73-4; Judith G. Propper, "A Job at Honest Pay: The Legacy of the Civilian Conservation Corps," *U.S. Forest Service Southwestern Region News* (December 1998): 37; Charles Clugston to the author, Monroeville, Pennsylvania, July 21, 1998.

¹³ Flynn, *Treasures*, 37; Kammer, *Historic and Architectural Resources*, 74; *El Paso Times*, January 27, 1935.

¹⁴ Gallegos and E.L. Partridge interviews, OHPB; Rothman, *Rims and Ridges*, 198; Harrison *et al.*, *Bandelier*, 21-49, 56-7, 68,70-4; *Santa Fe New Mexican*, December 11, 1983; *Los Alamos Monitor,* June 19, 1988.

¹⁵ James E. Reynolds to the author, Wheat Ridge, Colorado, June 12, 1991; Rupert Lopez interview, July 6, 1999; Walker interview; Vigil, "Blood, Sweat and Mud," 81-2; *NACCCA Journal,* 21 (November 1998): 1. Cecil J. Doty was the chief architect for the Park Service's new building in Santa Fe. The Park Service moved its regional headquarters from Oklahoma to Santa Fe in 1937. *Santa Fe New Mexican,* October 9, 1937, and August 5, 1939.

¹⁶ Vigil, "Blood, Sweat and Mud," 81-2; Jim Fulton and Brown interviews, OHPB; Harrison *et al.*, *Bandelier*, 21-8, 78-89; Flynn, *Treasures*, 20, 37; Paige, *CCC and the Park Service*, 125; Otis *et al.*, *Forest Service and the CCC*, 157; Richard West Sellars, *Preserving Nature in the National Parks* (New Haven: Yale University Press, 1997): 134. See Appendix C for a list of CCC projects listed on the National Register of Historic Places and the New Mexico State Register of Cultural Properties.

¹⁷ "Kivas Found in Quarai Monastery," *El Palacio*, 40 (May/June 1936): 122; Blake interview by Foote; Ele Baker interview by Cheryl Foote, August 30, 1988, included in Cheryl Foote to the author, Albuquerque, n.m.; Albert G. Ely, "The Excavation and Repair of the Quarai Mission" (Unpublished M.A. thesis, University of New Mexico, 1935): viii-ix; James E. Ivey, *In the Midst of Loneliness: The Architectural History of the Salinas Missions* (Santa Fe: Southwest Cultural Resources Center, 1988): 325; *Albuquerque Journal,* May 9, 1935, and July 28, 1938.

¹⁸ Ivey, *Midst of Loneliness*, 323; Martin Serna interview, March 12, 1991.

[19] Ely, "Quarai Mission," 6; E.L. Hewett and R.G. Fisher, *Mission Monuments of New Mexico* (Albuquerque: University of New Mexico Press, 1943): 208; Blake interview by Foote.

[20] *Albuquerque Journal,* August 2, 1936; *La Poliza,* December 1937; Hewett and Fisher, *Monuments,* 234.

[21] George P. Schneider interview and Carroll R. Kay letter, OHPB; Harrison *et al., Bandelier,* 15; *Santa Fe New Mexican,* December 11, 1983.

[22] Claire J. Mueller, "A Chaco Canyon Story," *NACCCA New Mexico Roadrunner Chapter #141 Newsletter* (September-October 1990): 5-6.

[23] *Ibid.,* 6.

[24] *Ibid.,* 6-7. Also see Robert H. Lister and F.C. Lister, *Chaco Canyon* (Albuquerque: University of New Mexico Press, 1981): 119-20.

[25] Mary I. Severns, "Tourism in New Mexico" (Unpublished M.A. thesis, University of New Mexico, 1951): 3, 63-4; *Albuquerque Journal,* August 2, 1938; Stanley M. Hordes and Carol Joiner, *Historical Markers in New Mexico* (Santa Fe: Delgado Studios, 1984): 37; Earl Shirley interview, June 9, 1996.

[26] Anabel Howell, *Ninety Miles From Nowhere* (Peralta, New Mexico: Pine Tree Press, n.d.): 94; *Forest Pioneer,* October 1933; Ares, *Jornada,* 43-4; Henry Arellanes interview, March 23, 1996; Gonzalez interview; Maynard W. Cummings to L.H. Laney, Albuquerque, July 14, 1938, U.S. Soil Conservation Service Papers, CSWR, UNM.

[27] Sherraden, "Effectiveness of the Camps," 241; *Pink Pebble Periodical,* June 15, 1936. Protests regarding rodent control in New Mexico continue today. See the *Santa Fe New Mexican,* April 2, 1998; *Albuquerque Journal,* May 23, 1999.

[28] Arellanes interview; *Mirager,* March 1936.

[29] *CCC Annual, Albuquerque District, 1936,* 51; Camp Inspection Report, Magdelena, November 23, 1938, CCC, NA.

[30] *Belen News,* May 31, 1934; *Albuquerque Journal,* July 4 and 14, 1937; Parham, "CCC in Colorado," 97; *Raton Range,* June 9, 1938; David Nichols, ed., *Ernie's America: The Best of Ernie Pyle's 1930s Travel Dispatches* (New York: Vintage Books, 1989): 118.

[31] Clyde Tingley to Dennis Chavez, Santa Fe, July 4, 1937, Senator Chavez Papers, CSWR, UNM; *Albuquerque Journal,* May 24-27 and June 8 and 13, 1938; *Albuquerque Tribune,* April 30, 1938.

[32] Fred Beck interview, May 29, 1991; Irene Fisher, *Bathtub and Silver Bullet* (Albuquerque: Albuquerque Historical Society, 1976): 66-7.

33 "Winter Work Will Develop La Joya Range," *New Mexico Magazine*, 11 (December 1933): 32; Kammer, *Historic and Architectural Resources*, 73-7; Oliver C. Payne, CCC Camp Report, Bosque del Apache, October-November 1939, Bosque del Apache National Wildlife Refuge, San Antonio, New Mexico (hereafter cited as BANWR); *Albuquerque Journal*, December 16, 1984; Cohen, *Tree Army*, 119. It is estimated that ninety percent of the whooping crane population had been lost between 1870 and 1900. Faith McNulty, *The Whooping Crane: The Bird That Defies Extinction* (New York: E.P. Dutton, 1966): 34.

34 Porter Memoirs, 11, 14-15; Harrison, *et al.*, *Bandelier*, 28.

35 Sam Chavez interview, May 20, 1993; *Dark Canyon Avalanche*, September 27, 1936; *Santa Fe New Mexican,* August 26, 1933.

36 Brown interview, OHPB; *Silver City Enterprise*, October 6, 1933.

37 H. Baca interview; Poorbaugh interview.

38 *Wasp*, December 31, 1936, and April 1937; *Mirager*, June 1936; *Dark Canyon Avalanche,* April 30, 1938.

39 Brown, *Heritage*, 180-1.

40 Gonzalez interview.

41 *La Poliza*, July 1937.

42 *Forest Pioneer,* 4th quarter, 1937; McEntee, *Final Report*, 22-3. For trucking fatalities in New Mexico, see the *Raton Range*, June 3, 1935, and CCC Press Release, May 18, 1937, and Camp Inspection Report, Santa Fe, August 14, 1937, CCC, NA; *Lincoln Lookout,* June 1937 and July 1937.

43 CCC Press Release on First Aid Training, Washington, D.C., January 21, 1935, CCC File, FDRL; Guadalupe P. Flores to the author, Victoria, Texas, November 24, 1991; *Camp Chatter*, April 1937; *Lincoln Lookout*, July 1937 and August 1937 and September 1937; Bryant, "Education," 98; *Lonely Pennsylvanian*, February 1940; *Dark Canyon Avalanche,* June 2, 1936; *Forest Pioneer*, 3rd quarter, 1938; Perea interview; Oliver C. Payne, CCC Camp Report, Bosque del Apache, July-August-September 1940, BANWR; *Kangarowl*, May 17, 1935.

44 *Dark Canyon Avalanche*, April 30, 1938; Baldridge, "Nine Years," 244.

45 *Ibid.*; Dawson interview; John Mooney interview, February 5, 1994; Harry Newbury interview, May 28, 1996; *Blue Buffalo*, April 30, 1938; *Silver City Enterprise*, May 14, 1937. For vehicle inspection forms, see Box 11, Folder 58, U.S. Soil Conservation Service Collection, CSWR, UNM.

46 *Organ Echoes*, May 31, 1937; *Mayhill Lookout,* June 1937;

*Gila Monster*, May 1937; Fred Poorbaugh, CCC Camp Report, Bosque del Apache, April-May-June 1942, BANWR; *Albuquerque Journal*, April 8, 1941.

[47] Flynn, *Treasures*, 275-6.

[48] *Ibid.*, 230; Ina Sizer Cassidy, "Art and Artists of New Mexico: Odon Hullendremer," *New Mexico Magazine*, 14 (April 1936): 21, 46. Other government-sponsored art was used to decorate the interiors of CCC-constructed buildings. At Bandelier, Pablita Velarde completed a series of eighty-four paintings depicting Pueblo Indian life, while Helmut Naumen did four pastels of similar Pueblo scenes. Harrison *et al.*, *Bandelier*, 286; Flynn, *Treasures*, 192. New Deal-sponsored paintings, lithographs, and Pueblo pottery from Cochiti, Santa Clara, and San Ildefonso are displayed in the lobby of the Park Service's headquarters in Santa Fe.

[49] Bennett interview, OHPB; Salmond, *CCC*, 139.

[50] Bassett, "Health and Culture," 54; E. Ricardo Garcia interview, July 12, 1996; Gelen 'Chester' Williams interview, May 21, 1998. James J. McEntee (assistant director of the CCC to 1939 and director from 1939 to 1942) listed these desirable characteristics the CCC helped to develop in enrollees in his *Now They Are Men: The Story of the CCC* (Washington, D.C.: National Home Library Foundation, 1940): 60-1, and his *Final Report*, 61-2, 81.

[51] See, for example, Williams interview, Jack O. Perry to the author, n.p., May 25, 1991.

*above*:  Retreat at the end of a work day was a regular part of camp life at Glenwood camp. *Courtesy: Levi Baca.*    *below:*  The most anticipated event of the day was dinner in the mess hall. This is the mess hall at the Tucumcari CCC camp. *Courtesy: Charles Clugston.*

# CHAPTER 6

## Evenings Off

Enrollees returned to camp tired and hungry after long days at work. Most looked forward to evening hours off when they could participate in a number of worthwhile activities. Good use of these leisure hours enhanced the average enrollee's experience in the CCC and, in many cases, their lives thereafter. Life lessons were learned after as well as during busy work days.

Once cleaned up, enrollees gathered for flag lowering ceremonies, much as they had gathered for flag raising ceremonies each morning. These daily events helped stimulate strong patriotism in young men like Gregorio Villasenor. As Villasenor later recalled

> We used to stand for retreat every day, five days a week
> ... and I thought it was a very fascinating thing ... . I
> was there with the rest of them, lined up and saluting
> the flag of the United States—no music, no nothing,
> just [everyone at attention] until the flag was [taken
> down].

Villasenor and his fellow enrollees could not have known that a high percentage of them would soon be called on to defend their country and the flag they honored each day of their service in the CCC.[1]

The enrollees' next activity was undoubtedly the most anticipated of the day: dinner at 5:30 p.m. In an informal survey conducted at the Glenwood camp in 1935, enrollees were asked to rank the "most vital part" of the CCC. The majority ranked mess call above all else, surpassing even payday on their list of top priorities. While breakfast was somewhat hurried and lunch was seldom more than sandwiches, dinner could be counted on to be substantial and relaxed.[2]

With food "probably the single most important indicator of enrollee satisfaction," one astute company commander declared that "a good mess made a good camp." Aware of this maxim, CCC inspectors carefully noted each camp's monthly expenditure on food, using these figures as a measure of not only good health and economy, but also of current or potential trouble.[3]

CCC rations were identical to army rations. Like enlisted soldiers, enrollees were served five thousand calories a day as required for muscular activity classified as either "hard" or "very hard." A typical dinner, costing about forty-nine cents a serving, consisted of meat, potatoes, vegetables, bread, fruit, dessert, and coffee. Provided ample portions, enrollees were normally allowed to return for seconds, if desired.[4]

Traditional New Mexican foods were conspicuously absent from most meals. According to Ray Hetzel, an experienced camp cook in New Mexico, this absence was due to the fact that he and his fellow cooks followed Army recipes, and few Army recipes included dishes like chile and beans. Aware that these foods were sorely missed by Hispanic enrollees, some cooks made them available at least occasionally. Their efforts were appreciated. A special enchilada dinner was served in the Gila camp in March 1937 and, while many Anglo enrollees "did not like the heat of the chili," almost everyone enjoyed the meal overall. The same dish was more frequently served at the Buckhorn camp where the commander, Lt. Henry Ehrlinger, was known to like New Mexican foods; most Anglo enrollees at Buckhorn learned to like them, too, as long as a good supply of ice water was available. P.F. Sanchez, editor of the Española camp newspaper, went so far as to include a recipe for Spanish rice and refried beans on the pages of *El Campo*, if only as a subtle suggestion to his camp's cook. An *Albuquerque Journal* reporter noted that several camps had revised their menus to include more beans as a way to "bolster up" the morale of New Mexican enrollees "accustomed to a heavy diet of frijoles."[5]

Enrollees generally praised camp cooking, if only because most enrollees had never eaten so regularly or so well in their young lives. Rookies were especially known for their appetites at meals. Cooks like Bill Bayer knew "to have plenty of extra food on hand" when new men were due to arrive. "Those guys would eat a lot for days" because "they really had empty bellies." But new arrivals had plenty of competition from veteran enrollees at mealtime. One camp of two-hundred reportedly consumed 2,200 pancakes at a single breakfast, for an average of eleven flapjacks per enrollee. Young men at the La Madera camp consumed no less than 4,500 potatoes, 4,000 pounds of bread, 560 dozen eggs, 1,860 quarts of milk, and 3,500 pounds of beef in December 1936, a typical month.[6]

Not surprisingly, the average enrollee in New Mexico gained as much as twenty pounds during his enlistment in the CCC; the average enrollee gained eight to fourteen pounds nationwide. Some enrollees gained so much weight that they acquired telling nicknames, including one fellow known as the 'Human Silo' at a Carlsbad camp. As early as August 1933 an anonymous poet contributed a verse entitled "Seconds" to *Happy Days*, the CCC's national newspaper:

> O Mother dear, did you hear
> The news that's going 'round?
> Another mess kit's empty
> And I've gained another pound....
>
> So Mother dear if you should hear
> When my six months are done,
> That I have joined the circus,
> Don't worry for your son.

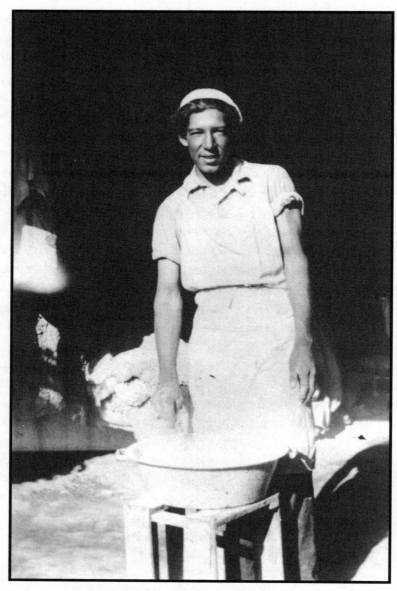

An unidentified camp cook using the facilities at hand.
*Courtesy: Margaret Espinosa McDonald.*

[For] I'll win [both] fame and fortune
My praises will resound,
As fat-man in the side-show
They'll pay me by the pound.[7]

Of course, the key to good cooking was not only high-quality food, but also well-qualified cooks. In a real sense, a good cook was as essential to the success of a CCC camp as an experienced chuck wagon cook was to a successful cattle drive in the Old West. Ramon F. Adams's words of praise for the cowboy cook rang equally true for each camp cook in the CCC: "If ever there was an uncrowned king on the cow range, it was the wagon cook ... . Too much credit cannot be given to the old wagon cook for the cowboy's contentment with life." Similar words of praise were uttered for CCC cooks like Joe Cardenas of the Mountainair camp in 1937. According to the Mountainair camp newspaper, "The camp is sure lucky in having a man like Joe for cook and we are sure proud of him."[8]

Cooking for over two hundred enrollees and officers was never easy. Young men naturally favored their mothers' home cooking, prepared with family or ethnic recipes passed down from one generation to the next. Satisfying diverse enrollee tastes could, in fact, drive a cook to distraction. In the opinion of the La Madera camp cook, the demands of his job had caused him to be "nominated for the No. 1 inmate of [the insane asylum at] Las Vegas." At least one kitchen manager waxed poetic in describing his challenging chores in a verse entitled "Punchin' the Dough." Other cooks were less benign, especially when faced with criticism of the quality or quantity of the food they served. When a young enrollee at the camp near Deming worried that he would not get enough pie, his company cook forced the youth to eat one whole pie and most of another at one sitting. Observers reported that the pie-eating enrollee "suffered considerably" from this dietary torture. Resorting to physical force, the same cook gave another enrollee a black eye when the young man insulted the cook's culinary skills by refusing to drink his coffee.[9]

Few cooks resorted to such extreme measures. Trained at special cooking and baking schools in Albuquerque and at New Mexico A&M in Las Cruces, most cooks took great care in their work. When cooks and bakers at the Gila camp first wore their 'whites,' they were justifiably proud of their new uniforms and were said to "look rather trim in their high hats cocked to one side."[10]

Veteran cooks were also proud of the strategies they used to prepare meals within their assigned budgets. Without careful planning, too much money could be spent early in a month, leaving little for later and causing major problems and discontentment. Bill Bayer, head cook at a Las Cruces camp, followed the dictum that "if you served a poor main dish [for supper], you better have a good dessert and plenty of it" if the enrollees were to be happy with their evening meal. On the other hand, Bayer advised that "if you had a good main dish, you could get by with a cheap dessert." Following this advice, cooks like 'Pop' Kent were known to make meals "faster and cheaper and better" than anyone in New Mexico. To prevent waste, good cooks directed kitchen helpers to inspect garbage cans to see what enrollees were not eating; consistently discarded items were cut from future menus. But not all cooks were this conscientious. Camp commander Fred Poorbaugh discovered that his head cook at the Bosque del Apache camp was selling beef in nearby Socorro and pocketing large profits for himself. Another officer in Las Cruces recalls a mess sergeant who was stealing hundreds of dollars from his camp's food budget until he was finally caught and summarily discharged.[11]

Fortunately, corrupt cooks were rare. The majority were honest, hard-working, highly valued enrollees. Indeed, good cooks were so valuable that enrollment requirements were eventually altered to attract and retain the best. Unlike other enrollees, these men could be married, could exceed the maximum age limit, and were not required to send their twenty-five dollar allotments home. Once recruited, cooks were sometimes granted special camp privileges as well. At the Sandia camp, a privileged mess sergeant was known to exploit his status by bringing cigars, liquor, and women into camp on weekends. A cook at Las Cruces was considered such an important resource that even his "Hitler[-like] constitution" was tolerated by fellow enrollees eager for good meals. The brutal cook at Deming who force-fed one enrollee and blackened the eye of another was disciplined, but not severely because capable cooks were always so "difficult to obtain."[12]

After dinner, enrolles were free to engage in a wide variety of activities. Those who received letters or packages at mail call often took time to respond with letters of their own. Out-of-state enrollees often received the most mail, if only because they seldom found the time or money for visits home. Girl friends were particularly good letter writers, although a sudden decline in correspondence often meant that a former sweetheart had discovered new male distractions closer to home. Other enrollees were so popular, as measured by the volume of mail they received, that they were the envy of all. The arrival of nineteen letters from nineteen different girls made Herman Levy a local legend and the subject of a special news item in his Ft. Stanton camp newspaper in September 1939.[13]

Responding to letters could be difficult. A reporter from the Redrock camp newspaper devoted an entire article to the problems of letter writing in camp, starting with the distractions of card games in his barracks and ending with power failures that suddenly killed one's source of light after dark. More seriously, many enrollees could not write home because they had never learned how to write. More literate staff members and fellow enrollees were often called on to assist. But even these helpful friends faced problems. When Fernando Reta wrote a letter home for an illiterate friend, he mentioned that the youth had been assigned to kitchen police (KP) duty. Confused, the enrollee's mother thought that her son had left the CCC and joined the police.[14]

When not writing home after dinner, many enrollees gravitated to their camps' recreation halls. Rec halls varied from the most basic to the quite elaborate. Most included a small library with an average of eight hundred books and as many as 2,300 volumes in the Roswell camp alone. With generous donations from local schools, colleges, civic organizations, and the Ft. Bliss Army base, camp libraries in New Mexico compared favorably with similar libraries across the nation. A camp inspector from Washington, D.C., described the reading room at Conchas Dam as "splendid" and the one at Carlsbad as nothing less than "superior" in 1942. Camp collections were supplemented with books from a traveling library furnished by the Army. With new and regular titles available, circulation reached as high as 353 volumes in a single month at the Glenwood camp.[15]

However, interest in reading was not as great at all camps, including the camp near Mountainair where a "pronounced lack of interest" was noted in 1937. With its high rate of illiteracy, it was not surprising that New Mexico as a whole ranked thirty-eighth of the forty-eight states in circulation of books per capita in 1930. Only ten Southern states ranked lower nationwide. By making books more readily available to enrollees, the CCC undoubtedly helped improve New Mexico's reading and circulation rates in the 1930s and early 1940s.[16]

Camp libraries also housed newspapers, with as many as six dailies and Sunday editions in each camp. Newspapers included the CCC's national, semi-official publication, *Happy Days*. Published in Washington, D.C., *Happy Days* reported news about camps throughout the country, including New Mexico. Newspapers from nearby towns were also made available to enrollees, helping to build ties between camps and local communities. But the most often read newspapers in camp were usually those sent from enrollee hometowns in New Mexico and elsewhere. Copies of the *Daily Oklahoman* and the *Dallas Morning News* were purchased for the large number of Oklahoma and Texas enrollees assigned to DG-43-N near Animas. In addition to informing and amusing enrollees, the availability of distant newspapers could be considered a strategy to reduce the number of desertions by young men far from home. Able to learn what was happening on the home front, these youths would be less likely to suffer homesickness and desert the CCC.[17]

*X* A standard list of about two dozen magazines could be found alongside newspapers and books in most rec halls. In keeping with the CCC's mission to help train the next generation of American workers and loyal citizens, most magazines focused on work (such as *Occupations, Opportunity*, and *Popular Mechanics*) and current events (such as *Time, Newsweek*, and *Life*). Controversial, radical periodicals like the *Champion of Youth* and *Spark* were strictly banned.[18]

Despite efforts to promote American ideals by the inclusion of some magazines and the exclusion of others, enrollees tended to simply read what interested them most. CCC officials need not have worried about enrollees reading subversive literature in government-run camps. An informal survey at the El Rito camp in mid-1935 showed that enrollees were far more interested in popular Western fiction than leftist propaganda. Three of the top five magazines favored by literate enrollees stressed Western themes, with *Western* number one, *Ranch Romance* number three, and *Wild West Weekly* number five. Only *Popular Mechanics*, at number seven, could be considered work-related among the top ten favorites, while *Time*, the most popular news magazine, ranked no higher than number seventeen.[19]

Energetic enrollees produced their own camp publications. Often written and edited by camp journalism classes, camp newspapers usually appeared once a month with as many as twenty pages in each issue. Circulation figures varied from about 180 to 250 copies per issue. Copies were often sent to enrollees' families (to help reassure them of their sons' well-being), to other camps (to exchange ideas or boast of achievements), and to key leaders like Governor Tingley (to assure their continued political support).[20]

Starting with *The Woodpecker*, one of the first camp newspapers in the entire United States, New Mexico enrollees created at least eighty-seven newspapers in forty-four different camps. Half of all newspapers ran less than a year, although one, the *Organ Echoes*, ran as long as five years. Great efforts were made to produce the best newspapers possible, despite limited resources and admittedly limited journalistic skills. Some publications received well-deserved praise, with ratings of as high as four stars (of a possible five) in the judgement of the *Happy Days* editors who rated camp newspapers across the United States.[21]

Like their counterparts elsewhere in the U.S., New Mexico's camp newspapers had unique, often comical names. Following the CCC's use of alliteration, enrollees at Redrock's SCS-2-N called their newspaper the *Pink Pebble Periodical*; this new designation was considered an improvement over the publication's original name, the *Dam News*, which "seemed a bit vulgar." Other attempts at alliteration included the *Buckhorn Buzzer*, the *Cactus Courier*, the *Lincoln Lookout*, the *Stanton Static*, and the *Tip Topper*. Some newspaper names referred to work (the *Pick and Shovel*) or an aversion to it (the *Goldbricker*). Enrollees also drew attention to their surroundings (the *Dust Bowl*) or to efforts to conserve them (*Save Our Soil*). A few camps favored Spanish names with such titles as *El Conejo* (The Rabbit) and *El Gallo de Pelea* (The Cockfighter).[22]

Most newspapers included similar features from one edition to the next. Many, in fact, borrowed freely from one another and from *Happy Days*. CCC-related humor, poetry, and cartoons were standard fare. But unique contributions could also be found. The *Cactus Courier's* March 1940 edition included a clever crossword puzzle with CCC answers. *Los Frijoles* at Bandelier reviewed movies shown in camp, while the *Mirager*, outside Deming, published a Western serial called "The Frame-Up" and ran a series of articles on New Mexico history. A column called the "Voice of Experience" offered advice to the love-lorn and similarly troubled souls at Conchas Dam.[23]

Most importantly, camp newspapers reenforced CCC values and life lessons. Entire editorials preached the virtues of honesty, consideration for others, and pride in achievement by individuals and their camps as a whole. Homilies served the same purpose, reminding enrollees that "Idleness introduces us to evil" and "The fellow who throws himself away seldom likes the place he lands." Reading much like a farmer's almanac, Mountainair's *Tip Topper* listed twenty-five "You can'ts," including:

"You can't sow bad habits and reap good character."
"You can't sow dishonesty and reap integrity."
"You can't sow deception and reap confidence."
"You can't sow cruelty and reap kindness."

Inspirational poetry, like Rudyard Kipling's "If," motivated enrollees while also raising group and individual morale. Editorials focused on the evils of alcohol, theft, going AWOL, and other troublesome behavior. Patriotism was emphasized with relevant editorials and articles on national holidays like Washington's birthday, Lincoln's birthday, and the Fourth of July. As the CCC's main benefactor, Franklin Roosevelt received special attention on his birthday as well. If a main purpose of the CCC was to help mold loyal, hard-working, cooperative Americans, CCC newspapers helped set the mold with words of instruction surrounded by words and images of diversion.[24]

Although successful for short spans, newspapers seldom lasted very long before they were beset by several typical problems. With short enrollment periods, newspaper staffs could suddenly disappear; the *Kangarowl* near Española lost its editor, assistant editor, managing editor, and cartoonist among the fifty-four enrollees discharged at the end of their enrollment period in April 1936. After several months in operation, many newspapers also suffered from a dearth of newsworthy items to report. Pleas for help took different forms. The *Pink Pebble Periodical's* editor thought to place a "news box" in the Redrock camp library so that enrollees could drop newsworthy items off at their convenience. The *Gila Monster* offered a cash prize of one dollar for the best news story of the month. In perhaps the most innovative (or sarcastic) approach, *The Yucca* left a space at the bottom of one of its pages and wrote, "This space is reserved for articles the boys never wrote." Little worked and newspapers often folded, but while they existed they served the CCC and its larger purpose well. CCC leaders could seldom complain.[25]

Other rec hall activities included shooting pool, playing board games, throwing darts, and playing musical instruments when they

*above*: This camp canteen with pool tables at the Tucumcari CCC camp was typical of the canteens in all the camps. *below*: Army Reserve officers serving as commanders at the Tucumcari camp. *Photos courtesy: Charles Clugston.*

were available. At least one camp, near Magdelena, boasted a Wurlitzer music machine in its rec hall; enrollees at Capitan enjoyed a player piano that had been generously donated for their entertainment.[26]

Many rec halls also housed canteens or camp exchanges. Here enrollees could purchase small items such as candy, magazines, cigarettes, stationery, toiletries, and footlockers. With many camps far from town, enrollees needed these small-scale stores to buy treats as well as necessities. As one enrollee later put it, with some exaggeration, canteens sold "everything a young man would want." Even condoms were sold, although only at cost to "preclude parents or agitators [from] saying [that] enrollees were encouraged in illegitimate sexual practice in order to help make financial profit in the camp exchange." While most purchases were put to good use, others were not. Some enrollees learned that they could purchase lye soap at their canteen, rub it vigorously on their skin, and raise their body temperature high enough to warrant sick leave for at least a day.[27]

Enrollees could also purchase souvenirs of their CCC experience in the form of company photographs sold at many canteens. Professional photographers, like A.W. Newman of Silver City, often visited camps, took photos of camp scenes, and made them available for sale. Some photo collections were put together in small albums called 'lookies.' Official yearbooks, with shots of each camp, were likewise produced on the district-wide level. Much like high school yearbooks, they left ample room for enrollee autographs, photos, and personal comments.[28]

But of all the photos taken, wide-angle pictures of whole companies were most popular, selling for a dollar each. Normally taken in camp with enrollees and their officers smiling broadly, some camps insisted on less traditional settings and poses. One group had its photo taken at its work site with enrollees dressed in fatigues or shirtless in October 1934. In an even more unusual shot, enrollees at the Glenwood camp posed with everyone looking in different directions and most not smiling.[29]

Enrollees who managed camp canteens learned much from this business experience and responsibility. To help increase sales, ambitious canteen stewards sometimes advertised in their camp newspapers, taking out full-page ads in sheets like the *Stanton Static*. A canteen in northern New Mexico went so far as to advertise that "we have the finest little store this side of Chama." They neglected to mention that their's was about the only store between their CCC camp and Chama.[30]

Canteen prices were generally low. At the Mayhill camp, cigarettes sold for eleven cents a pack, while candy bars were four cents, a bar of soap went for eight cents, and shaving cream cost twenty cents in November 1936. Mayhill's canteen averaged five hundred dollars worth of business per month, with fifteen percent of all profits contributed to a fund to buy equipment and sponsor activities to benefit the camp as a whole. Enrollee customers lacking cash to purchase items could always draw credit. Introducing many young men to their first use of credit, if only on a small scale, the CCC issued coupon books or aluminum tokens refundable at the camp exchange. Canteen debts were due on payday each month.[31]

Evening hours were also consumed with camp meetings. Many companies held regularly scheduled weekly meetings at which camp leaders lectured on both camp- and work-related topics. Their speeches were usually in English, but occasionally in Spanish for "the Spanish boys who do not understand English too well." Attendance at meetings was usually high. Roll call was often taken with those who were absent assigned additional duties, such as KP. More positively, most enrollees attended if only because they looked forward to the food and entertainment that frequently followed. Singing and the playing of musical instruments were especially popular. Anglo enrollees preferred hill-billy songs, while Hispanics played Spanish tunes at the El Rito camp's meeting in September 1935.[32]

Less official gatherings were held on other nights of the week. Smokers were always popular events. Used to reward companies or on special occasions like the departure of long-serving enrollees, smokers included food, beer, athletic competition, singing, and, of course, "smokes for everyone." Officers at the Española camp gave a pack of cigarettes to each enrollee at a smoker held for departing camp members in September 1937; ironically, enrollees at this event elected Sammy Shays the "most valuable man in the company" because he was well liked, well respected, and never smoked.[33]

Despite this tribute to Sammy Shays, smoking was unofficially encouraged in an age when the dangers of nicotine were hardly realized or usually ignored. Cigarettes were sold at camp canteens, advertised in *Happy Days*, given as gifts by officers, and used as rewards for every imaginable form of camp competition. At one time or another, cigarettes were offered as prizes in bingo games, short story contests, surprise inspections, and even track meets. Encouraged in these ways, many enrollees developed an unhealthy habit of smoking while serving in the CCC; the average enrollee spent twenty percent of his five dollars spending money on cigarettes each month. Some rolled their own cigarettes to save money, while others smoked pipes or chewed tobacco, depending on what was popular in camps from year to year.[34]

Other evening gatherings were generally more wholesome. Organized debates often drew good crowds, especially when a debate topic was of interest to a large part of a camp's population. A favorite topic in 1937 posed the question "Should the CCC be made a permanent institution?" Crowds also gathered in rec halls to listen to (and bet on) major sporting events broadcast over camp radios. Enrollees across the nation listened intently when Joe Lewis won the heavyweight boxing championship by knocking out James J. Braddock in the eighth round of their match in June 1937. Important college football games and the baseball World Series received similar attention.[35]

Enrollees participated in amateur nights held as often as once a week in some camps. One such amateur hour at the BR-39-N camp near Las Cruces headlined serious and humorous readings, cartoon drawing, a whistling performance, a minstrel act, and two violin solos. The "crowning event" of the evening was a singing trio, led by camp commander Heywood C. Bailey and accompanied by BR-39-N's camp doctor on the piano. Prizes, such as merchandise from the camp canteen, were often given to the best acts, as measured by audience applause.[36]

But the greatest rewards of such events were usually intangible. Earning the applause of their fellow enrollees gave young men a sense of worth and self-respect they may or may not have enjoyed at work or in other phases of camp life. Comedy and music also helped to unite diverse, sometimes hostile, factions. As one educational advisor recalled, Spanish songs played by Hispanic enrollees were often so "irresistible" that out-of-state enrollees would gather around, listen, and "vigorously" call for encores. "Enemies," wrote M.P. Bryant, "were transformed into friends and a fine feeling of comradeship developed." Music served as a "common denominator" for enrollees serving with strangers far from home.[37]

Camp plays were seldom as popular as musical events, although some camps enjoyed at least brief periods of theatrical activity and success. Short-lived drama clubs were organized in camps near Grants, Hot Springs, Lordsburg, Carlsbad, and Jemez. Plays performed included the blatantly racist "Harlem Minstrels," the mysterious "Midnight Murder," and the comic "Kangaroo Court." Interest clearly waned by 1940 when a CCC report showed that no more than one percent of all enrollees in New Mexico participated in acting or vaudeville groups.[38]

A procession of colorful entertainers traveled from camp to camp in the Southwest. Magicians, with their usual fare of card tricks, vanishing rabbits, and daring escapes, were consistent rec hall favorites. Vaudeville shows were staged at dozens of camps in the region. The Lewis Family, performing before their seventy-third CCC audience by March 1936, were said to "sure have what it takes to hilariously entertain the tree army." The Lewises' show included music, dance, a one-man band, and Madam Alberta, billed as "America's Greatest Ventriloquist." The Virginia Varieties boasted a piano player who deftly played his keyboard with boxing gloves on his hands and a blindfold over his eyes. A group calling itself the Royal Northwest Mounted Police was known to give "a first class performance," complete with manly songs, humorous skits, and reenactments of how "the Mountie gets his man." An exotic troupe from South America, Holland, and Hawaii entertained enrollees with skits and songs from their native cultures. Reports that Sally Rand performed her famous fan dance before an audience of enrollees in the a Rio Puerco camp were never confirmed, although a Sally Rand look-alike was undoubtedly just as enthralling to a camp full of admiring young men.[39]

But live shows were expensive and rare in most camps. Old movies were less costly and far more frequently shown. Films of varying quality and content were presented at least once a week. Some were work-related and educational; the Forest Service showed fourteen conservation films to a total of 2,480 New Mexico enrollees in July 1934 alone. But as valuable as these documentaries were to the training of future American workers, none could compare in popularity to Hollywood-produced big-star productions. Using proceeds from sales in their camp canteens, most camps acquired new or used movie projectors. Enrollee projectionists like Chester Williams rolled as many as six reels per show; Williams earned an extra dollar a week for his efforts. Admission to rec hall "theaters" was usually free, although some camps charged patrons ten cents a week or fifty cents a month to help cover the cost of film rentals. Local residents were often invited to movie showings in an effort to improve camp-community relations. Locals who attended shows at F-52-N were charged fifteen cents each, but were so grateful for entertainment that many said they would be willing to pay twenty-five cents since the nearest theater was sixty-five miles away in Glenwood.[40]

New Mexico enrollees clearly favored certain actors, actresses, and movie themes. Mae West movies, such as *Belle of the '90s* (1934), were always hits in camp; as a movie reviewer at the Buckhorn camp noted in his camp newspaper, anyone could "imagine how Mae West would go over in a CCC camp." Only movies on the Old West challenged those starring Miss West. The first movie shown on the Mayhill camp's new projector was *The Covered Wagon* (1940), with Wallace Berry in the leading role. Other Westerns, like the *Texas Gun Fighter* (1932), were shown with appropriate—and sometimes inappropriate—cat calls from the audience. Cowboy stars like Gene Autry and the Hispanic Pinto Pete were always well received. Only a sudden power failure could ruin the fun of an action-packed Western for a cheering crowd of enrollees and their appreciative local guests.[41]

Exhausted after full days of work and evening activities, enrollees retired to their barracks in time for lights out at 10:00 p.m. Taps were played (in camps with bugles) and camp commanders made brief bed checks about 11:00 p.m. An enrollee's day passed quickly, but his hours of sleep went faster. Most enrollees slept soundly until the sound of reveille awoke them all too soon the following morning.[42]

## Endnotes - Chapter 6

[1]    Holland and Hill, *Youth*, 41; Gregorio Villasenor interview by Dorothy Cave, August 7, 1985, included in Dorothy Cave to the author, Roswell, June 3, 1991.

[2]    Salmond, *CCC*, 139; *Kangarowl*, February 27, 1935.

[3]    Poorbaugh interview; *Save Our Soil,* April 1936; *Glenwood News*, August 1936; Camp Inspection Report, Magdelena, August 3, 1937, CCC, NA.

[4]    *Albuquerque Journal*, August 17, 1936; Bassett, "Health and Culture," 9-12, with sample menus, 13-16. The cost of an average serving was calculated from twenty sample New Mexico Camp Inspection Reports, 1935-42, CCC, NA. Thanksgiving and Christmas menus were especially elaborate. See, for example, the Thanksgiving menu, DG-41-N, Lake Arthur, November 24, 1938, CCC Papers, NMSRCA.

[5]    Ray Hetzel interview, March 8, 1996; *Gila Monster*, March 15, 1937; *Buckhorn Buzzer,* August 1937; Johnson interview; *Albuquerque Journal,* May 22, 1936.

[6]    Serna interview; Rivers interview; Noah C. Gibson, Jr., interview, September 7, 1990; "Feeding the CCC," *Food Industries,* 8

(February 1936): 59. A 200-man camp consumed three thousand gallons of water per day. Otis *et al., Forest Service and the CCC,* 29.

⁷ Salmond, *CCC,* 129; *Camp Cactus Carrier,* October 1939; *Happy Days*, August 26, 1933.

⁸ Casaus interview; Ramon F. Adams, *Come an' Get It: The Story of the Old Cowboy Cook* (Norman: University of Oklahoma Press, 1952): 5, 170; *Tip Topper*, March 1937. For examples of praise given to other cooks, see *Follies of 1830,* June 1935; *Gila Monster*, October 26, 1934, and May 1937; *Albuquerque Journal*, August 6, 1941.

⁹ *Tip Topper*, September 1937; *Kangarowl*, March 29, 1935, and January 1937; Camp Inspection Report, Deming, January 6, 1939, and Major General H.J. Bees to Adjutant General, Ft. Sam Houston, March 1, 1939, CCC, NA.

¹⁰ *Organ Echoes*, September 1936; *Tip Topper,* March 1937; Simon F. Kropp, *That All May Learn: New Mexico State University, 1888-1964* (Las Cruces: New Mexico State University, 1972): 241; Cohen, *Tree Army,* 134; Educational Advisors Report, Las Cruces, October 4, 1940, CCC, NA.

¹¹ Barela interview; Logan, "Golden Memory," 5-6; Huffman interview; Poorbaugh interview; Dawson interview.

¹² Graham Hennington interview, July 3, 1991; *Organ Echoes,* May 1936; Camp Inspection Report, Deming, January 6, 1939, CCC, NA. Some CCC cooks made cooking their lifelong career. Gilbert Solis cooked at the Bandelier camp and then continued in this field for more than forty years. *Santa Fe New Mexican*, December 11, 1983.

¹³ Sanchez interview; *Lonely Pennsylvanian*, September 1939.

¹⁴ *Pink Pebble Periodical,* January 15, 1938; Reta interview.

¹⁵ Camp Inspection Reports, Roswell, August 14, 1940; Redrock, October 1, 1935; Carlsbad, February 12, 1942; Conchas Dam, February 19, 1942, CCC, NA; Dawson interview; Salmond, *CCC,* 139; Holland and Hill, *Youth*, 155-7; Bryant, "Education," 85, 104; *Kangarowl*, August 12, 1935; *Belen News*, August 8, 1940.

¹⁶ *Tip Topper*, May 1937; Sanchez, *Forgotten People*, 29; William S. Gray and Ruth Monroe, *The Reading Interests and Habits of Adults* (New York: Macmillan, 1930): 19.

¹⁷ Educational Advisor's Report, Las Cruces, October 4, 1940, and Camp Inspection Report, Roswell, January 30, 1940, CCC, NA; Bryant, "Education," 86; Dawson interview; *Whirlwind*, July 1937.

¹⁸ Bryant, "Education," 86, Salmond, *CCC,* 140; *Gila Monster,* August 25, 1934; Gower, "Censorship," 283.

¹⁹ *Kangarowl*, June 14, 1935.

²⁰ *Camp Cactus Carrier*, October 1939; *Gila Monster,* April 15, 1935; *Camp News*, October 24, 1935; *Animas Announcer*, February 20, 1936; *Kangarowl*, September 4, 1935; John H. Veale to Clyde Tingley, Elephant Butte, March 21, 1935, Governor Tingley Papers, NMSRCA.

²¹ *Socorro Chieftain,* July 15, 1933; Bryant, "Education," 123. The April 1940 edition of the *Lonely Pennsylvanian* received a four-star rating. *Lonely Pennsylvanian*, May-June 1940.

²² *Happy Days*, June 9, 1934; *Pink Pebble Periodical*, February 12, 1935.

²³ *Cactus Courier*, March 1940; *Los Frijoles*, November 1936; *Mirager*, March and August 1937; *Un-Conchas*, June 1940.

²⁴ *Organ Echoes*, July 30, 1936, September 1936, and February 1937; *Tip Topper*, November 1936; *Save Our Soil,* April 1936; *Goldbricker,* May 30, 1935, and October 31, 1935; *Gila Monster,* July 1936 and April 15, 1937; *Velarde Views*, February 29, 1940; *Mal Pais,* February 1937.

²⁵ *Kangarowl,* April 10, 1936; *Pink Pebble Periodical*, December 12, 1935; *Gila Monster*, October 1936; *Yucca,* November 1937.

²⁶ *Organ Echoes*, May 1936 and July 1936; Green interview.

²⁷ Emery Smith interview, October 18, 1991; Camp Inspection Report, Silver City, September 10, 1936, CCC, NA; Jones interview.

²⁸ *Black Ranger*, March 20, 1936. Yearbook examples include *CCC Annual, 1936, Albuquerque District, and Civilian Conservation Corps: Official Annual, 1936, Ft. Bliss District, 8th Corps Area* (n.p.: Direct Advertising Company, 1936).

²⁹ *Kangarowl*, September 19, 1935; *Peñasco Pennant*, January 23, 1936; *Tumbleweed*, March 1939. The unusual photo of F-25-N, Glenwood, is from MS. #84, CCC Files, Rio Grande Historical Collection, New Mexico State University, Las Cruces, New Mexico.

³⁰ James E. Reynolds to the author, Wheat Ridge, Colorado, June 12, 1991; *Stanton Static*, April 1937; *Ghost Talks*, February 1937.

³¹ *Mayhill Lookout*, November 1936; Serna interview; Huffman interview; Salazar interview, OHPB. Paul Manderscheid, who has collected CCC tokens for years, reports that at least three camps in New Mexico used tokens: Buckhorn, Ft. Stanton, and Carlsbad. About twenty millimeters in diameter, tokens were usually round, as at Buckhorn and Ft. Stanton, or octagonal, as at Carlsbad. Paul Manderscheid to the author, Okemos, Missouri, February 1999; *NACCCA Journal*, 22 (January 1999): 5.

³² *Truchas Echo*, February 22, 1939; *Kangarowl*, July 12 and September 19, 1935; *Dark Canyon Avalanche,* June 2, 1936.

<sup>33</sup> *Camp News*, January 23, 1936; *Tumbleweed*, June 1939; *La Poliza*, January 1937; *Wasp,* September 1937.

<sup>34</sup> *Fresnal Ranger,* March 8, 1935; *Kangarowl,* January 1937; *Glenwood News*, February 1937; *Stanton Static*, December 1936; *Truchas Echo,* February 22, 1939; *Hoot Owl*, September 14, 1936; *Goldbricker,* February 11, 1935; *Lonely Pennsylvanian*, April 1940; *Dark Canyon Avalanche*, May 15, 1937; Theodore V. Nelson interview, October 16, 1992; Perea interview.

<sup>35</sup> Recreational activities for a typical week at the Bandelier camp appeared in Camp Inspection Report, Bandelier, November 14, 1938, CCC, NA. On debates, see *Goldbricker,* February 11, 1935; *Kangarowl,* May 1937; *Organ Echoes*, December 1937; *Rio Chicito*, December 1937. On radio broadcasts of major sporting events, see *Gila Monster*, October 26, 1934; *Camp News*, October 10 and November 21, 1935; *Kangarowl,* May 1937; *Los Frijoles,* May 1937.

<sup>36</sup> *Organ Echoes,* May 1936 and July 30, 1936, and October 1936; *Organ View Optic*, July 6, 1936; *Pink Pebble Periodical,* December 12, 1935; *La Poliza*, April 1937.

<sup>37</sup> Bryant, "Education," 120-1; Robert H. True to the author, n.p., June 13, 1991. Helen Chandler Ryan, director of New Mexico's Federal Music Project, "emphasized music education and music recreation in the rural villages and CCC camps." Suzanne Forrest, *The Preservation of the Village: New Mexico's Hispanics and the New Deal* (Albuquerque: University of New Mexico Press, 1989): 121.

<sup>38</sup> Camp Inspection Report, Redrock, September 23, 1936, and Educational Advisor's Report, Hot Springs, September 1935, CCC, NA; *Fresnal Ranger*, February 22, 1935; *Pink Pebble Periodical*, March 12, 1935; *El Conejo*, December 1936; *La Poliza*, December 1936; Bryant, "Education," 119-20.

<sup>39</sup> *Los Frijoles*, May 1937; *Save Our Soil*, March 1936 and June 1937; *Gila Monster*, June 15, 1937; *Kangarowl*, February 25, 1936, and March 25, 1936; *Mirager,* February 1937; Kemp interview. Sally Rand did travel through New Mexico, visiting her aunt in Tucumcari before continuing on to the West Coast, in 1938. *Albuquerque Journal*, June 23, 1938.

<sup>40</sup> Bryant, "Education," 186; *Forest Pioneer*, July 1934; Williams interview; Camp Inspection Report, Glenwood, October 1, 1937, CCC, NA.

<sup>41</sup> *Save Our Soil*, March 1936; Barela interview; *Peñasco Pennant*, March 12, 1936, and March 26, 1936; Felix Vega interview, October 16, 1992.

<sup>42</sup> Salmond, *CCC*, 141.

Front cover of a newspaper from the Las Cruces, BR-29-N camp. The
marks and smudges are reminders of mimeograph reproduction.
*Courtesy: Rio Grande Historical Collections, New Mexico State
University Library, Las Cruces, NM.*

# CHAPTER 7

## The 3 R'S in the 3 C'S

In addition to all they learned about work values and life skills at work sites and in camp, enrollees spent much of their spare time in the pursuit of more formal knowledge. Interested enrollees could take a wide range of evening classes offered in camp and at nearby schools. This opportunity was especially appealing to those who had had to quit school at an early age to help support their poverty-stricken families.[1]

Most New Mexico enrollees were eager for more schooling, realizing that it would take an education as well as work experience to land good jobs once their enrollment in the CCC was over. Those not already convinced of the connection between school and work were frequently reminded. Camp newspapers preached the value of education in articles and editorials. In a typical editorial, enrollee Andrew Candeleria listed the many benefits of additional schooling, ending with the assertion that "We all know very well the material benefits that are derived from an education ... . A man with schooling, whether it be in a vocation or profession[,] will earn more money than one without training." Candelaria's remarks were specifically directed at new enrollees who were urged to grow "mentally [as well as physically] to perform all kinds of work and thus be better citizens of the United States." Camp commanders reiterated this message at camp meetings, setting high goals for enrollee participation in evening classes; Captain Heyward Bailey set a goal of no less than one hundred percent at his Las Cruces camp in September 1936. Although enrollees were not punished for refusing to attend classes, incentives were sometimes offered to encourage those who were hesitant. Enrollees who attended two classes per evening at an Albuquerque camp were relieved of fatigue duty on Saturday mornings in March 1939.[2]

Educational advisors were often the key to the success or failure of each camp's educational program. Applicants for this essential job were required to be U.S. citizens, possess college degrees, have two years of teaching experience, and have "sufficient commercial or practical experience to insure [their] ability to teach vocational subjects." The salary was two thousand dollars a year, a favorable sum compared to the eight hundred dollars earned by most rural teachers and the average eleven hundred dollars earned by urban faculty in New Mexico.[3]

Unofficially, the best applicants for educational advisor jobs had several additional qualities and qualifications. According to M.P. Bryant, who served in this capacity at several camps in New Mexico, the ideal advisor had teaching experience at both the elementary and high school levels, since he would undoubtedly be teaching at both levels in camp. Sixteen of New Mexico's thirty-nine advisors in 1940 had such a background; advisors averaged about a year's experience in grade schools, almost three years experience in high schools, and four years experience overall. Bryant also favored advisors with military experience. The latter were desirable because although "there is absolutely no militarism in the CCC camp," advisors worked under Army and Navy camp commanders and needed to know military methods to complete military forms and get along with those in charge. It was essential to get along with camp officers because some in the military expressed a strong mistrust of "long-haired men and short-haired women" who might teach enrollees unsettling liberal ideas. Bryant reported that two-thirds of New Mexico's advisors had had either military service or had trained in the National Guard or reserves.[4]

But of all the desirable characteristics for an educational advisor to possess, his ability to be innovative and flexible were considered most important. In fact, according to Bryant, "men accustomed to routine and formalized programs simply do not function well in a CCC camp atmosphere where the work is largely a plan-as-you-go type and where all procedures are decidedly informal." Planning-as-you-go often meant literally starting at ground level by building a camp schoolhouse. Classroom space in camps like BR-39-N near Las Cruces was judged inadequate when two classrooms and a shop were outgrown and plans for a six-room adobe-style building were made in 1938. A similar twenty-by-forty-foot adobe structure was built with enrollee labor at the Buckhorn camp; it was proudly christened Buckhorn University upon completion in 1936. But an enlarged building could not guarantee an educational program's success when essential equipment failed to function adequately. Such was the case in the Redrock camp where classes had to be canceled for ten consecutive nights when the camp's power plant broke down in early 1935.[5]

Recruiting teachers with adequate training and experience was also trying. Advisors often turned to a "ready-made faculty" of camp officers, doctors, and technical personnel with consistently good results. Fifty percent of all camp doctors plus eighty percent of the all technical staff members in New Mexico "gladly and willingly assumed this extra burden of teaching" in their respective fields of expertise. In addition, qualified Works Progress Administration workers were assigned to teach special crafts or vocational skills. WPA teachers taught such varied skills as wood-carving, carpentry, leathercraft, and welding.[6]

Local volunteers were also available to teach single classes or whole courses. Renowned naturalist Ross Calvin spent time in several CCC camps while collecting plants in the New Mexico wilderness. Calvin's log books record that appreciative enrollees responded to his lectures with hearty applause. Professors from nearby colleges did similar duty. Seven professors joined Dean Hugh Milton of New Mexico A&M in visiting a Las Cruces camp in February 1937. After dinner and a tour of the camp, an obliging

professor gave a "demonstration of electrical and chemical phe-
nomena" in laymen's terms. Later that evening, enrollees expressed
their appreciation for Professor John W. Clark's work in teaching
a diesel mechanics class over several months. Clark received a
hand-tooled billfold (made in the camp's leathercraft class) for his
efforts. Local public school teachers were likewise recruited for
camp classes; twenty-one teachers moonlighted in mostly academic classes during the spring of 1940.[7]

X Despite help from many sources, there never seemed to be
enough teachers, especially when camps were located in remote
areas of New Mexico. The departure of educational advisors for
opportunities elsewhere often meant not only fewer teachers, but
also long periods when no classes were organized and offered at
all. Eager to learn, the enrollees themselves pitched in. Using
methods typical of rural, one-room schoolhouses, enrollees with
some high school education taught elementary school subjects,
while those with high school diplomas taught beginning high school
studies. Enrollees at the Redlands camp were without an educational advisor for so long in 1934 that they took the matter into
their own hands by setting up their own "college," naming it Yuma
University, and teaching each other "whatever skills and knowledge they possessed." By 1940, of 924 camp teachers in New
Mexico, thirty-nine percent were enrollees, teaching thirty-one
percent of all courses.[8]

Once recruited, novice teachers faced many challenges with
few resources. One resource, a *Manual for Instructors in Civilian Conservation Corps Camps*, was prepared in Washington,
D.C., and distributed throughout the nation in 1935. The manual
provided both good and bad advice. Admirably, it urged teachers
to develop independent critical thinking skills in their students by
encouraging the "exchange of experience" and the "introduction
of different points of view." Ironically, the same manual gave
advice on how to "avoid dangerous issues" and "handle heated
arguments." If dangerous issues arose in class, instructors were
told to either declare that the "issue is not part of the lesson" and
"refuse to discuss it" or promise to return to the issue later in

hopes of "the topic being forgotten." To defuse heated arguments, instructors were told to either tactfully deal with leaders on both sides of the conflict, "sham[e] those who are making the disturbance," or simply call a recess. No suggestions were made regarding physical fights that might occur when heated arguments continued during recess outside the classroom.[9]

𝑋 Despite problems, most camps had good advisors and hardworking teachers most of the time. Drawing on their ingenuity and plan-as-you-go skills, advisors developed their own educational programs in relation to the abilities and interests of the enrollees in their charge. Innovation was especially important because many enrollees had had bad experiences in school. Hispanic students faced particularly difficult circumstances. According to a perceptive study of New Mexico education in the 1930s, the average Hispanic child entered school

> not only without a word of English but without the environmental experience upon which school life is based. He cannot speak to [his English-speaking] teacher and is unable to understand what goes on about him in the classroom. He finally submits to rote learning, parroting words and processes in self-defense. To him, school life is artificial. He submits to it during class hours, only partially digesting the information which the teacher has tried to impart.

Often discouraged by their grammar school experiences, a large number of Hispanic children dropped out of school at an early age with no intention—or desire—to ever return. Others dropped out simply because their families could not afford to send them to school when they were needed to work at home. A 1929 study estimated that fifty percent of all Hispanic children left school before reaching the seventh grade. Even those who remained in school received less of an education when many school districts went bankrupt and were forced to drastically shorten their school years for lack of funding during the Great Depression.[10]

Given the average enrollee's poor memories of school, educational advisors worked hard to counteract the image of classrooms as confining, highly structured environments where unappealing subjects were taught, rote learning was encouraged, and countless rules were enforced. As a result, CCC courses were typically designed to be short, informal, and as practical as possible. Presented with more traditional school settings, most enrollees would have simply "voted with their feet" and refused to attend at all.[11]

Educational programs therefore varied from camp to camp. Despite some fear of a nationally-controlled curriculum, a uniform CCC program was never imposed in New Mexico or elsewhere in the United States. However, there were similarities in camp offerings, especially at the grammar school level where reading, writing, and math skills were emphasized. Of 370 classes offered at the grammar school level in 1940, over seventy-three percent focused on the "3 R's."[12]

Literacy courses were especially important. Many Hispanic enrollees had never learned to read and write in Spanish, no less English. Even enrollees who had attended several years of school were often evaluated as illiterate because many had forgotten much of whatever reading and writing skills they had acquired years before.[13]

As the New Mexico state director of literacy, Nina Otero-Warren visited CCC camps to make suggestions on how reading and writing instruction could be improved. She often focused on the special problem of teaching literacy in English to a population whose first language was usually Spanish. Otero-Warren urged the use of several teaching tools she herself had developed. One such pamphlet, entitled *Writing a Letter: A Bi-lingual Reading Lesson*, taught everything about letter writing in English and in Spanish. The pamphlet's cover featured two drawings: of an enrollee confidently writing home and of his shawled mother receiving the welcomed letter in a rural mailbox. For more advanced readers, Otero-Warren suggested her illustrated classic, *Old Spain in Our Southwest*. A highly romantic view of New

Mexico history and culture, *Old Spain in Our Southwest* was meant not only to help teach reading skills, but also to create pride in traditional Hispanic customs, from religious practices to folk stories and songs.[14]

While Otero-Warren criticized some camp literacy classes as "makeshift" and "inadequate," she praised others as well organized and productive. Enough camps fit the latter description to make a significant difference in the lives of many young men. Although no data exists to compare literacy rates before and after enrollment in New Mexico's camps as a whole, CCC inspection reports attest to the progress made in individual camps. At BR-3-N near Carlsbad, inspector Matthew J. Bower found that of thirteen beginning readers at the end of 1941, eleven could be counted in the ranks of the literate by early 1942.[15]

Only half as many academic courses were taught at the high school level, as compared to the grammar school level, because few enrollees were prepared for advanced study in the CCC. Of the four high school subjects most often taught in camp, Math classes were first, History classes were second, and English courses were tied with Spanish classes for third in 1940. Spanish and other courses related to the Southwest were in high demand as out-of-state enrollees hoped to learn more about their new surroundings and New Mexicans sought to learn more about their native state and culture. In addition to Southwest history and Spanish language classes, archeology classes were taught in camp, with popular field trips to ancient Indian ruins, including Frijoles Canyon in northern New Mexico and Mimbres pottery sites in southern New Mexico. Enrollees in a Southwest literature class visited Lincoln to interview two octogenarians, one of whom claimed to have fought alongside Billy the Kid and the other who claimed to have fought against the legendary outlaw in the Lincoln County War. Students from the Ft. Stanton camp's photography class went along, "snapp[ing] pictures of everything in sight."[16]

A wide range of arts and crafts classes were also offered so that young men could learn "constructive use of leisure time," not only in camp, but later when they reached adulthood. The 1938

Enrollee clerks often used the typing skills learned in evening classes for their work in CCC camp headquarters. *Narrative Report, Bosque del Apache Camp, July-August-September 1940.*

edition of the CCC's *Educational Manual* for New Mexico listed no fewer than twenty-eight suggested arts and crafts classes, including both the usual, such as wood working, and the unusual, such as marionette making. As with academic classes, arts and crafts classes often stressed Southwestern themes. Enrollees at the Ft. Stanton camp made benches in Spanish designs for use in their rec hall. Further north, students learned to weave blankets in the Chimayo style; their success was partly measured by the sale of their attractive handiwork. Students at the Whitewater camp could sign up for instruction in rock carving and "Yucca craft" in 1937. As with many New Deal programs, a major goal of the CCC was to validate and preserve traditional arts and crafts already threatened by extinction by the 1930s. Justifiably proud of the fruits of their labor, enrollees often displayed their arts and crafts at open houses in camp and in nearby forts and towns.[17]

While other courses were popular and well-attended, few were more valued and appreciated than the many vocational classes taught in camp. Most enrollees realized that vocational training was essential for their future employment and personal success. Much could be learned on the job in the CCC, especially if an enrollee worked in a skilled or semi-skilled field like surveying or heavy equipment operation. But much could be learned in vocational classes as well. As a result, thirty-nine percent of all CCC courses taught vocational skills. The CCC camp near Santa Fe taught so many vocational classes that it was the only camp in the United States designated as a "full-blown trade school."[18]

A wide range of skills were taught as vocational fields, from blacksmithing to taxidermy. However, of the seventy-three skills taught in New Mexico's camps in 1940, five clearly dominated. Of these five, woodworking led the list with forty-five classes, auto mechanics was second with thirty-five classes, truck driving was third with thirty-four, typing was fourth with thirty-three, and cooking was fifth with thirty-two.[19]

Lacking large budgets to purchase equipment for specialized classes, educational advisors resorted to a number of plan-as-you-go measures. Typewriters, for example, were often rented from suppliers at a rate of fifty to seventy-five cents a month for each student; while some enrollees complained of this expense, most valued the training and enrollment in typing classes was always high. Camps located near high schools or colleges made arrangements to use teaching equipment after regular school hours. Enrollees stationed near Tucumcari learned typing on machines at the local high school in 1939. Socorro and Ft. Sumner high schools opened their machine shops to enrollees, while Albuquerque High School did the same for welding students in the early 1940s.[20]

Securing able vocational instructors was often as difficult as finding adequate equipment. The task of finding a qualified person to teach taxidermy in the Corona camp literally backfired when the assigned instructor accidently shot himself in the leg while hunting for specimens for his students to mount. Enrollees had to wait eight months for J.W. McCarley's leg to heal and their long-awaited class to begin.[21]

Enrollees who completed high school and showed exceptional academic promise were given the golden opportunity of attending college while still in the CCC. By 1936, New Mexico A&M developed a special program for enrollees stationed at two nearby camps, BR-39-N and SCS-16-N. Qualified corpsmen not already assigned to these camps could be transferred from camps elsewhere in New Mexico; as many as four young scholars transferred from the Redrock camp in early 1938. Once in Las Cruces, selected enrollees lived and worked like any other enrollees, with some exceptions. All lived in barracks, for example, but most lived in specific barracks more conducive to the quiet needed for study. Like other enrollees, they worked each week day, but usually in the morning and at less strenuous jobs so that they would be ready for their afternoon classes on the New Mexico A&M campus. Most student enrollees were assigned to work crews that trapped or poisoned prairie gophers in nearby fields; one 'Gopher Gang' trapped 2,348 gophers in October 1936 alone.[22]

Their daily labor completed, student enrollees rode Army trucks to New Mexico A&M, arriving in what was undoubtedly the most unusual student transportation on campus. Corpsmen took from six to ten credit hours per semester, with classes held between 1:00 p.m. and 4:00 p.m., four days a week. Enrollees paid their own tuition, although it was reduced from $25.50 to only $10.00 a semester, a substantial savings for members of the CCC. Most enrollees pursued engineering degrees.[23]

Student success in the New Mexico A&M program varied. Enrollment averaged about thirty students a semester, with as high as sixty-two in the spring of 1937. Most enrollees did well academically, despite the challenge of juggling studying, work, and camp responsibilities. BR-39-N proudly announced that its college students out-performed SCS-16-N's students in the program's first semester, with six of its enrollees earning B averages and only one youth disqualified for the following semester. Earning all A's, BR-39-N's Clyde Cook did so well in the spring of 1937 that he received a full-scholarship at A&M for the 1937-38 academic year.[24]

Few completed their four-year degrees while still in the CCC if only because most were freshmen when they entered the program and the average CCC enrollment in New Mexico equaled less than a year. But an estimated twenty-five percent of those who began their studies while in the CCC continued their college education at A&M or elsewhere after leaving the Civilian Conservation Corps. In what could be considered a forerunner of the G.I. Bill following World War II, the special enrollee program at A&M mirrored similar college programs designed for talented enrollees on campuses across the nation.[25]

Other qualified enrollees registered at public colleges and private business schools near their camps in several parts of New Mexico. Within five months after the CCC's creation in 1933, over thirty enrollees from the Gila camp registered for night classes at the New Mexico State Teachers College in Silver City. University of New Mexico President James Zimmerman specifically encouraged at least two enrollees to register for night classes at the Albuquerque campus. A number of enrollees attended the New Mexico Normal School at Las Vegas, the Spanish-American Normal School at El Rito, and business schools in both Albuquerque and Tucumcari.[26]

But without programs designed to meet their unique circumstances, enrollees seldom enjoyed the same rate of success at these institutions as their CCC colleagues enjoyed at A&M. Andres Hernandez's experience at the New Mexico State Teachers College was typical. Hernandez registered for two afternoon classes at the college and, along with other student enrollees, received transportation to the campus in Army trucks, much like enrollees at A&M. But as the semester wore on, fewer and fewer enrollees attended classes until only Hernandez remained. With his camp unwilling to send a truck and driver for only one student, the young man had to walk six miles each way on his own. Studies were difficult enough without this additional burden, especially in inclement weather. Faced with similar problems in distant camps, many enrollees signed up for correspondence courses at low costs from schools like UNM and the normal school at Las Vegas.[27]

Enrollees who achieved their educational goals despite hardships were deservedly honored with special recognition and ceremonies. Some were praised in camp newspapers for the number of courses they completed. Others, like Neff Meskiman, were commended for studying diligently in camp and landing a "civilian" job as a "reward for his work in school." Proficiency certificates were awarded at the conclusion of many courses. Enrollees who completed their elementary, eighth grade, or high school studies received diplomas, often in public ceremonies and often with considerable pomp and circumstance. Thirty-four enrollees, including twenty-one elementary school, ten eighth grade, and three high school graduates, were honored at special exercises in the Santa Fe camp in 1940. The ceremony included a traditional commencement address and music by Los Villeros Alegres. Ten eighth grade graduates were similarly honored at a ceremony held at the Odean Theater in Tucumcari.[28]

At the college level, Ray Dawson and Henry R. Johnson were among the handful of enrollees who completed their degrees while still enrolled in the CCC. Dawson had started college at the University of Iowa, had moved to the Southwest for health reasons, and had joined the CCC in New Mexico. Enrolling at New Mexico A&M, he graduated in the top ten percent of his senior class. Johnson, who began his studies as an enrollee in 1936, was lauded as a success story by CCC leaders when he graduated from the University of New Mexico with a Bachelor's degree in economics just three years later.[29]

But most enrollees never expected or received public accolades for their educational achievements. Thousands were simply rewarded with the personal gratification of attaining new knowledge and acquiring new job skills. Juan Otero, for example, was so determined to learn to type that he practiced ten times a week when he was only required to practice four times a week at his camp in Bandelier. Years later, former enrollees looked back and appreciated their schools in the woods even more. Felix Cabrera spoke for hundreds when he recalled that he learned a great deal of English, math, typing, blueprint reading, and estimating skills in the CCC, all of which served him well in the military and in the rest of his professional career. While the success of the CCC's educational program varied from camp to camp, many enrollees benefitted from it with sharper mental skills to match the stronger bodies they had developed while serving in New Mexico. In the judgement of an historian of education in New Mexico, "CCC classes may have been the most successful of all ... New Deal educational programs" because they provided truly "useful skills that broadened [each enrollee's] occupational opportunities" and brightened each enrollee's vocational future.[30]

## Endnotes - Chapter 7

[1]    Bryant, "Education," 66-7. On education in the CCC nationwide, see the *New York Times*, July 28, 1935; Salmond, *CCC*, 47-54;

Hill, *School in the Camps*; George P. Rawick, "The New Deal and Youth: The CCC, the NYA and the American Youth Congress" (Unpublished Ph.D. dissertation, University of Wisconsin, 1957): 117-31.

² *Pink Pebble Periodical*, June 15, 1936; *Organ Echoes*, September 1936; *The Ripple*, March 1939.

³ Bryant, "Education," 18-19; Sanchez, *Forgotten People*, 75.

⁴ Bryant, "Education," 32; Hill, *School in the Camps*, 17-21; Dan K. Utley and James W. Steely, *Guided With a Steady Hand* (Waco, Texas: Baylor University Press, 1998): 68.

⁵ Bryant, "Education," 26; *Organ Echoes*, March 1936, August 1937, October 1937, and December 1937; *Save Our Soil*, April 1936; Robert Thomas interview, May 17, 1991; *Pink Pebble Periodical*, February 12, 1935.

⁶ Bryant, "Education," 15, 40, 42-5, 47-8, 99; Holland and Hill, *Youth*, 151-3; Dawson interview; *Tip Topper*, July 1937; Camp Inspection Report, Deming, January 25, 1940, CCC, NA.

⁷ Ross Calvin, Log Book, entries of August 8 and 19, 1936, Ross Calvin Papers, CSWR, UNM; *Organ Echoes*, February 1937; Bryant, "Education," 48.

⁸ Bryant, "Education," 16, 33, 46; Hendrickson, "CCC in the Southwest," 23; Forrest, *Preservation*, 117. Problems faced by educational advisors nationally are summarized in Everett L. Edmonson, "Some Nation-Wide Educational Problems of the Civilian Conservation Corps" (Unpublished Ph.D. dissertation, Northwestern University, 1940).

⁹ *Manual for Instructors in Civilian Conservation Corps Camps* (Washington, D.C.: U.S. Government Printing Office, 1935): 22-3, 27-9.

¹⁰ Sanchez, *Forgotten People*, 31-2; Harlan Sininger, "New Mexico Reading Survey" (Unpublished M.A. thesis, University of New Mexico, 1930): 89; Lynne Marie Getz, *Schools of Their Own: The Education of Hispanos in New Mexico, 1850-1940* (Albuquerque: University of New Mexico Press, 1997): 104.

¹¹ Bryant, "Education," 69, 74; Hill, *School in the Camps*, 41; Lacy, *Soil Soldiers*, 42-3, 45.

¹² Calvin W. Gower, "The Civilian Conservation Corps and American Education: Threat or Local Control?" *History of Education Quarterly*, 7 (Spring 1967), 58-70; Bryant, "Education," 90-1.

¹³ Johnson interview; Williams interview; Platt L. Welker interview, OHPB; Logan, "Golden Memory," 5; *Fresnal Ranger*, February 1, 1935; Educational Advisors Association Minutes.

¹⁴ Nina Otero-Warren, *Writing a Letter: A Bi-Lingual Reading Lesson* (Santa Fe: n.p., n.d.), Alfred M. Bergere Papers, NMSRCA; Nina Otero-Warren, *Old Spain in Our Southwest* (New York: Harcourt,

Brace and Company, 1936); Charlotte Whaley, *Nina Otero-Warren of Santa Fe* (Albuquerque: University of New Mexico Press, 1994), 146-52. *Old Spain in Our Southwest* was also used in the New Mexico public schools.

[15] *El Campo*, March 1937; *La Piedra Lumbre*, November 1936; Camp Inspection Report, Carlsbad, February 12, 1942, CCC, NA; Merrill, *Roosevelt's Tree Army,* 49.

[16] Bryant, "Education," 90-2; Welker interview, OHPB; Harrison et al., *Bandelier*, 15; *Pink Pebble Periodical*, April 16, 1935; *Albuquerque Journal*, May 18, 1935; *Save Our Soil*, April 1936; *Lonely Pennsylvanian*, April 1940.

[17] *Glenwood News*, August 1936 and October 1936; Bryant, "Education," 116-17; *Stanton Static*, April 1937; *La Piedra Lumbre*, September 1936; Forrest, *Preservation*, 117; *Save Our Soil*, July 1937; *Organ Echoes*, July 30, 1936, and September 1936; *Organ View Optic*, August 11, 1936.

[18] Bryant, "Education," 90-4, 96; Camp Inspection Report, Carlsbad, November 1936, CCC, NA; Forrest, *Preservation,* 117.

[19] Bryant, "Education," 92-4; *Mayhill Lookout*, January 15, 1937; *El Gallo de Pelea*, August 31, 1936; *Organ Echoes*, September 1936; Sanders Memoirs, 112.

[20] *Organ Echoes*, September 1936; *Camp News*, October 24, 1935; *Tumbleweed*, May 1939; *Ft. Sumner Bugler,* April 1941; Oliver C. Payne, Camp Report, Bosque del Apache, October-November-December 1940, BANWR; Gibson interview.

[21] *El Gallo de Pelea*, January 1936.

[22] *Organ Echoes*, September 1936, October 1936, November 1936, and June 30, 1937; Nelson interview; Lopez interview; *CCC Annual, 1936, Ft. Bliss District*, 57, 59; CCC Headquarters, Ft. Bliss District, CCC Bulletin #72, Ft. Bliss, August 6, 1936, CCC Papers, NMSRCA (hereafter cited as CCC Bulletin #72); *Pink Pebble Periodical,* January 15, 1938; Mooney interview; Vega interview.

[23] Dawson interview; Smith interview; *Organ Echoes,* August 31, 1936, April 1937, and September 1937; CCC Bulletin #72; *New Mexico State College of Agriculture and Mechanic Arts College Record: Catalog Issue for the Sessions of 1935-36*, 29 (June 1936), 36; Kropp, *All May Learn*, 241; Camp Inspection Report, Las Cruces, December 1, 1938, CCC, NA.

[24] *Organ Echoes*, October 1936, November 1936, December 1936, January 1937, February 1937, April 1937, July 31, 1937, and September 1937; Educational Advisor's Report, Las Cruces, October 4, 1940, CCC, NA.

[25] Average enrollment calculated from a sample of CCC enrollment cards, 1936-42, CCC Papers, NMSRCA; Educational Advisor's Report, Las Cruces, October 4, 1940, CCC, NA; CCC Press Release on Cooperation of Schools, Washington, D.C., February 12, 1940, CCC File, FDRL; Howard W. Oxley, "Colleges and CCC Camp Education," *School Life,* 21 (December 1936): 106, 120; *School and Society*, 44 (December 12, 1936): 772-73; Gower, "CCC and American Education," 62. Other colleges and universities offering special programs for enrollees included such diverse institutions as Baylor University, Georgetown, the Tuskegee Institute, the University of Maryland, Oklahoma A&M, Northeastern University, and the University of Chicago.

[26] *Silver City Enterprise*, September 15 and 22, 1933, and October 6, 1933; *Forest Pioneer*, October 1933 and October 1935; Chacon interview; *Wasp*, September 1937; *Tumbleweed,* September 1938.

[27] Hernandez interview; *Save Our Soil*, August 1937; *El Gallo de Pelea*, August 31, 1936; *New York Times*, October 17, 1937. At least forty colleges and universities in the U.S. offered low-cost correspondence courses to enrollees by 1936. Oxley, "Colleges and CCC Camp Education," 120.

[28] *Rio Chicito*, December 1937; *Fresnal Ranger*, January 18, 1935, and February 22, 1935; *New Mexico Daily Examiner*, May 30, 1940; *Tumbleweed*, June 1939; Westwood interview.

[29] Dawson interview; CCC Heroes' Stories File, July 6, 1939, CCC, NA.

[30] Camp Inspection Report, Bandelier, October 2, 1935, CCC, NA; *Gila Monster,* January 1936; Felix Cabrera interview, July 24, 1993; *CCC Annual, 1936, Ft. Bliss District*, 49; Henderick, "CCC in the Southwest," 23; Getz, *Schools of Their Own*, 106. Camp educational programs received a less favorable review in Utley and Steely, *Guided With a Steady Hand*, 68 and 70-1.

*above*: Enrollees like Lee Roy Jones and five of his friends from the Carlsbad camp gladly shed their uniforms for 'civilian' clothes in preparation for weekends in local towns.    *below*: Enrollees often fraternized with local girls, despite the initial fears expressed by the females and their families. *Photos courtesy: Lee Roy Jones.*

# CHAPTER 8

# Weekends in Town

Like workers everywhere, CCC enrollees looked forward to weekends off with great anticipation. After a long week of work, study, and in-camp duties, enrollees enjoyed time on their own to relax and just have fun, especially when given opportunities to explore their new surroundings. With few exceptions, trips to nearby attractions enhanced the enrollees' lives, creating some of the most vivid memories in their CCC experience.

Unfortunately, weekends usually began with some additional duties, at least on Saturday mornings. While enrollees seldom traveled to their weekday work sites, they were often required to do light work around camp, such as cleaning their barracks and policing (picking up) camp grounds. Although some performed these tasks begrudgingly, others willingly helped to improve the looks, and hence the image, of their temporary homes. At BR-39-N near Las Cruces, enrollees took great pride in planting lawns and flower beds (including a cactus garden) throughout their camp. As a result of their labor, the *Las Cruces Daily News* declared BR-39-N a model camp that had transformed a "backyard nobody wanted" into an attractive spot with "more fresh, green grass ... than any lawn in town." At the Bosque del Apache camp "every possible effort" was made to improve the camp site with gravel walks, trees, shrubs, and even a lily pond. Neat signs and careful landscaping could make camp entrances look more like entries to well-groomed parks rather than back roads into work camps. Camp beautification contests were held, as at Ft. Stanton where a five dollar prize went to the barracks with the best surrounding landscape by Independence Day 1937.[1]

Landscaping efforts contributed to the enrollees' improved morale, while drawing favorable comments from average visitors and public officials alike. State and national leaders were consistently impressed by what they saw. Although President Roosevelt and his wife Eleanor never visited CCC camps in New Mexico, as they sometimes did back East, CCC director Robert Fechner visited camps in New Mexico and Arizona in 1934. Governor Andrew Hockenhull (1933-34) visited state camps, as did Clyde Tingley during his two terms as New Mexico's governor (1935-38). Enrollees at the Elephant Butte camp (BR-8-N) were so honored by Clyde and Carrie Tingley's visit in early 1935 that they dedicated an issue of their camp newspaper, the *Rock Hound*, to the governor and sent him sample copies.[2]

Overnight guests stayed in special guest rooms built in many camps; the room built at Polica Canyon (F-31-N) was filled with furniture made by the camp's carpentry class and decorated with paintings produced by the camp's oil painting class. All camps were known for their hospitality and willingness to help travelers, especially in emergencies on back roads and in the wilderness.[3]

Great efforts were made to maintain camp buildings and grounds not only to impress high officials and occasional guests, but also to prepare for periodic camp inspections. District inspectors were said to check everything imaginable, including "latrines, literacy, lice, and literature." Camp commanders went to great lengths to prepare for such scrutiny, especially when notoriously strict inspectors were expected. Surprise inspections were particularly dreaded, as reflected in a 1937 poem:

> Now once or twice it's very nice
> To entertain inspectors;
> To show them how we're doing now
> And count the truck reflectors.

But it's not wise for all these guys
To come so unexpected.
They always find our work behind
And things to be corrected ... .

It sure is tough, the kind of guff
We have to take while grinning.
But pitch the ball, we'll take it all
And play another inning.[4]

Camp commanders developed coded messages to warn each other of impending reviews. When a commander knew that an inspector was en route to a neighboring camp, he would make a collect call to the targeted camp and ask for a specific CCC dentist by name. If one dentist's name was used, it meant that the inspector was two camps away; if another dentist's name was used, it meant that the inspector was only one camp away. A call announcing that "stormy weather is on its way" meant that the inspector might arrive at any time. Some supervisors were particularly worried about their inventories, noting that running a CCC project could be "a hell of a bookkeeping nightmare." Six worried officers went so far as to meet once a month in a bar in Socorro to discuss common problems and exchange camp property and supplies so that each commander had no more or less than he was supposed to for inspections. Willing to go to great lengths to please fastidious inspectors, one commander learned that a district inspector liked trees. Expecting a visit by this inspector, the commander had his enrollees cut long branches from nearby salt cedar trees and "plant" 160 of them along the road into camp. The salt cedars impressed the inspector, but "died" soon after, having succeeded in their very temporary decorative mission. Despite anxieties, most camps passed inspections with high grades. After one such evaluation in September 1937, inspector A.W. Stockman described the camp near Carrizozo as "splendid" in appearance, "exactly maintained and administered in a superior manner."[5]

Enrollees were just as intimidated by inspections made by their own supervisors on Saturday mornings. Similar to Saturday Army inspections, CCC inspections required enrollees to have perfectly-made bunks, clean uniforms, shined shoes, and overall neat barracks. Those who did well could expect praise and even rewards. In competitions between barracks, residents of the cleanest barracks could win everything from a best barracks banner to field trips to favorite destinations like Conchas Dam and Carlsbad Caverns. Using carrots as well as sticks, officers in the El Rito camp (F-36-N) rewarded those in the cleanest barracks with relief from Saturday morning chores, while enrollees in the dirtiest barracks at Carlsbad (BR-3-N) were confined to camp and given extra weekend assignments.[6]

Enrollees who finished their chores and passed inspection were on their own by early Saturday afternoon. Those with money and cars enjoyed the most options regarding recreation for the weekend. Unfortunately, few enrollees had much money and fewer owned their own cars. Each youth earned thirty dollars a month, but with twenty-five of their thirty dollars automatically sent to help their families back home, enrollees had only five dollars a month of actual spending money. True, everything from food and shelter to clothes and work transportation was provided by the CCC, but enrollees still had obligations to cover with their few dollars of profit. Those enrolled in typing classes, for example, paid fifty to seventy-five cents a month to rent the machines they practiced on. Others had debts to pay on coupon books or tokens used in the camp canteen. Haircuts cost twenty-five cents, and the average enrollee spent a dollar a month on cigarettes. Additional funds were needed to pay off bets on games of chance, like poker and dice, or on hotly-contested athletic competition, like boxing bouts. More benignly, enrollees could be counted on to contribute money in national emergencies, like floods back East in 1937, or when a fellow enrollee's family needed funds to cover the cost of an unexpected tragedy, like funeral expenses. When all these expenses were added up, little remained for weekend sprees.

As a result, most enrollees declared themselves "broke" within hours on payday. A 1936 poem in the Deming camp newspaper only half factiously told of a "sad buckaroo" who had joined the CCC without "dinero" and left the 3Cs in much the same condition.[7]

Not all enrollees ran short on cash so quickly. Many were even frugal enough to send part of their five dollars home each month to further help their families or to save for their own futures. One enrollee became famous when he bought only one coupon book during his first three months in camp, and then spent only three cents of it for a stamp to mail a letter home. Noah Gibson, Jr., proudly saved two-hundred dollars during his twenty-seven months in the CCC. In other cases, enrollees' families saved much of the twenty-five dollars they received each month to create a nestegg for their sons when their time in the CCC was up. Enrollees at the Glenwood camp were so impressed (or annoyed) by James Raleigh's refusal to spend money that they took a survey and gave him the dubious distinction of being considered the "tightest man in camp."[8]

Enterprising enrollees not only saved, but also invested money while serving in the CCC. Operating in-camp businesses, they offered goods and services of many expected—and unexpected—kinds. Nearly every camp had at least one enrollee who was willing to extend credit in either cash or canteen coupon books. Noah Gibson was able to save as much as he did largely based on his ability to collect fifty cents on payday for every twenty-five cents in coupon books he lent during the month. Bernardo Lujan claimed that by collecting twenty to twenty-five percent interest on loans to fellow enrollees at his Bandelier camp, "I was making more money than the officers."[9]

Entrepreneurial enrollees made additional money by offering other camp services. Photo developing was provided if dark room facilities were available; four clever young men at the Corona camp advertised that they could "develop your roll of film free, providing you will make a donation of not less than twenty-five cents to [our] firm." Most camps also had at least one enrollee who could cut hair for a small fee; barbers were kept so busy that they sometimes cut hair until ten or eleven o'clock at night. With plenty of practice in the CCC, several, including Bernardo Lujan at Bandelier and Emery Smith at Las Cruces, made this craft their life-time work in New Mexico. Less skilled, but no less ambitious enrollees were willing to wash clothes and even substitute for fellow enrollees assigned to KP duty to earn extra cash. For an extra twenty-five dollars a month, selected enrollees could serve as 'dog robbers' (or orderlies) for camp officers. Another group served as 'firemen' who, for a fee collected from each enrollee in a barracks, kept a fire going on cold nights in their barracks' pot-belly stoves.[10]

But the prize for the most innovative camp service offered in New Mexico must go to two enrollees at the Redrock camp in 1935. In a variation on the mail order bride business, these young businessmen sold envelopes with the names and addresses of young women in Wyoming who were willing and able to become pen pals with subscribers "or your money back." As an ad in the Redrock camp newspaper put it, a boy simply had to buy a pre-addressed envelope "and presto, you establish a sweet ... romance with one of Wyoming's most beautiful maidens." No investigations were held to reveal if these maidens were as attractive as advertised or if they were only a few females willing to correspond with a long list of gullible male customers.[11]

The variety of goods sold in camp matched or surpassed the variety of available services. Clothes were always popular merchandise; like soldiers, enrollees were eager to shed their weekday uniforms for finer civilian garments on weekends. Entrepreneurs like Henry Arellanes sold suits for a mail order firm that provided him with sample material and instructions on how to measure fellow enrollees for a good fit. For every three suits that Arellanes sold, he received either cash or a new suit of his own. Leo Valdez promoted a similar business with an ad in the Española camp newspaper that read, "Suits to order—guaranteed to fit." Working for a Chicago-based clothing firm, Alex Salazar sold tailor-made suits for as much a fifty dollars each at Bandelier. In addition, Salazar sold gaberdine shirts with pearl snap buttons; "the more buttons you ordered, the more the shirt cost." Ties, shoes, and other accessories were also for sale in most camps.[12]

Ambitious salesmen peddled other goods, including greeting cards in the case of Johnny Hargrove at Redrock and piñon nuts in the case of Mel Montoya. Some enrollees crossed the legal line and sold camp equipment and supplies in town or, if their camps were near the international border, in Mexico. Undoubtedly the most ambitious enrollee salesman served at the Glenwood camp and confidently advertised, "If you are thinking about buying or selling anything SEE BUTLER. I pay better prices and sell below cost. Ask any CCC boy. Honesty is my policy."[13]

Perhaps inevitably, some enrollees caught the gold bug while living in the wilderness. Several panned for gold in the Sacramento River, hoping that this river in New Mexico would yield the same riches as the famous river by the same name in California. Although enrollee miners claimed success, their yield was small and was really only fool's gold, according to skeptics on the scene.[14]

Despite their extra income, even relatively affluent enrollees could seldom afford large purchases like cars. Having cars in camp was, in any case, against CCC rules. Those caught with private vehicles faced immediate discharge because cars were considered unsafe on most wilderness roads; those who could afford cars probably didn't belong in the CCC anyway. The CCC also restricted the use of cars as a means of reducing unauthorized leaves or prolonged absences from camps.[15]

But the rule that banned cars was not always obeyed. Enrollees like Roy Huffman and Bernardo Lujan soon realized they could park their cars at a distance from camp and camouflage them quite well under branches or behind shrubs. Others were encouraged to follow suit when officers winked at the no-car regulation. Harold Davis's captain at the Magdelena camp officially refused Davis's request to keep a car, but subtly pointed out a woodpile behind which a car could be easily hidden near camp. Unable to afford cars of their own, John Mooney and his fellow enrollees simply waited for the right moment, pushed a CCC vehicle from the camp garage, and got it started down the road, knowing that the man who ran the garage was too hard of hearing to detect their after-hours mischief.[16]

With little money and few cars, enrollee trips home were rare. Some never returned home during their enrollment periods. Others, like Levi Baca, only went home once or twice during up to two years of enrollment. A faction preferred to stay in camp because the food was often more plentiful than in their poverty-stricken homes. Another faction feared that if they went home and got spoiled by their mothers' cooking, they'd never return to camp. Trips home and back could be hazardous for other reasons as well. Although against CCC rules, many enrollees hitchhiked, leaving themselves at the mercy of unpredictable drivers and even less predictable weather conditions. Roy Lemons tells of hitching a ride through New Mexico on his way home to Texas. All went well until the driver of a car Lemons had hitched a ride in discovered that his young passenger was an enrollee in the CCC. Clearly opposed to the CCC, or perhaps the New Deal in general, the driver stopped his vehicle in the middle of nowhere and refused to take Lemons any further. Four other Texan enrollees en route home from New Mexico were even less fortunate when the car they were in collided with a truck loaded with pipes. The crash was so severe that the truck driver was killed and all four enrollees required transport to a hospital where they eventually recovered. Elsewhere, Tony Roybal took hours to hitch a rode from Bandelier to Española, eventually arriving home safely despite three feet of snow on the ground.[17]

Hitching rides on freight trains was also prohibited by the CCC, but regularly practiced by experienced youths. Some, like Lee Roy Jones in Carlsbad and Tony Sanchez in Las Cruces, were so skilled at this inexpensive, rapid form of transportation that they regularly made it home and back to camp in plenty of time for Monday morning roll call. Jim Johnson discovered a far safer form of railroad travel: reduced fares for CCC enrollees on the Santa Fe Railroad line. Johnson recalls a porter who was so kind and cooperative that he arranged for Johnson's train to make a special stop at his destination in Maxwell rather than make Johnson travel sixteen miles back from the next scheduled stop at 1:00 a.m. A fortunate few enrollees had families so close to their camps that they could even count on camp trucks to drop them off and pick them back up on weekends.[18]

But, given the possible obstacles and dangers of long distance travel, most enrollees limited their trips home to emergencies and holidays. Accumulating one day of leave time for every month of service, enrollees usually had enough leave to travel home in the event of a family illness or death; sympathetic officers regularly granted additional time off if needed. Two of the biggest holidays of the year, Christmas and New Years, left many camps largely deserted. Fifty percent of the enrollees at SCS-4-N at El Rito were granted five-day leaves to go home for Christmas in 1936, while the remaining fifty percent took their five-day leaves during the New Years holiday. Aware that a large percentage of all desertions occurred following major holidays, prudent officers took this opportunity to remind enrollees of the dire consequences of going AWOL. Although sometimes late, most enrollees returned to camp out of a personal sense of duty as well as a sincere desire to continue helping the loved ones they had just visited back home.[19]

While few enrollees ventured home on weekends, many planned trips for rest and recreation in nearby towns. Still lacking cash and cars, most relied on transportation provided by the CCC. Army trucks, used for transport to and from work sites during the week, were now employed for transport to and from local communities. Dressed in street clothes and ready for experiences far from camp and home, enrollees began their weekend 'liberty parties' with great expectations.[20]

Exuberant enrollees were dropped off at central locations in their urban (or at least quasi-urban) destinations. In Albuquerque, they were left at McClellan Park on Central Avenue. In Carlsbad, they were left at the local post office, while in Española it was the train depot. Enrollees were reminded that they would be picked up at the same spots later that Saturday or on Sunday afternoon.[21]

Enrollees scattered in search of entertainment, with most seeking good, clean fun. Movies drew large crowds; Gregorio Villasenor remembered seeing Gary Cooper in *Beau Geste* (1939) at a theater in Deming. Villasenor was so "fascinated by the notes of the bugle" in this film about the Foreign Legion that he vowed to become a bugler, a goal he later achieved in the Army. Enrollees who went to railroad towns like Albuquerque and Belen could also hope to see movie stars and well-known celebrities when passenger trains stopped at depots and Harvey Houses along the tracks. Other enrollees frequented pool halls, shooting galleries, bowling allies, and skating rinks. Several hundred from three different camps attended the Middle Rio Grande Rodeo in Bernalillo in August 1933. At least one adventuresome enrollee from back East accepted the challenge of riding a bronco at a New Mexico rodeo, lasting only moments before he was thrown to the ground with only wounded pride and wounded limbs to show for his Wild West escapade.[22]

But of all the diversions offered in towns, dances understandably held the greatest interest for most young men. Whether hosted at private dance halls or in public places, the color, music, and feminine companionship of local festivities stood in stark contrast to the rest of an average enrollee's workweek experience. The interior of the Mountainair community building, for example, was decorated in red, white, and blue bunting for a 1937 dance described as "the social event of the season." The main street of Belen was equally colorful for the street dances held during the annual Belen fiesta. Enrollees at the Santa Fe fiesta were said to have so many girls to chose from that they could dance every dance all night. Couples at local gatherings danced to the music of Spanish, country, and popular songs of the day. Those at the Capitan grade school gym danced to jitterbug tunes at what was billed as a Jitterbug Jamboree; a favorite song at the jamboree was entitled "Jim Jam Jumpin' of the Jumpin' Jive." Tickets to dances were inexpensive, and some dance halls, like the Palader Pavilion in Lordsburg, offered special discounts to CCC customers.[23]

Most enrollees enjoyed themselves at dances and were praised by their host communities as "a very orderly lot of young men," in the words of the *Grant County Bulletin*. Unfortunately, not all town residents felt the same way about members of the CCC. This was especially true of young males who saw enrollees as unwanted competition for female attention. Feelings of jealously and fear were typical in small communities from the first news that a CCC camp might be established in an area. 'Si' Porter described these fears when he and his fellow residents of Corona, New Mexico, heard rumors that a CCC camp was about to be built.

> [The] rumors were very upsetting to a lot of people. The country folks believed the CCC boys would come from big city areas back East ... . Most of the single boys and some of the married ones expected to have to whip all the CCC boys and run them clear out of the state. Most of the girls and women thought they would be raped and mistreated by the type of boys that would come into the CCC camp. They were sure they would never speak to any of them.

Porter's single, eighteen-year-old sister was particularly nervous, vowing that she would learn to shoot a gun or use a butcher knife to defend herself against unwanted attention. She would definitely not let any enrollee "get close enough to even talk to her" and "she would be sure to stay away from them and never speak to them." Porter's sibling and "all the natives" prepared for the worst. "It was sure to be bad."[24]

Local fears were realized with tragic results in the case of Samuel Griego, a CCC worker, and Federico Maestas, a married resident of Rio Arriba County. Returning home after two years of labor in Wyoming, Maestas discovered that his wife had been having "improper relations" with Griego and was, in fact, about to give birth to a child. Enraged, Maestas killed Griego. Maestas was sentenced to up to ten years in the state penitentiary when he pled guilty in his trial for murder.[25]

Fortunately, such disasters were the exception rather than the rule. Most residents in small towns discovered that CCC enrollees were not as bad as they had originally imagined. Even 'Si' Porter's sister in Corona eventually changed her mind, going so far as to date and then marry the supply clerk serving at camp F-41-N. And the Porter girl's case was not unique. Countless enrollees met and dated New Mexico girls. Some, like Emery Smith, Chester Williams, and Robert Michaeli, returned from distant states to marry in New Mexico after their enrollment periods ended, since CCC rules banned marriage during one's time of service.[26]

Budding romances were regularly reported on the pages of camp newspapers. One publication listed enrollees who reported to sick call when they were supposedly struck by a local strain of "love sickness." Other newspapers reported on the strange, love-sick behavior of enrollees who were known to spend less and less of their free time in camp and more and more time in town. A cartoon in *The Yucca,* produced at the Whitewater camp, showed an enrollee named Fergy requesting additional leave time. When the camp commander asked if Fergy wanted "two more days of grace," the young man replied, "No, sir. Two more days of Edith." CCC enrollees were so popular with the girls of El Rito, New Mexico, that the girls supposedly began sending them Christmas cards shortly after the Fourth of July in 1936. The camp newspaper advised, "Go to it boys[;] there's your chance to get a nice bride."[27]

News of fresh romances made good stories for camp newspapers, but they were less well received by jealous local males. Tempers flared, especially at dances and especially when those in attendance had had too much alcohol to drink. Fist fights at a dance in Cliff led to several visits to the Gila camp doctor in 1934. In November 1935 a fight broke out between local men and CCC enrollees at a dance in Grants; a week later over ninety combatants battled in a follow-up fray that temporarily halted traffic on Route 66 and left two enrollees in their camp infirmary with "bruises and lacerations." Knives were employed in fights near Ruidoso; one seriously wounded enrollee had to be transported to the Army hospital at Ft. Bliss for additional treatment. A.B. Barela recalls that a riot broke out between local males and enrollees from Pennsylvania when the latter arrived at a dance in Socorro. Roy Huffman and a friend never even left their car before they encountered trouble one night in Pecos. Driving up to a sidewalk, they were greeted by a local resident who pointed a gun in their window and informed the enrollees that they should not plan to compete for female interest that evening. Huffman and his fellow enrollee saw the wisdom of this less-than-subtle suggestion.[28]

Tomás Brown faced similar resistance as he and an enrollee friend, Pat Rainwater, walked down a poorly lit street on their way back to camp on the outskirts of Santa Fe. When the enrollees heard some "youths make a very derogatory statement about us foreigners coming in and trying to steal their girls," Brown objected to "the adjectives ... used to describe us." A fight ensued. Although proud of their fighting skills (Rainwater was a welterweight boxer), the two enrollees were outnumbered and quickly defeated. Later, while nursing their wounds in camp, Brown for once regretted his knowledge of Spanish that had allowed him to understand the rough remarks that had gotten him and Rainwater in so much trouble.[29]

Anglos like Brown tasted the bitter pill of racism in some towns, but Hispanic enrollees experienced discrimination far more often. This was particularly true in the southern and eastern counties of New Mexico where Southern, Jim Crow racism sometimes prevailed. In one instance, a bar in southern New Mexico hung a sign that warned "No Mexicans Allowed." When Hispanic enrollees were refused service in the establishment (ironically called Casa Mañana), they returned to camp and told their Anglo commander of their poor treatment. Angered, the captain led truck loads of revenge-minded enrollees back to the bar where he assisted them in turning over cars, wreaking the interior, and closing the place down. The bar reopened later, but with its offending sign removed. Not as readily intimidated, Anglo cowhands near Animas refused to allow Hispanic enrollees to enter their dance halls at any time. At Cliff, public dances were segregated, with Anglo dances held on certain days and Hispanic dances held on other occasions. But as harsh as such discrimination could be, it was relatively rare in New Mexico and seldom as bad as in neighboring states. As one Hispanic enrollee remembered, the Hilton Hotel in El Paso, Texas, went so far as to hang a sign declaring "No Dogs or Mexicans Allowed."[30]

While most fights involved racism or competition for local girls, other conflicts were caused by jealousy in general. In Alex Salazar's words, enrollees "were kind of big shots when we'd come to town. We'd go to the dance and we'd have money. The other poor guys, they were broke." Local envy could lead to thefts. In one incident, Robert Reed of the Gila camp was relieved of twenty dollars and stripped "to his nature suit" after a 1934 Halloween party in Cliff. Three years later, Rosendo Pacheco of the Mountainair camp was confronted by two local men who started a fight and robbed him of seven dollars of his hard-earned cash.[31]

Thefts could occur in the courts as well as in the streets. Fred Poorbaugh remembers a Justice of the Peace in Mora, New Mexico, who was notorious for fining enrollees for petty misdemeanors. In fact, the judge had a habit of fixing fines at whatever amount enrollees had in their possession at the time of their arrest. Outraged by this robbery from the bench, camp commander Poorbaugh called on a federal attorney to protest the mistreatment of his men. Sufficiently reprimanded, the magistrate returned most of the collected fines and was known to treat enrollees more fairly thereafter.[32]

Although some charges against enrollees were petty or contrived, others were not. Fighting was the major cause for enrollee arrests in New Mexico, and the major cause of camp-community friction in the United States as a whole. Additional trouble resulted from too much drinking, too much gambling, and too many visits to local houses of ill-repute.[33]

Underage enrollees bought liquor illegally in bars or, more commonly, from local bootleggers at dances or in back alleys. Drinking often led to fights or illness, especially if a particularly bad batch of moonshine liquor was purchased and consumed. Tony Sanchez recalls that beer cost five cents a glass in Silver City, while a half gallon of homemade wine, known as *vino de la pata* (wine made with grapes crushed by feet), cost $1.25. Local whiskey, called *mula* (because it had a kick like a mule), was sold on the street in mason jars. Steve Zavocky, Jr., remembers a watering hole in Lordsburg that was "an appealing establishment if you were of age." Of course, anyone "passed the age test if you had a quarter." Those with too many quarters often drank too much and experienced trouble avoiding obstacles in or near their path. John Mooney recalls a fellow enrollee who consumed so much beer that he stumbled and fell into a hotel cactus garden. The fallen victim's wounds were so severe that he needed help to reach a nearby hospital for medical attention.[34]

Other vices proved equally damaging to one's health and wealth. Enrollees certainly lost far more than they gained at local gambling halls. And brothels could be expensive in more ways than one. While services in these establishments cost as little as twenty-five cents, the venereal diseases caught from prostitutes could be far more expensive in the long run. Despite repeated warnings about VD by camp officials, some enrollees were careless. Enrollees at least had the advantage of weekly examinations, known as "short arm inspections," and appropriate treatment if VD was detected. Following treatment, enrollees with venereal disease were routinely given dishonorable discharges from the CCC, a stigma that caused at least some young men to be more cautious in their sexual encounters on their trips into town.[35]

Some communities were so notorious for their vice and violence that they were declared off limits by camp commanders. The commanding officer at Deming ended liberty parties to Las Cruces in 1939 after a civilian was killed during a "gun battle" in a dance hall frequented by enrollees. The commander at SCS-20-N curtailed liberty parties to Silver City "in view of the 'wide-open' practices and exuberancy of holiday celebrants—cowboys, ranchers, etc.—who congregate in Silver City on festive occasions." Prostitution was so prevalent in Gallup that President Roosevelt himself learned of it and ordered an investigation in the interest of the CCC enrollees and Navajo Indians who frequented the town. A special investigator dispatched to Gallup in 1935 confirmed that all suspicions were true. Prostitution ran rampant because members of the "underworld assert influence on persons in politics and civic positions and as a result [they] are not molested." Prosecutions in state and local courts were "insufficient in number," while "convictions are few, [and] fines and sentences [are] frequently too light." In these and similar circumstances in other towns, trouble could always be found by enrollees who looked for it. Like a faction of youth in every generation, some enrollees erroneously perceived drinking, gambling, and womanizing as legitimate rites of passage to manhood rather than as dangerous routes to larger problems in adult life.[36]

As great as temptations could be to enrollees on leave in New Mexico, they were said to be many times greater for those who traveled to towns along the border with Mexico. Towns on the Mexican side of the border were famous—or infamous—for the potent tequila they sold, the marijuana they peddled, and the VD their prostitutes spread. Henry Arellanes remembers that he and his fellow enrollees at the Columbus, New Mexico, camp were repeatedly reminded that Mexican laws were different than U.S. laws; while a camp commander could bail an enrollee out of jail in the United States, he could do little for those arrested across the border. But not all enrollees heeded such warnings. The smoking of marijuana obtained in Palomas across the border from Columbus became so prevalent that the Columbus camp doctor was instructed to search for the drug and, in an odd choice of words, "weed out all marijuana smokers" among enrollees. Conditions became so bad in Palomas that the town was eventually banned to all enrollees serving in Columbus.[37]

While youths in Columbus simply had to walk across to Mexico, most camps were many miles from the international border. One Saturday, two enrollees from the Ft. Stanton camp took nine hours to hitchhike to Juárez and so much longer to return that they missed Monday morning roll call and had to pay a dollar each in fines for going AWOL. The best that could be said of their excursion was that they had spent so much time on the road that they had had little time left for mischief in Juárez. The same could not be said for Tomás Brown. On a trip to Juárez, Brown attended his first bullfight, but invited trouble when he started yelling "Viva el toro." The enrollee tourist was "informed in no uncertain terms that I was supposed to be yelling for the bullfighter, not the bull." Joseph Delfine and six fellow enrollees from the Conchas Dam camp waited twenty-four hours to catch a freight train to Juárez. After a seventeen-hour trip to the border, they discovered that it cost money to cross the bridge into Mexico and slightly less to return to the United States. Six other enrollees brought back more permanent memories of a trip to El Paso, Texas, in 1940. The group returned to their camp at Ft. Stanton in plenty of time for roll call, but with their bodies decorated with tatoos of all shapes and sizes. The editor of their camp newspaper predicted that their tatoos would be "souvenirs from the West that they will never lose."[38]

What life lessons did enrollees learn on their weekend trips to town? Although few had much money, enrollees learned to budget what little they had or face the consequences of debt or reduced activity until their next payday. A judicious few discovered their own business skills, running small enterprises that not only gave them more cash at the time but more confidence in their futures. Once in town, most enrollees passed their free hours in innocent, enjoyable activities. More adventuresome types also learned about the opposite sex, leading to marriages in healthy relationships or social diseases in unhealthy ones. Hopefully, a few early experiences were enough to teach most youths that womanizing, gambling, and drinking were vices to be avoided rather than cultivated in life. Tragically, Hispanic enrollees in some southern and eastern communities of New Mexico also faced ugly racism in town, if not usually in camp. While some resisted this treatment, most realized that they lived in an era when little was done to deal with, no less eliminate, unfair racism.

Enrollees learned large and small lessons in their quest for rest and relaxation in nearby towns. But while officers, advisors, and older boys could caution enrollees before they ventured far from camp, it was up to the youths themselves to live and, hopefully, learn on their own. It was a credit to their families, the CCC, and themselves that most tested their adult wings and returned to their camp nests unharmed and, in most cases, far wiser.

## Endnotes - Chapter 8

[1]    Jones interview; *Organ Echoes*, May 1936 and July 30, 1936; *Las Cruces Daily News* quoted in *Organ Echoes*, September 1937; CCC Annual, 1936, Fort Bliss District, 59; Oliver C. Payne, Camp Report, Bosque del Apache, July-August-September 1941, BANWR; *Camp News*, November 21, 1935; *Stanton Static*, April 1937.

[2]    Oliver C. Payne, Camp Report, Bosque del Apache, July-August-September 1941, BANWR; Eleanor Roosevelt, *The Autobiography of Eleanor Roosevelt* (New York: Harper and Brothers, 1961): 203-4; Paige, *CCC and the Park Service*, 128; *Albuquerque Journal,* July 25, 1934; *Lincoln Lookout,* June 1937; John H. Veale to Clyde Tingley, Elephant Butte, March 21, 1935, Governor Tingley Papers, NMSRCA.

[3]    *Fresnal Ranger,* February 22, 1935; *Rio Chicito*, February 1938; *Glenwood News*, August 1936.

[4]    Stephen J. Leonard, *Trials and Triumphs* (Boulder: University Press of Colorado, 1993): 63; Dawson interview; *Forest Pioneer,* 4th quarter, 1937.

[5]    Casaus interview; Poorbaugh interview; Dawson interview; Collins interview; Camp Inspection Report, Carrizozo, September 15, 1937, CCC, NA.

[6]    *Lonely Pennsylvanian*, April 1940; *Organ View Optic*, April 10, 1936; *Kangarowl*, September 19, 1935; *Tumbleweed*, September 1938; *Camp Chatter*, May 1937.

[7]    Newbury interview; Harold Davis interview, June 9, 1996; Serna interview; Casaus interview; Kemp interview; Perea interview;

*Kangarowl*, January 1937; *Organ Echoes*, August 31, 1936; *Mirager*, April 1936.

⁸  Huffman interview; *Kangarowl*, March 15, 1935; Gibson interview; Logan, "Golden Memories," 6; *Glenwood News,* August 1936.

⁹  Huffman interview; Beck interview; Gibson interview; Bernardo Lujan interview, OHPB.

¹⁰  *La Poliza*, January 1937; *Lincoln Lookout*, September 1937; Sanders Memoir, 112; Lujan and Salazar interviews, OHPB; Smith interview; Newbury interview; Serna interview.

¹¹  *Pink Pebble Periodical*, June 18, 1935.

¹²  Huffman interview; Arellanes interview; Green interview; Serna interview; *Wasp*, April 1937; *El Campo*, April 1937; Salazar interview, OHPB.

¹³  *Pink Pebble Periodical*, December 12, 1935; Serna interview; Westwood interview; Porter Memoirs, 18; *Glenwood News*, August 1936.

¹⁴  *Mayhill Lookout*, June 1937.

¹⁵  Manual of Instructions, Selection of Men for the CCC, CCC Papers, NMSRCA; *The Ripple*, April 1939.

¹⁶  Lujan interview, OHPB; Huffman interview; Davis interview; Mooney interview.

¹⁷  Hennington interview; Casaus interview; L. Baca interview; Jones interview; Gibson interview; Roy Lemons interview, September 1, 1990; Lucero and Roybal interviews, OHPB.

¹⁸  Jones interview; Sanchez interview; Johnson interview; Gallegos and Joe Martinez interviews, OHPB.

¹⁹  Baldridge, "Nine Years," 290-1; *Wasp*, December 31, 1936; *Gila Monster*, December 25, 1935; Porter Memoirs, 32.

²⁰  Newbury interview; *Bi-Weekly Blast*, July 15, 1940; *El Gallo de Pelea*, August 31, 1936.

²¹  T. Montoya interview; Jones interview; Salazar interview, OHPB.

²²  Rivers interview; Villasenor interview by Cave; Porter Memoirs, 1; *Lonely Pennsylvanian*, August 1939; Sanchez interview; Camp Inspection Report, Glenwood, September 16, 1936, CCC, NA; Camp Inspection Report, Redrock, September 23, 1936, CCC, NA; *Albuquerque Journal,* August 30, 1933; *Lincoln Lookout*, July 1937.

²³  *Tip Topper*, September 1937 and October 1937; *La Piedra Lumbre*, October 1936; *Lonely Pennsylvanian*, May-June 1939 and September 1939; *Pink Pebble Periodical*, May 21, 1935.

²⁴  *Grant County Bulletin* quoted in the *Gila Monster*, September 1935; Porter Memoirs, 2, 5.

[25] *Santa Fe New Mexican*, October 11, 1933.

[26] Porter Memoirs, 8, 38; Smith interview; Williams interview; *Carlsbad Current-Argus*, January 11, 1998; Draves, *Builder*, 245.

[27] *Pink Pebble Periodical*, March 15, 1937; *Yucca*, November 1937; *Wasp*, December 31, 1936.

[28] Garcia interview; Gonzalez interview; James E. Reynolds to the author, Wheat Ridge, California, June 12, 1991; *Gila Monster,* September 21, 1934; *Grants Review*, November 28 and December 12, 1935; Sanchez interview; Barela interview; Huffman interview.

[29] Brown, *Heritage*, 180.

[30] Hernandez interview; Arellanes interview; Williams interview; Vega interview.

[31] Salazar interview, OHPB; *Gila Monster,* November 3, 1934; *Tip Topper*, February 1937.

[32] Poorbaugh interview.

[33] Sherraden, "Effectiveness of the Camps," 114; Holland and Hill, *Youth*, 215-19.

[34] Shirley interview; Huffman interview; Blake interview by Foote; Chavez interview; H. Baca interview; Sanchez interview; Steve Zavacky, Jr., entry in M. Chester Nolte, ed., *The Civilian Conservation Corps: The Way We Remember It, 1933-42* (Paducah, Kentucky: Turner Publishing Company, 1990): 223; Mooney interview.

[35] *Organ Echoes*, May 31, 1937; Baldridge, "Nine Years," 251; Camp Inspection Report, Mountainair, October 8, 1935, CCC, NA; Camp Inspection Report, Hot Springs, November 25, 1938, CCC, NA; *Albuquerque Journal*, July 19, 1934.

[36] Major General H.J. Brees to Adjutant General, Ft. Sam Houston, March 1, 1939, CCC, NA; Camp Inspection Report, Silver City, January 9, 1939, CCC, NA; Harold Ickles to Franklin D. Roosevelt, Washington, D.C., August 1, 1935, and Summary of the Report of Special Agent Shipley Relating to Prostitution and Other Vices in Gallup, New Mexico, Washington, D.C., August 1, 1935, CCC File, FDRL; Parman, "Indian CCC," 85.

[37] Casaus interview; Chavez interview; Green interview; Steve Zavacky, Jr., entry in Nolte, *We Remember*, 223-4; Arellanes interview; Special Investigative Report, Columbus, May 20, 1941, CCC, NA.

[38] *Lonely Pennsylvanian*, October 1939 and May-June 1940; Brown, *Heritage*, 197-98; *NACCCA Journal,* 22 (May 1999): 5.

# CHAPTER 9

## Weekends in Camp

*X* Enrollees on liberty parties in town were provided rides back to camp in the same trucks that had brought them on Saturday afternoons. Most trucks left from designated locations in town at 11:30 p.m. each Saturday evening. Tony Sanchez remembers that three whistles were blown as a reminder for latecomers. Tomás Brown recalls "making the rounds in an army truck to the many bars in Capitan on Saturday night[s] helping to round up some of the group who had overindulged."[1]

When camps were located far from towns and trips were rare, enrollees often spent Saturday nights away from camp, returning by truck on Sundays. This was usually the case with enrollees from the camp at Conchas Dam, a three-hour trip from Tucumcari. Enrollees who stayed over Saturday nights had the benefit of extra time in town, if their funds held out. Those visiting towns with nearby camps took the opportunity to stay in camp, using the bunks of boys on leave at no extra cost. Santa Fe was an especially attractive destination for this reason, among others.[2]

Rides back to camp were generally subdued, if only because enrollees were exhausted from too much of everything in town. Unfortunately, the trip home could be among the most dangerous in an enrollee's week, especially on Saturday nights when poor lighting, bad weather, and rough roads could lead to terrible

Enrollee pranksters at the Little Walnut camp, 1933, amuse themselves during off hours. *Courtesy: Andres Hernandez.*

accidents. The road to Silver City was considered so hazardous in 1939 that trips to that town were sharply curtailed; crashes on this treacherous route had left one enrollee dead and several others seriously injured during the previous year. In a particularly bad crash, a CCC truck returning to camp with twenty-five enrollees on board collided with a sedan just north of Española on a Saturday night in 1939. Six enrollees suffered injuries when their truck rolled on its side. The twenty-one-year-old driver of the sedan was killed instantly. The CCC truck's driver was exonerated of any guilt, although the nightmare of this accident undoubtedly haunted everyone involved for years.[3]

Less tragically, Ricardo Garcia and a fellow enrollee went to Silver City on a Saturday, but lacked money for a hotel room when they opted to stay overnight. Finding a boxcar on some nearby tracks, they decided to spend the night on board, courtesy of the unsuspecting railroad. To their surprise, the boxcar was attached to an outbound train, which started moving in the middle of the night. When their "sleeper car" finally stopped, the friends found themselves in far-off El Paso. It took the rest of the weekend for them to hitchhike back to camp before they were reported for inadvertently going AWOL.[4] Most return trips to camp were far less eventful.

Glad to be back in camp, exhausted young revelers crawled into their beds for a good night's sleep. But their rest was not assured. Pranksters, many of whom had not ventured into town, lurked in the shadows, ready to exploit their tired colleagues' vulnerability. A favorite trick was to place all kinds of items, both living and dead, in an enrollee's bed so that he would discover them just as he got comfortable. Buried treasures included everything from rocks and brooms to snakes and lizards. Adding a New Mexico ingredient to this prank, one enrollee put ground red chile in Agustiano Gallegos's pillow, causing Gallegos to suffer much discomfort through the night at his Bandelier camp. When Gallegos retaliated by throwing a bucket of water on his adversary, the boy responded by pouring pepper all over Gallegos's bed. Ready to concede defeat, Gallegos realized that "if you would get mad, [barracks pranksters] would never get off your back."[5]

*above*:  Jim Johnson exploring the Indian ruins at Bandelier
National Monument.     *below*: Jim Johnson (l.) and a fellow
enrollee enjoying a weekend at the Bandelier National Monument.
Many lasting friendships were established in the CCC.   *Photos
courtesy:  Jim Johnson.*

Enrollees practiced a bag full of other nocturnal tricks. Sound sleepers, and especially those with bad hangovers, awoke to find their beds in any number of places, from the shower room to a freshly dug latrine pit. Those who did not shower often, as proven by persistent body odor, could also expect a rough scrubbing with harsh lye soup. But the most frequent and popular CCC prank of all involved short sheeting, or 'Frenching,' enrollees' beds. As described on the pages of the *Gila Monster* in 1935, short sheeting was accomplished by folding a bed sheet in the middle and covering the tampered bed with a blanket so that everything looked quite normal. An unsuspecting victim would attempt to crawl under his sheet and blanket, only to find that it was "impossible to push his feet more than half way in the bed." A more intricate folding of sheets made it impossible to get into the bed at all. The *Gila Monster* reported that "On finding their beds in this condition, [enrollees] give vent to their feelings with unprintable 'verbals,' and by making enough noise to wake the dead." Tired of this rude interruption of their sleep, the *Monster's* editors declared open season on all jokesters, an odd declaration after giving such exacting instructions on how to cause trouble and friction in camp. But most enrollees never needed to read camp newspapers to learn new tricks to play. Victims of such mischief expressed their anxiety in an oft-quoted "prayer":

> Now I lay me down to sleep,
> While CCCs around me creep;
> May no other CCC take
> My shoes and shirt before I wake.

> Dear Lord, grant me my slumber,
> That my bunk be not torn asunder,
> May no legs and springs give way
> And smash my dome before I awake.[6]

Unfortunately, enrollees engaged in misconduct beyond mere barracks pranks. Gambling was prevalent in many camps, especially on payday. Craps and poker games could be found in nearly every barracks in camps where officers were known to be lenient. Careful players hung blankets to shield games or placed lookouts to warn gamblers of approaching authorities. George 'Midge' Green recalls a highly moral captain who allowed enrollees to play poker and other card games in their rec hall as long as they bet with chips rather than with cash. The well-meaning officer never realized that his card playing enrollees waited until after lights out to exchange their chips for money in the camp latrine. Some enrollees, like Pee Wee Broadick, grew famous for their skills with cards or dice, while others lost nearly everything they owned on bets. Manuel Jaramillo, for one, tried his hand at gambling to raise money for a gift for his girl friend, but did so poorly that he "lost everything but his long handle drawers." A reporter for SCS-4-N's newspaper cautioned Jaramillo not to send this last possession to the girl as his gift. When short on cash, enrollees gambled with coupons from their canteen books. Some even bet their CCC supplies. Paul Porter was said to have won so much in supplies that he "had enough shoes, pants, shirts, socks, coats and army blankets to last him for years" after he left the CCC.[7]

Enrollees may have owed gambling debts when they engaged in far worse criminal activity: camp theft. Much to the credit of CCC enrollees, theft was rare in New Mexico's camps, but it did occur occasionally. Personal belongings, like shoes or jackets, were most vulnerable. Government property was taken with more serious results. On May 31, 1939, the company safe at a camp near Lordsburg was stolen in the middle of the night. With all enrollees accounted for, a thorough search of the area was begun. The safe was finally discovered four miles from camp at 8:30 the following morning. Its contents, including $297.00, were gone. Four enrollees were eventually charged with the crime and faced dishonorable discharges, although the FBI continued its investigation of the incident for another month. An FBI investigation was hardly needed at 'Midge' Green's camp when cakes and pies began disappearing from the mess hall kitchen after dark. The mystery was easily solved when the camp cook added an extra diarrhea-causing ingredient to a new batch of baked goods. Camp authorities simply waited at the latrine to identify the obvious culprits as they rushed by about dawn.[8]

The illegal use of drugs and alcohol caused additional trouble in camp. Drug use was most common in camps near the Mexican border where drugs could be easily acquired and transported into camp. Marijuana was the drug of choice, but few enrollees indulged and most others looked down on those who did. Alcohol was far more prevalent. Liquor could be brought from town, purchased from local bootleggers, or manufactured by enterprising enrollees. With skills often learned prior to joining the CCC, enrollees used grapes, apples, peaches, or raisins to make moonshine liquor in makeshift stills hidden near camps. Some enrollees were bold enough to operate stills within the confines of their camps, although the odds of discovery by camp officers were far greater. As his camp's cook, Roy Huffman had access to all the surplus raisins he could use in a still he brazenly assembled under his mess hall's floor. Huffman recalls that the wine he produced was almost as bad as the idea of operating a still in camp. Both his liquor and his still were eventually discovered, putting Huffman permanently out of business. There is no record that Huffman's still (or any other in New Mexico) was investigated by Department of Justice agents masquerading as enrollees, as happened in a Virginian camp in 1934.[9]

Consuming homemade or cheap liquor could cause other adverse consequences. Jim Johnson remembered sharing the cost of a cheap bottle of wine with three fellow enrollees at their camp at Bandelier. They consumed the entire bottle, only to face a week of illness. To try to control the flow of liquor in camps, some officers allowed beer to be sold at camp canteens. Angered by this concession, the Womens Christian Temperance Union (WCTU) wrote hundreds of letters to CCC headquarters in Washington, protesting the sale of beer in camps across the United States. Their letters had little impact on CCC policy.[10]

* * *

With some exceptions, most enrollees who chose to stay in camp on weekends avoided trouble as they enjoyed their leisure hours far from work or town. Imaginative, energetic youths, they seldom lacked for activities to keep them entertained. A group at Radium Springs even created a 'Stay At Home Club.' Enrollees told their favorite jokes or stories at club meetings, although the camp newspaper soon suggested that "It wouldn't hurt ... if some would wash their yarns before spinning them" in public. When not telling tall tales or sordid jokes, enrollees read, wrote letters, made friends, or simply relaxed. The *Lincoln Lookout* congratulated those who participated in such worthwhile activities, pointing out "the money you are saving and Monday morning headache you are avoiding" by remaining far from the temptations of town.[11]

The largest number of enrollees who did not go to town on weekends looked forward to outdoor activities near their wilderness camps. Long hikes in the countryside promised beautiful scenery and some unexpected adventures. Leslie Clark reported that enrollees hiked along the Sacramento River nearly every weekend in the summer of 1933. Enrollees at Bandelier hiked through canyons, swam in creeks, and explored nearby Indian ruins. Many collected ancient arrowheads and pottery shards. George Schneider claimed to have found enough arrowheads in a single day to fill not only the four pockets in his jeans, but also his cap and shirt, used as makeshift knapsacks; conscientiously, he later turned his collected artifacts over to a museum. Enrollees near Ft. Selden explored the old military site in search of discarded Army treasures. Twenty-three enrollees from the Redrock camp inspected Tyrone, a recent ghost town and former mining community. White Sands, Gran Quivira, Look-Out Point, and Red Cloud Canyon were also favorite destinations for hikes and excursions.[12]

Caves were particularly alluring. Hundreds of enrollees visited Carlsbad Caverns; trucks left the Corona camp nearly every weekend in mid-1936 so that every enrollee could visit the world famous caves at least once during his enrollment period. Enrollees were admitted as guests of the Parks Service in gratitude for the CCC's work in the caverns and at hundreds of other Park Service sites across the country. Those who worked in Carlsbad were afforded the pleasure of exploring new sections of the underground caverns, according to Amadeo Quintana.[13]

Other enrollees discovered caves while hiking on their own. Enrollees from the Radium Springs camp located a new cave on a Sunday in March 1936. The cave had four large rooms and was about one hundred yards deep. Samples of stalagmite were carried back to camp as souvenirs and proof of the boys' great find. Three years later, another group of Sunday explorers found a cave in Lincoln County. Attempting to leave, they realized that "they were going around in circles." After an anxious night below ground, the group finally found the cave's exit, surfaced, and returned to camp the next morning. In a near-tragic episode, James Garrett and Charles Tracy found a small opening in an isolated area south of Animas. The opening turned out to be the mouth of a large cave whose inhabitants included six diamondback rattlesnakes, ranging in size from four and a half to six feet long. Recovering from their shock, the enrollees attempted to take the snakes out alive; with youthful bravado, they vowed to send them to the Albuquerque zoo as "wards of Governor Tingley." When removing the snakes proved impossible, Garrett and Tracy managed to kill all six reptiles. They returned to camp without captives or skins, but with many tales that may well have grown taller in the telling.[14]

Adventuresome enrollees near Hillsboro climbed Star Mountain in search of a weekend challenge in October 1935. Climbing slowly, with frequent rests and drinks from their canteens, the group made steady progress with only two mishaps: when a novice mistook the sound of a grasshopper for a rattlesnake and when another hiker stumbled onto a cactus. The group proceeded with caution, knowing that "one little slip and down you would go for hundreds of feet." On reaching the peak, the hikers were struck by the view in every direction. "Nature had painted the scene purple, gold and silver. This was a picture that will linger in our minds for years ... because it was a picture not painted by the hand of man" but by the power of a far higher authority.[15]

In addition to real or imagined snakes, enrollees observed many other species of animals in the wilderness. Deer, wild turkeys, mountain goats, chipmunks, and fish were plentiful, while coyotes, mountain lions, bobcats, and eagles were seen, but rarely. So many kinds of birds were spotted in northern New Mexico that the Española camp newspaper printed a guide on how to identify major groups. A rookie enrollee from Pennsylvania reportedly chased down a roadrunner, catching it with a headlong dive. Walter Swalgo released his prey after nearly all of his fellow Easterners had had an opportunity to inspect New Mexico's state bird at close range.[16]

Wild animals visited camps out of curiosity or, more often, in search of food. Most frighteningly, bears were known to sort through trash cans when prey in the wild was scarce. Generally, enrollees prudently gave hungry bears a wide berth, as when a night watchman came across a mother bear and her two cubs at 4:00 a.m. in the Bandelier camp. Other enrollees at the same camp were less cautious when a hungry bear was discovered with his head stuck in a small garbage pail. A brave enrollee freed the bear from his metal helmet before a crowd of enrollees chased the confused animal to the edge of camp and up a fir tree. Showing no mercy for their cornered victim, the enrollees retrieved an old single-shot rifle and shot the intruder dead. The company enjoyed bear meat for several meals. Local livestock were handled more mercifully, if only because they were usually someone's property. When runaway horses and cattle destroyed gardens and shrubs in two camps, fences were built around the camps' periphery to keep the culprits out while also keeping peace with nearby farmers and ranchers. Enrollees erected a fence around the monument at Bandelier for a similar purpose.[17]

Although CCC regulations prohibited the use of guns by enrollees, tempting game in the surrounding wilderness led some young sportsmen to ignore this particular rule. Mostly novices, few enrollees had much success in hunting. The *Pink Pebble Periodical* reported that three aspiring hunters went turkey hunting in the Burro Mountains on a weekend prior to Thanksgiving in 1935. Despite long hours in the field, the enrollees came back empty-handed. In their camp newspaper's words, "all they killed was time." Enrollees at Bandelier were more successful hunters, but only because they shot wild turkey and deer with small box cameras rather than guns. Most hunting was, therefore, left to camp officers and better-trained civilians like Lee Evans, a famous mountain lion hunter who traveled through the Corona camp on a hunt in early 1936.[18]

But most camp animals were treated as pampered pets rather than wildlife intruders. Some camps were venerable zoos with everything from homing pigeons and Shetland ponies to gold fish and lizards as unofficial residents. Enrollees at one camp found a fawn with a broken leg; they nursed the wounded animal back to health until it grew too large and had to be returned to the wild. Baby animals were frequently born in camp confines. 'Tex,' a stray cat rescued by enrollees on a visit to El Paso, gave birth to three kittens at the Mountainair camp in 1937; 'Tex,' her offspring, and all other cats provided the additional service of keeping mice at bay. Enrollees at the Buckhorn camp proudly claimed to have set a national CCC record when their dog had ten puppies in one litter; a mother dog at the Ft. Stanton camp tied this unofficial record in February 1939.[19]

CCC camps became well known for their care of young animals. In fact, locals often dropped unwanted pups near camp sites, hoping that enrollees would show mercy and care for the discarded dogs. Chester Williams recalls having as many as twenty-five pups in camp at one time. Not knowing what to do with so many dogs, enrollees in Williams's company loaded the twenty-five animals onto a truck and unceremoniously dumped them near another CCC camp as a prank.[20]

Some camps kept less traditional creatures as pets. Julian Shish fed grasshoppers to the four large-mouth bass he kept in a cement pool he had built at his camp in Tucumcari. Leon Blake brought a coyote into the Mountainair camp where it slept in the barracks, played catch with enrollees, and "stood out in the road every evening just waiting for the trucks to come [home] with the

*above*:  Enrollees at the Redrock camp captured a Gila monster
with a Corn Flakes box.  The Gila monster became the camp
mascot.  *Courtesy:  Stewart Henry Robeson Papers, Rio Grande
Historical Collection, New Mexico State University, Las Cruces, New
Mexico.     below*:  Members of the district championship basketball
team visit Apline, Texas, 1934.  *Courtesy:  Andres Hernandez.*

CC boys." One day Torrance County Sheriff Rex Miller drove by and spotted the animal as it patiently waited for the enrollees' return. Mistaking it for a wild coyote, Sheriff Miller killed the unorthodox pet with his rifle. A side camp near Carlsbad kept a pet rabbit until an enrollee repeated Sheriff Miller's mistake and killed it, employing a brick as "the fatal weapon." A better fate awaited a cub bear that was kept at the Magdelena camp until it was fully grown and finally released. At least two camps captured gila monsters, using an empty Corn Flakes box for the lizard's capture at the Redrock camp. Appropriately, the gila monster in residence at the Gila camp was soon declared its company's mascot.[21]

X Nearly every camp had its own mascot, with mixed results. The El Rito camp, commanded by a reserve naval officer, used a goat as its mascot and gave it the fitting name of 'U.S. Navy.' Not far north, enrollees at the Abiquiu camp used another goat as their mascot until it was found guilty of eating the camp's flowers and braying "at ungodly hours." The uncooperative goat was soon replaced by a porcupine. A miniature burro, said to be the smallest in the CCC, represented the Berino camp. 'Miss Ana of Doña Ana' was so much a part of camp A-4-T that she was listed on the camp's (unofficial) roster in 1936.[22]

But by far the largest number of camp mascots were dogs of all shapes and sizes. Each dog, from a Chihuahua at Ft. Stanton to a Great Dane at Hillsboro, was admired for his or her unique characteristics. 'Buck,' at the Buckhorn camp, was said to have the qualities of an ideal enrollee: "He doesn't swear. He doesn't smoke. He doesn't drink and we don't think he stays out at night very late. Furthermore, Buck is always on time and never misses the truck." Few could ask for more of man or beast.[23]

Mascots like 'Miss Ana' and 'Buck' Navy represented their camps on various occasions, but most consistently at athletic events. Although original plans for the CCC did not include athletics, it was inevitable that sports became a major part of CCC life: young men in the prime of their physical lives often used athletic competition to help prove their masculinity as another rite of passage. The CCC also acknowledged the value of sports in helping to develop a generation of disciplined, cooperative, team-spirited workers. In addition, the CCC realized the benefit of having enrollees amuse themselves with games rather than with problem-causing mischief. These diversions were especially important for morale in camps located so far from the nearest town that regularly scheduled liberty parties were impractical and rare.[24]

Enrollees competed in informal as well as in formal competition. Informally, baseball or basketball games were organized on the spur of the moment. Holidays like the Fourth of July were often celebrated with baseball games, as when the 'Hurricanes' (consisting of Hispanic players) played the 'Tornados' (consisting of Anglo players) at the Mountainair camp on July 4, 1940. The 'Hurricanes' won by the lopsided score of 41-10 when the 'Tornados' were said to be "handicapped by wild pitching and ragged fielding." Whole camps often challenged one another in hotly-contested games: the Whitewater camp played the Deming camp in baseball, losing 16-1 on June 27, 1937. Ever the optimist, Whitewater's sports reporter declared "we're getting better" when his team lost to Deming again, but by a 15-2 margin two weeks later.[25]

Beyond single-game competition, enrollees organized leagues with full schedules or tournaments at several levels of play. In many camps, enrollees created leagues with barracks competing against one another in short seasons; Barracks #2 won the inter-barracks tournament at BR-39-N in Las Cruces with a case of beer as its prize in May 1936. At a higher level, district-wide competition took place in baseball, basketball, and track and field. About 250 enrollees from Albuquerque district camps challenged one another in at least five sporting events on the University of New Mexico's athletic fields in May 1935.[26]

More typically, camp teams played local town, business, school, and college teams, including the freshmen and varsity teams at New Mexico A&M. Healthy rivalries developed, as between the CCC and the Española Browns. On May 5, 1934, the Browns got the better of a CCC team, winning an exciting victory in the bottom half of the ninth inning. Some CCC teams joined city leagues if their camps were located near enough to town for enrollees to play in regularly scheduled games. Three CCC teams played in the Las Cruces softball league, with the 'Broncos' of BR-39-N winning the ten-team league championship in 1936. In the process, the 'Broncos' "won the respect and admiration of the entire community for their excellent play and gentlemanly conduct."[27]

But not all CCC teams could equal the success of the champion 'Broncos.' Losing teams identified legitimate or contrived reasons for their misfortunes on the playing field. Members of a Carlsbad camp's basketball team accused their Hagerman, New Mexico, foes of winning "only when professional players were run in" to dominate a hard-fought game in 1937. The Glenwood camp's basketball team ran into similar difficulties when it accused its Silver City rivals of using former college players as well as football and wrestling techniques such as "the body slam, full nelson, and ... flying tackle." Glenwood lost 28 to 25. Weather conditions prevented victory on other occasions. A spring dust storm was identified as the cause of the Mountainair camp's baseball team loss to their local rivals, although it was not explained why the storm was more bothersome to CCC players than to local community players on the same field. Health problems prevented other victories. The Gila camp's baseball team had to postpone a late season game when the entire camp was placed under quarantine with an undisclosed illness for several days in 1934.[28]

Few enrollees required excuses when it came to their favorite sport of boxing. Inspired by boxing heroes like Joe Lewis, Gene Tunney, and Jack Dempsey, many enrollees used every spare moment to hone their fighting skills. Boxing instruction was regularly provided behind Barracks A at the Mayhill camp. At Hillsboro, a dozen pugilists checked out boxing equipment "quite steadily." Enrollees "rustled, begged, stole, and borrowed" enough material to build their own boxing ring at the Buckhorn camp. Many camps even installed lights for evening workouts and bouts. The punching bag at the El Rito camp was used so often that it broke, only to be broken a second time shortly after it was repaired in Santa Fe.[29]

Once trained, self-confident boxers believed they could beat all challengers. Arturo 'Dynamite' Munoz at the Glenwood camp went so far as to print a challenge in his camp newspaper: "All challengers welcome," specifying only that his competitors be between the ages of two and 105. The best fighters from one camp often challenged the best from a neighboring camp for bragging rights in a particular region of New Mexico. These fights were usually held in camp, but were sometimes scheduled in nearby towns to draw larger crowds and greater attention. A fight card with matches in five different weight classes was offered at the armory in Silver City on August 19, 1933. Enrollees with nicknames like 'Champ,' 'Speedy,' and 'Kid' fought bravely in three-round contests. The evening's finale pitted heavy-weights 'Battling' Ferguson of the Mimbres camp against 'Steamboat' Bilbrey of the Walnut camp. Enrollees also fought non-enrollee challengers, as when six boxers from the Sandia camp met six youths from a government-run transient camp in an Albuquerque ring. Some enrollees even fought in Golden Gloves competition. Tecumseh Boone, "that hard hitting Oklahoma Indian," joined four other fighters from his Whitewater camp in a Golden Gloves tournament held in Silver City in early 1938. Although they didn't win, the CCC boxers "put up a fight that anyone should be proud of."[30]

Enrollees were rewarded for their athletic prowess in both conventional and unconventional ways. At Glenwood, winning teams in basketball, volleyball, and softball won free canteen books. The Mayhill camp's basketball team earned a large steak dinner after securing a victory over their arch rivals, the CCC camp in Roswell. First place winners at a CCC track meet held in Silver City won gold medals; second place finishers each received a package of cigarettes. The victorious barracks in a baseball tournament held at Whitewater received free movie tickets as their reward. Reminiscent of high school awards, the Elephant Butte camp offered felt letters to deserving enrollees who participated in athletics and other camp activities. A pitcher from the La Madera camp was named to the *Happy Days* national All-CCC baseball team in 1935. Ambitious ball players were motivated to excel by reports that major league scouts watched CCC games and signed standout players to professional contracts, if only in the minor leagues. But most enrollees played sports for the pure enjoyment of the competition. Awards and prizes were tangible bonuses. Intangibles, like fun and personal satisfaction, were reward enough for most.[31]

A healthy, competitive spirit was also sparked in non-athletic contests. Like many Americans of their era, enrollees were always ready to enter contests and win prizes at a time when larger economic opportunities and rewards were limited by the Depression. In addition to competition on talent nights, in safety contests, and during camp inspections, enrollees challenged one another in everything from answering the most trivia questions to receiving the most mail. In town, enrollees were tempted to enter community drawings, including one held at a Silver City movie theater each Thursday night; the theater's jackpot grew to four hundred dollars, creating a "show epidemic" at the Gila camp in late 1934.[32]

On a national scale, *American Forests* magazine sponsored a contest that offered publication and prizes for the best enrollee answers to the question "What the CCC Has Done for Me." K. Edd Teston's essay about the impact of the CCC on his family in New Mexico was one of only thirty-seven chosen for publication from two thousand entries submitted from across the United States in 1934.[33]

In another effort to boost morale and avoid the perils of liberty parties in town, CCC officers often allowed enrollees to hold weekend dances in camp. Officers saw many advantages to camp dances, including an opportunity to train young men in the art of socially accepted behavior in the presence of young ladies. At least one camp, near Tucumcari, prepared enrollees for such events with free dancing lessons in its rec hall. Prior to dances, enrollees were routinely advised to "conduct yourselves in a gentlemanly manner." They were later praised for their "splendid conduct" if all went well in the course of an evening.[34]

Camp dances were held on various occasions, including on holidays, to welcome newcomers, or to bid farewell to departing enrollees. Great efforts were made to clean up and decorate facilities for these special events; enrollees at a Las Cruces camp even turned their tennis court into a dance floor for summer dances. The price for tickets was normally fifteen cents, with female guests admitted free.[35]

But how could enrollees hope to invite female guests to camp dances when CCC camps were often located in isolated, distant parts of New Mexico? This seemingly insurmountable problem was solved in two main ways: either CCC-sponsored dances were moved into town and held at local community centers, as in Mountainair, or enrollees actively recruited female guests to come to their camps from nearby communities. News of upcoming dances went out to residents in outlying towns, farms, and ranches. X "Young maidens" lacking transportation to camp could often count on CCC trucks dispatched on this special mission. In this manner, guests from Ft. Stanton, Capitan, and Lincoln were driven to a dance at a Ft. Stanton camp, compliments of the CCC, in late 1936. Guests to a Cloudcroft camp dance came from Tularosa and Alamogordo, despite the distance and some heavy rains; the girls from Alamogordo rated the camp "tops in everything but accessibility." With understandable trepidation about sending their daughters off to remote camps inhabited by eager young males, parents often accompanied their daughters, arriving and departing on their own or with their daughters in less-than-elegant, but functional CCC trucks. With so many watchful chaperons present, decorum was all but guaranteed.[36]

At least two local women did not feel they needed older chaperons to accompany them to a dance at a remote CCC camp. Ada Berniece Coyner had been attracted to a teaching job in the Lordsburg public schools by a "princely sum" of seventy dollars a month in pay, compared to the fifty dollars a month she had previously earned in rural Nebraska schools. Finding little social activity in Lordsburg, Ada and a fellow female teacher decided to attend a Saturday night dance held at the CCC camp at Redrock. Such an outing was "quite a risque adventure" for single women, but the two teachers felt safe enough because they were convinced that as self-described "old maids" in their thirties they no longer required chaperons. Arriving at the dance, Ada and her friend were introduced to Lt. Stewart Henry Robeson and another camp officer. Getting along well, each couple eventually dated, became engaged, and got married within a few years.[37]

In another ironic twist, enrollees from the Ft. Stanton camp were often transported in trucks to a dance held at a nearby National Youth Administration (NYA) camp for young women after that facility opened in the fall of 1936. Following a leap year dance at the girls' camp in 1940, several male enrollees were said to have leaped into new relationships, causing mail sent between the CCC and NYA camps to suddenly double.[38]

Enrollees and their female companions danced to music provided by radios, jukeboxes, or live bands at camp gatherings. Using alliteration (as enrollees often did in naming camp newspapers), camp bands went by such imaginative names as the 'Frolicsome Foresters' and the 'Mountain Music Men.' Other musical groups were known as the 'Mountain Boosters,' the 'Hill-Billy Clod Hoppers,' and the 'Gloom-Chasers.' Band members made up for poor equipment and little musical instruction with strong motivation and enthusiasm. Camp bands played a variety of music, from "peppy" Spanish songs to popular Jitterbug tunes. Bands played and couples danced for hours. Little trouble occurred, if only  because liquor was seldom served and jealous local males were excluded. Camp dances usually ended about midnight with "everyone ... smiling in spite of sore toes and feet."[39]

Depending on the nature of their Saturday night entertainment, enrollees normally experienced restful sleep until Sunday morning. Many slept late on Sunday, the only day when they had no early morning duties. Others rose in time to attend religious services in camp or in nearby community churches. Unlike some parts of the country where officers required their enrollees to attend church, enrollees in New Mexico were never ordered to participate, but often did.

Enrollees in camps near towns were provided transportation to churches, using the same Army trucks that had transported boys to work sites during the week and to liberty parties just hours before. Local churches usually welcomed these newcomers with open arms. Methodist and Baptist churches in Carrizozo, for example, invited enrollees to join their Sunday School classes in 1937. Other churches recruited enrollees to sing in church choirs. Few enrollees felt unwanted, although one recalls an embarrassing moment when he was asked to sit toward the back of a church, leaving room for the town's more privileged citizens in the pews up front.[40]

Eager to reenforce enrollee religious beliefs and moral behavior while they lived far from the influence of families and home communities, the CCC did more than supply Army trucks for church-going enrollees on Sunday mornings. The Corps recruited Protestant and Catholic chaplains to serve in camps across the country, including New Mexico. Many chaplains were reserve officers, called to duty in the CCC much like camp commanders had been called to serve by the mid-1930s. Other chaplains were local ministers or priests who extended their ministries to include camps in their area, with contracts that specified duties and provided a small stipend plus travel expenses. A third group of chaplains were volunteer clergymen from nearby towns who simply wanted to help out. Nationally, the total number of CCC chaplains equaled over 3,900 by 1936. Plagued by a shortage of camp chaplains in New Mexico, only seven CCC chaplains were listed in the state in early 1941.[41]

Each CCC chaplain was responsible for about eight camps. Constantly on the move to serve the spiritual needs of enrollees dispersed over large areas, chaplains compared their lives to old-time circuit riders. Like circuit riders, they often faced both harsh weather and great isolation. One chaplain wrote in his log book of spending a cold night "between icy blankets" with only the "song of the coyote" to interrupt the "intense silence" of an evening near Saddle Mountain.[42]

With so much ground to cover, it was impossible for chaplains to be present in every camp on every Sunday morning. Services were therefore held whenever a chaplain arrived in camp, or about twice a month. Catholic masses at the Gila camp were conducted in the rec hall on Saturdays, while Protestant services were often held during the work week. Chaplain Clay Oakes once arrived at the Abiquiu camp on a Friday when enrollees were still at work. Rushed for time, Oakes went to the enrollees' work site and spoke to them during a break. Two months later Oakes spoke to a crowd of enrollees after "upwards of an hour of boxing matches" at the Española camp. More distant camps, like the one at Conchas Dam, went whole months without seeing a minister or priest. Left on their own, enrollees did the best they could. Mr. Horn, a blacksmith at the Buckhorn camp, was recruited to teach a Bible study class on Sunday mornings. Enrollees met outside under the trees for the same purpose at the Glenwood camp in the summer of 1935.[43]

When available, the CCC expected chaplains to deliver uplifting, non-sectarian messages, rather than fire-and-brimstone evangelical sermons. Character building, not mass conversion, was the religious goal of the secular CCC. A Methodist minister therefore preached on "Building the Character of Man" at the Carrizozo camp on Sunday, July 10, 1937. A Catholic priest spoke to enrollees assembled at DG-40-N near Carrizozo about "The Spirit of American Youth Toward the Government We Now Have." When Chaplain Oakes spoke to enrollees at Española after their evening of boxing exhibitions, he preached about the Protestant work ethic. According to Oakes, if each man used his abilities "to their full extent, courageously doing his best with what he has and trusting to Providence to supply any deficiencies, he will inevitably accomplish what is laid out for him to do." Pleased with the theme of this message for CCC enrollees and future American workers, the Española camp newspaper translated much of the chaplain's message into Spanish "for the benefit of those ... who are not completely familiar with the English language."[44]

Despite many hours of contact with enrollees, some chaplains had little faith in the impact of their spiritual labors. Attendance at camp services and in Sunday School classes often suffered. Appealing to the CCC's competitive spirit, one chaplain went so far as to offer a trophy to the camp on his circuit with the best Sunday School attendance in early 1937. Ross Calvin, an Episcopal minister based in Silver City, noted poor attendance at camp services, but continued to distribute prayer books, visit sick enrollees at the Ft. Bayard hospital, and befriend those who seemed destined to go "down the lonesome road that leads to the penitentiary door."[45]

Most chaplains were as eager as Ross Calvin to serve the young souls in their care. Of all the hard-working chaplains who served the spiritual needs of New Mexico's camps, Father Albert Braun was probably the longest-serving and most famous. After sixteen years as a Franciscan missionary among the Mescalero Apaches, Braun, an Army reserve officer, was called to duty as a CCC chaplain in May 1933. From this date until November 1940, when he was called to regular Army duty, Father Albert drove hundreds of miles to say mass and counsel enrollees at numerous camps. Attendance at mass was normally good, but it was especially high in camps when the Franciscan priest brought five attractive local girls to sing in the choir during services. As a young educational advisor from Iowa, Ray Dawson admired one female member of the choir in particular. Traveling by car with the group, Dawson was accused of sitting closer and closer to Eliza Baldonado, described as a "beautiful and charming girl." Father Albert helped the budding romance by driving no faster than thirty-five miles per hour. In one of the many love stories in CCC history, Ray and Eliza were eventually engaged and married. Indirectly responsible for this match-making, Father Albert was clearly pleased. Typically, he "would give all of himself to make things a little bit better for the young men enrolled in the camps."[46]

Some enrollees practiced a form of Catholicism that did not require the services of priests like Father Albert or other CCC clergymen. Taking part in Holy Week ceremonies dating back to at least the late eighteenth century, these enrollees belonged to the highly secretive Brotherhood of Our Father Jesus, or Penitentes. Tomás Brown had heard about this devoutly religious organization during his boyhood days in Maxwell, New Mexico, but "it didn't take long to discover who were active participants" among the enrollees in his CCC camp near Santa Fe. As Holy Week approached, several Hispanic enrollees "took off on leave with various explanations about being needed at home." When Holy Week ended and these same enrollees returned, Brown could not help but notice in his camp's none-too-private showers that "their backs looked as though they had been beaten to a pulp." Brown and others were impressed by how sincere these young men were "in practicing what they believed was necessary for the atonement of their sins."[47]

It is well to remember that while enrollees took large strides toward adulthood in the CCC, most were still adolescents during much of their six- to twelve-month enrollment periods. CCC leaders had to expect and, within limits, tolerate adolescent behavior from their charges. Most of this behavior was good-natured and seldom malicious; even camp pranks were usually meant to amuse rather than do harm. Other behavior involved typical adolescent exploration of the world, its mysteries, and its parameters. The surrounding wilderness provided ideal opportunities for such exploration of nature and its wildlife. Athletic competition allowed enrollees to explore physical challenges beyond their daily work and camp duties. And religious services gave young men the chance to contemplate spiritual matters, including the existence of a higher authority whose grand creation they witnessed on hikes and other outdoor excursions. In these ways, the Civilian Conservation Corps gave its adolescent enrollees the off-duty time and relative serenity to understand the world around them as they matured to adulthood. Such time and serenity would seldom have been possible outside the CCC as New Mexico and the rest of the  nation continued to suffer the agony of the Great Depression.

## Endnotes - Chapter 9

[1]    Sanchez interview; Brown, *Heritage*, 191.
[2]    Camp Inspection Report, Conchas Dam, February 12, 1942, CCC, NA; Lucero interview, OHPB.
[3]    Gonzalez interview; Camp Inspection Report, Mangas, January 9, 1939, CCC, NA; *Albuquerque Journal,* February 12, 1939; *Truchas Echo*, February 22, 1939.
[4]    Garcia interview.
[5]    Henington interview; Maestas interview; Cabrera interview; Gallegos interview, OHPB.
[6]    Johnson interview; *Gila Monster*, January 31, 1935; *Wahoo*, November 1, 1937; Beck interview; Kemp interview; Casaus interview; Hall interview; Maestas interview; Arnellanes interview; H. Baca interview; Cabrera interview; Green interview; *Animas Announcer,* May 20, 1936; *Pink Pebble Periodical*, November 15, 1936.
[7]    *Tumbleweed*, September 1938; Maestas interview; Barela interview; T. Montoya interview; Sanchez interview; Smith interview; Newbury interview; Jones interview; Chavez interview; Green interview; Dawson interview; *Wasp*, December 31, 1936; Gibson interview; Henington interview; Johnson interview; Porter Memoirs, 10.
[8]    Dawson interview; Camp Inspection Report, Hot Springs, June 21, 1939, CCC, NA; Green interview.
[9]    Vega interview; Thomas interview; Sanchez interview; Dawson interview; Beck interview; Maestas interview; Quintana interview, OHPB; *Pink Pebble Periodical*, October 4, 1935; Huffman interview; Otis *et al.*, *Forest Service and the CCC*, 101.
[10]    Johnson interview; *Pink Pebble Periodical,* February 12, 1935; *Glenwood News*, June 1936; Sherraden, "Effectiveness of the Camps," 221, 325.
[11]    Radium Springs camp newspaper (unnamed), September 29, 1935; *Lincoln Lookout,* July 1937.
[12]    *Farmington Times-Hustler*, August 11, 1933; Clay Smith to the author, San Antonio, Texas, April 19, 1980; Schneider interview, OHPB; *Organ View Optic*, January 14, 1936, and March 12, 1936;

*Pink Pebble Periodical,* September 15, 1936; *El Gallo de Pelea,* August 31, 1936; Coker interview; Porter Memoirs, 1.

¹³ *El Gallo de Pelea,* June 26, 1936; *Fresnal Ranger,* October 5, 1934; Shish interview; Quintana interview, OHPB.

¹⁴ *Organ View Optic,* April 10, 1936; *Lonely Pennsylvanian,* September 1939; *Whirlwind,* February 1937.

¹⁵ *Black Ranger,* November 1, 1935.

¹⁶ *Kangarowl,* September 25, 1936; *Lonely Pennsylvanian,* February 1939.

¹⁷ Brown and Partridge interviews, OHPB; *Mirager,* June 1936; *Save Our Soil,* May 1937; Harrison *et al., Bandelier,* 314-15.

¹⁸ Draves, *Builder,* 212; *Pink Pebble Periodical,* November 14, 1935; Brown interview, OHPB; *El Conejo,* January 1937 and May 1939; *El Gallo de Pelea,* February 1936.

¹⁹ Oliver C. Payne, Camp Report, Bosque del Apache, July-August-September 1940, BANWR; *Hoot Owl,* September 14, 1936; Jones interview; *Lonely Pennsylvanian,* February 1939 and May-June 1940; Barela interview; *Tip Topper,* March 1937; *Buckhorn Buzzer,* July 1937.

²⁰ Williams interview.

²¹ Shish interview; Blake interview by Foote; *Dark Canyon Avalanche,* June 2, 1936; *Gila Monster,* June 1936.

²² *Kangarowl,* July 12, 1935; *La Piedra Lumbre,* September 1936; *CCC Annual, 1936, Ft. Bliss District,* 70, 72.

²³ *Lonely Pennsylvanian,* November-December 1939; *Black Ranger,* February 12, 1936; *Save Our Soil,* August 1936.

²⁴ The Army had made similar use of sports during World War I. See Captain John L. Griffith, "The Value of Athletics As Part of Military Training," *American Physical Education Review,* 24 (April 1919): 191-5.

²⁵ *Bi-Weekly Blast,* May 15, 1940; *Save Our Soil,* July 1937.

²⁶ *Organ Echoes,* May 1936; *Albuquerque Journal,* May 20, 1935.

²⁷ Newspaper clipping, May 5, 1934, in Camp Inspection Report, Santa Fe, n.d., CCC, NA; *Organ Echoes,* July 30, 1936, August, 31, 1936, and December 1936.

²⁸ *Camp Chatter,* February 1937; *Goldbricker,* January 28, 1935; *Tip Topper,* May 1937; *Gila Monster,* September 5, 1934.

²⁹ *Peñasco Pennant,* February 6, 1936; *Black Ranger,* March 20, 1936; *Save Our Soil,* April 1936; Bryant, "Education," 114-15; *Hoot Owl,* September 14, 1936; *Kangarowl,* September 4, 1935.

³⁰ *Goldbricker,* May 30, 1935; Serna interview; T. Montoya interview; Perea interview; *Yucca,* March 1938; *Silver City Enterprise,*

August 18 and September 1, 1933; Blake interview by Foote; Harrison *et al., Bandelier,* 17.

[31] *Glenwood News,* March 1937; *Mayhill Lookout,* January 15, 1937; *Hoot Owl,* September 14, 1936; *Save Our Soil,* July 1937; *Winds,* March 1939; *CCC Annual, 1936, Albuquerque District,* 23; *Happy Days,* October 2, 1937. Ed Musial, a brother of the famed St. Louis Cardinal outfielder Stan Musial, served in the CCC camp at Conchas Dam in 1940. *NACCCA Journal,* 21 (December 1998): 5.

[32] *Gila Monster,* November 16, 1934.

[33] Mooney interview; Otis *et al., Forest Service and the CCC,* 15; K. Edd Teston, "The Shanty on the Claim," in Ovid Butler, ed., *Youth Rebuilds: Stories from the C.C.C.* (Washington, D.C.: American Forestry Association, 1934): 55-8.

[34] *Pink Pebble Periodical,* June 18, 1935; *Wasp,* June 1937; *Tip Topper,* April 1937.

[35] *Pink Pebble Periodical,* May 7, 1935, and October 4, 1935, and October 17, 1935; *Kangarowl,* May 17, 1935, and January 1937; *Hoot Owl,* September 14, 1936; *La Poliza,* December 1936; *Tip Topper,* February 1937 and October 1937; Mooney interview.

[36] *Tip Topper,* May 1937; *Kangarowl,* November 1936; *Tumbleweed,* February 1939; *Pink Pebble Periodical,* August 15, 1936; *La Poliza,* December 1936; *Camp News,* October 10, 1935.

[37] Eva Jane Matson, "A CCC Romance" included in Eva Jane Matson to the author, Las Cruces, August 5, 1998.

[38] *Stanton Static,* December 1936 and January 1937; *Lonely Pennsylvanian,* February 1940 and March 1940; *El Gallo de Pelea,* June 26, 1936; Delores Bogart interview, February 14, 1992; Gonzalez interview; Green interview. Thanks in part to Eleanor Roosevelt's influence, a CCC-like program was created for girls. With only forty-five camps for 8,500 girls, the program was considered "pathetically meager." The camp at Ft. Stanton was one of the best in this limited effort. See Susan Ware, "Women in the New Deal" in Sitkoff, *Fifty Years Later,* 124-5; *Albuquerque Journal,* March 12, 1941.

[39] Mooney interview; *Lonely Pennsylvanian,* September 1939; *Kangarowl,* November 1936; *Fresnal Ranger,* March 8, 1935; *La Poliza,* December 1936; *Save Our Soil,* September 1936; *Mal Pais,* March 1937; *Pink Pebble Periodical,* June 18, 1935; *Stanton Static,* December 1936.

[40] *Dark Canyon Avalanche,* November 21, 1936; *Mal Pais,* February 1937 and July 1937; *Camp Cactus Carrier,* October 1939; *Lonely Pennsylvanian,* February 1940; Gibson interview.

⁴¹ Camp Inspection Report, Carrizozo, December 22, 1936, CCC, NA; Baldridge, "Nine Years," 292, 296; Holland and Hill, *Youth*, 213-15; Alfred C. Oliver, Jr., and Harold M. Dudley, *This New America: The Spirit of the Civilian Conservation Corps* (London: Longmans, Green and Co., 1937): 111-31; Station List and Roster of Civilian Administrative Personnel, Contract Physicians, Camp Physicians, Educational Advisor, and Project Superintendents, New Mexico District, CCC, February 14, 1941, CCC Papers, NMSRCA (hereafter cited as Station List and Roster, 1941); Salmond, *CCC*, 142.

⁴² Poorbaugh interview; Baldridge, "Nine Years," 291; Bassett, "Health and Culture," 49-51; Ross Calvin, Log Book, entries of November 14-16, 1933, Ross Calvin Papers, CSWR, UNM.

⁴³ Bryant, "Education," 126; *Gila Monster,* September 12, 1934; *La Piedra Lumbre*, November 1936; *Ghost Talks*, January 1937; Matthew J. Bower to Charles H. Kenlen, Conchas Dam Camp, August 10, 1940, CCC, NA.

⁴⁴ Baldridge, "Nine Years," 292; Renwick C. Kennedy, "Military Interlude," *Christian Century*, 50 (September 13, 1933): 1144-5; *Mal Pais*, July 1937; *Ghost Talks*, January 1937.

⁴⁵ *Kangarowl,* April 1937; *Truchas Echo*, February 22, 1939; *Mal Pais*, February 1937; Ross Calvin, "Ministrations in the C.C.C. Camps," *Silver City Enterprise*, August 11, 1933. Ross Calvin later wrote one of the most insightful descriptions of the Southwest, *Sky Determines* (New York: Macmillan, 1934; Silver City: High-Lonesome Press, 1993).

⁴⁶ Dorothy Emerson, *Among the Mescalero Apaches: The Story of Father Albert Braun, OFM* (Tucson: University of Arizona Press, 1973): 153-5, 161; *Dark Canyon Avalanche*, June 2, 1936, and February 15, 1937; *Mayhill Lookout*, February 22, 1937; *Lonely Pennsylvanian,* September 1940; Casaus interview; Barela interview; Dawson interview.

⁴⁷ Brown, *Heritage*, 182-3. On the Penitente movement in New Mexico, see Marta Weigle, *Brothers of Light, Brothers of Blood: The Penitentes of the Southwest* (Albuquerque: University of New Mexico Press, 1976).

# CHAPTER 10

# Town & Camp

On March 12, 1934, the Grant County Chamber of Commerce responded to rumors of local CCC camp closings by sending an urgent telegram to President Franklin D. Roosevelt. County leaders "respectively protest[ed]" the removal of CCC camps from the Gila and Apache National Forests of New Mexico because there was so much "unfinished constructive work to be done." The chamber wired a similarly insistent telegram to CCC director Robert Fechner the following day. Grant County community leaders were not alone in their protests to save threatened camps in New Mexico. In fact, the smallest hint of a camp's closing moved most towns to apply intense grassroots pressure in behalf of their endangered neighbors. After their initial opposition, what caused these communities to react so vehemently to defend threatened camps? Why did most towns seek to save CCC camps after many had expected nothing but trouble when camps were first built near their families, homes, and business enterprises?[1]

The first reason was political. While most enrollees were too young to vote, they were not too young to attend campaign rallies and similar political events. Some of the same leaders who had wired President Roosevelt to rescue Grant County CCC camps in March 1934 invited enrollees to attend Democratic Party rallies and dances in Silver City and Cliff later that election year. The Gila camp newspaper reported that the entire camp "stopped work long enough [on an October] afternoon to help the Democrats have a big time at Silver City." In Santa Fe, Park Service supervisor George Collins remembers getting everyone from the local CCC camp to attend a political rally during Jack Dempsey's campaign for the U.S. Congress. Many enrollees also volunteered to participate in political events staged by Democrats in Torrance County during President Roosevelt's reelection campaign of 1936.[2]

Meanwhile, enrollees over twenty-one years of age were encouraged to vote in some, but not all camps. A "truckload" of eligible youths from the Gila camp voted in the November 1936 elections; for most, it was their first experience in a voting booth. While election officials in other states challenged enrollee votes based on residency requirements, such resistance seldom occurred in New Mexico. Enrollees who were old enough to vote but were not state residents were simply urged to vote by absentee ballot. Educational advisor Merrell Hatch and twenty-five eligible enrollees from the Mountainair camp cast their absentee ballots in the 1936 election with the cooperation of a local judge at Mountainair's town hall. Educational advisor S.E. Gould at the Animas camp prompted enrollees to vote in a similar fashion, writing an editorial that appeared in the *Whirlwind*. At Gila, the Democratic Party took "full charge" of the camp's rec hall, "issuing ballots to those who would not be able to be home to vote." Enrollees close enough to their home communities were often given time off to go vote, as in the case of enrollees from Socorro County serving at the camp near Mountainair.[3]

How much pressure did enrollees feel to participate in politics and vote for the Roosevelt administration's Democratic Party? Most enrollees recall little or no pressure, although Democratic leaders would have preferred more opportunities to influence enrollee voters. Camp commander Fred Poorbaugh recalled that Senator Dennis Chavez once asked to address the enrollees in Poorbaugh's CCC company. Lt. Poorbaugh refused, telling the senator that his political speech would have to be made outside camp grounds or not at all. When Forest Service supervisors resisted Governor Tingley's efforts to conduct voter registration drives in CCC camps, Tingley vowed to take the issue to higher authorities in Washington, D.C. Rosters of eligible enrollee voters were eventually furnished to leaders of both major parties, and "immediately before election time [party operatives] were allowed inside the camps to 'interview' the men whose names appeared on [their respective party's lists]."[4]

It is debatable how these efforts affected enrollee political behavior. Certainly, acceptable voting behavior was no more a requirement to remain in the CCC than party membership had been to join the organization. And, as one historian has suggested, even enrollees who were old enough to vote often did not because they were "preoccupied with subjects that always absorb the thoughts and remarks of young males—the job, girls, sports, movies, and cars." While most enrollees were grateful to Franklin Roosevelt and his administration for creating the CCC, their gratitude did not necessarily translate into political action for FDR's Democratic Party.[5]

Adult beneficiaries in enrollee families were more likely than their sons to vote for Democratic candidates in general elections. A 1936 political ad in the *Taos Valley Review* reminded readers in northern New Mexico to

> Remember What [sic] Roosevelt has done for New Mexico! [He] provided jobs for the unemployed [and] took the jobless boys and young men off the highways and gave them gainful employment in CCC Camps.

There were few camps in close proximity to Taos, but there were many grateful families with "gainfully employed," regularly paid young men in the CCC. LEMs and other camp personnel who owed their jobs to political patronage were likewise indebted to the Democratic Party. The political payoff for such economic aid could be considerable.[6]

Party candidates reaped additional political capital by taking credit for the creation or retention of CCC camps in their districts or in the state as a whole. Although not from New Mexico, Lyndon Johnson in neighboring Texas was known for his "frantic, frenzied, almost desperate aggressiveness" in seeking and keeping New Deal programs for his Congressional district. In fact, Johnson's district had so many CCC camps by 1936 that when the federal government set limits on the number of camps per district, LBJ's district was a "distinct embarrassment."[7]

Clyde Tingley was almost as aggressive in his efforts to secure camps and other New Deal programs for New Mexico. Despite his rather course personal manner, the governor became friends with President Roosevelt and traveled to Washington, D.C., at least twenty-three times to seek federal projects for his impoverished state. Local leaders often mentioned the political benefits of these efforts in their correspondence with Tingley and other political chiefs. Clarence Wiggs wrote to the governor in 1935, declaring that he knew "of no other locality that is in need of ... [a CCC] camp more than Hatch. I trust you will give this your attention ... [because] I want 'old man Tingsley' [sic] to get all the votes around here" next election. Senators Chavez and Hatch were similarly besieged by requests for camps accompanied by promises of reciprocated votes. Tingley, Chavez, and Hatch were not always successful in their efforts; some towns never got camps, despite years of trying. But they were the exception rather than the political rule. In fact, several politically important towns, including Española, Albuquerque, Carlsbad, and Las Cruces, had two or more camps at one time or another from 1933 to 1942.[8]

Tingley, Chavez, and Hatch were also reminded of the political need to compete with other states for Civilian Conservation Corps camps and high enrollment totals. In 1935 State Senator A.O. Steyskal of Grant County told the governor that "unless the State of New Mexico gets busy 'much pronto' ... [we] will not have [our] proper share of [CCC] camps" compared to competing states, including neighboring Arizona. Senator Steyskal need not have worried: more new CCC camps were opened in New Mexico in 1935 than in any year of the CCC's history in the state. Compared to its neighbors in the Southwest, New Mexico had an average of thirty-two camps each year, while Colorado had thirty-four, Arizona had thirty-one, and Utah had twenty-seven. New Mexico's enrollment numbers were even more impressive. The state's total enrollees often surpassed all other states in proportion to quotas based on population; with a quota of only 509 enrollees, the state's enrollment equalled 2,249 in 1941. New Mexico's total enrollment over nine years equaled 54,000, of which 32,300 (or sixty percent) were native New Mexicans. State leaders consistently proved their political mettle and just as consistently reaped their political rewards.[9]

The economic benefits of CCC camps were crucial to communities in the depths of the Great Depression. Each camp represented a source of needed employment and steady income for many formerly destitute families. Local workers often helped in the construction of new camps and later served as Local Experienced Men hired to assist or supervise enrollees in their daily work assignments. By mid-1933, 427 LEMs worked in camps across New Mexico; three years later the number had nearly tripled to 1,279. This income benefitted many individual families, but also helped whole communities. As the county with the largest number of Local Experienced Men in 1933, Grant County's 141 LEMs could be counted on to pump over $42,000 a year into the ailing local economy. As a contemporary observer put it, early misgivings about CCC camps "had a tendency to cool off" when local men were hired and CCC funds began to flow into private pockets and, ultimately, into business coffers.[10]

CCC payrolls also benefitted communities when twenty-five dollar monthly allotments began flowing home from young residents enrolled in distant camps. This was clearly true in the case of the Teston family of eastern New Mexico. Once successful cotton farmers, the Testons had lost their farm in west Texas and had filed for a government homestead in New Mexico by 1932. But their first crop in New Mexico had failed due to harsh conditions, leaving the family "broke, stock-poor, and not able to get back to Texas." It was only when their son, Edd, enrolled in the CCC at Portales and was sent to F-19-N near Los Alamos that family finances improved. Sending home his regular pay plus his extra compensation as an enrollee Leader, Edd helped his family and its struggling farm at a crucial moment. The young enrollee returned home on a three-day leave to be greeted in "the happiest reunion I have ever witnessed." After inspecting their family's fields, Edd and his father predicted a plentiful harvest of cotton and corn. Edd could have been describing the personal impact of CCC labor and income on thousands of families across New Mexico when he declared that "Out of chaos and ruin had come plenty."[11]

By mid-1941, $5,481,078 had been sent home to New Mexican families and towns, priming local economies much as New Deal spending primed the nation's economy as a whole. Seen another way, the CCC removed young workers who would have competed for scarce jobs and income if they had stayed at home. Enrollees helped reduce local unemployment by leaving whatever jobs existed to those who remained at home. As early as October 1934 the *Silver City Enterprise* asserted that the CCC had helped keep the "wolf from the door of thousands."[12]

Enrollees could be counted on to spend some of their hard-earned money in towns near camps. However, with only five dollars in actual pay per month, their payroll could not be expected to make a great impact on business, no less on business recovery. Their few dollars were nevertheless appreciated by the businesses they patronized. Food vendors, for example, could expect additional trade from enrollees in town on weekend excursions. R.L. Coker's father ran a short-order restaurant in Hot Springs near where CCC trucks picked up enrollees after weekend trips to town; some of the restaurant's best customers were enrollees who attempted to sober up with coffee before returning to camp. Enrollees visiting Silver City could eat at a restaurant appropriately called the New Deal Lunch Room. Young men like Charles Clugston fondly recall the Flag Ranch Cafe in Tucumcari. On another level, John Mooney remembers a street vender named Juan who walked from Las Cruces to Mesilla, selling the best tacos "for miles around." Juan's selling price was "a minuscule five cents" a taco.[13]

To advertise their quality goods and low prices, local businesses went so far as to run ads in camp newspapers. The Lordsburg Cafe's ad enticed new enrollees to "make yourselves at home" and enjoy good meals in "the coolest place in town." Grant County stores like the Broadway Bakery, Cosgrove's Sporting Goods, and the Glenwood Trading Post advertised in the *Goldbricker*, promising not only good prices, but also "service with a smile."[14]

Local businesses realized greater profits by helping to supply goods and services for entire camps. Although most supplies were distributed from CCC regional headquarters, certain commodities were purchased locally whenever possible. This was especially true of perishables like fruits, vegetables, and dairy products. Estimates on the average monthly purchases made by camps varied from as low as three thousand dollars, or about a hundred dollars a day, to as high as five thousand dollars, or about 166 dollars a day.[15]

Local services were also in demand. Responsible for their own laundry, enrollees often paid fellow enrollees to wash their clothes, but sometimes sent this work out to local businesses or nearby families. 'Si' Porter reported that his poverty-stricken family was happy to help the Corona camp with both food and laundry services. Camp F-41-N bought green beans, corn, and other vegetables from the Porter's small farm, making the camp's cook "glad to get the [fresh] produce and my folks glad for the pay." The family was also glad to profit from the enrollees' dirty laundry. Lacking electricity or a water well on their property, the Porters had to do all their CCC and personal cleaning by hand, using lye soap, a washboard, and water collected from rain or snow in a cistern. The labor was never easy, but the money was always appreciated.[16]

Store merchants appreciated the impact of CCC projects that generated new economic activity and income. Two examples illustrate this point. In Grant County, residents living north of

Silver City had "dreamed for years of a highway giving them an outlet to the south." With crews working from both directions, the CCC made this dream a reality by building a new road through rugged terrain. The road's completion was good news not only for formerly isolated residents, but also for Silver City merchants who soon saw more shoppers and greater profits. Across the state to the east, CCC efforts to improve access to Carlsbad Caverns brought many more tourists to the area and many more tourist dollars into the local economy.[17]

Enrollee labor in national forests brought similar results in tourism, spending, and renewed business prosperity. In 1937 appreciative campers fastened a note to a tree in the Santa Fe National Forest. Written on a piece of brown wrapping paper, the message read: "CCC Boys—You keep the campground in first-class condition. We wish to extend our gratitude and thanks to you for an enjoyable two days' outing." A year later, another enthusiastic vacationer told the director of the New Mexico Tourist Bureau that she thought that Carlsbad Caverns were "just too wonderful." Giving enrollees even more credit than they deserved, the effusive visitor inquired if the caverns had in fact been dug by the CCC. The Tourist Bureau director replied that despite all the enrollees' labor, they had not yet accomplished such a feat in New Mexico. Regardless of such misconceptions, tourists were return-ing to the state in greater numbers, for longer stays, with addi-tional cash to spend. The value of expenditures by tourists in out-of-state vehicles equaled approximately eighty million dollars in 1939. With an average stay of four and a half days, a typical car of tourists spent $50.34 during their time in New Mexico. It is impossible to say how much of this increase in tourism resulted from CCC efforts in the National Forests, Carlsbad Caverns, the Catwalk, and elsewhere, but state residents were willing to give a fair share of credit to the hard-working enrollees encamped near their communities.[18]

Hundreds of farmers and ranchers also appreciated CCC labor, especially in the conservation of soil and water resources. While much work was done on public land, a great deal was done on badly depleted private land as well. By 1940 a Soil Conservation Service official in De Baca County wrote that the "greatest problem" was not too little work for the CCC, but too much, given the "enthusiastic cooperation" of rural residents. Similar votes of confidence were heard all across New Mexico.[19]

Local businessmen and citizens demonstrated their appreciation for the direct and indirect benefits of CCC spending and labor by quickly defending CCC enrollees in need of in-town assistance. In one case, several enrollees were accused of causing mischief from stealing cars to smashing furniture during altercations in a local saloon in Bloomfield, New Mexico. Justice of the Peace J.M. Thomas attempted to crack down on this disorderly conduct, but met resistance from the Bloomfield camp commander, Robert L. Maddox. According to Maddox, community officials like Thomas had no jurisdiction over CCC personnel. Maddox added, "It is a known fact that Justice Thomas has absolutely no use for CCC enrollees, or anything else that President Roosevelt has inaugurated." Nonplused, Justice Thomas responded, "If there is such a law defining these boys as preferred citizens [outside local jurisdiction], kindly give me the book, chapter and verse." This legal dispute was soon resolved, but only after sixteen local merchants signed a petition attesting to the enrollees' general orderliness. The merchants' motivations were not stated, but were clearly understood: if criticized and unwelcome, the CCC might retreat from this or any community, depriving local businesses of needed customers and essential cash flow during hard economic times.[20]

However, not all businessmen enjoyed the best relations with their local camps. Businessmen were never pleased when out-of-state competitors, rather than local companies, were given the opportunity to supply nearby camps. In fact, some merchants were even anxious about business competition from within their neighboring camps. In mid-1935 private newspaper publishers complained to the New Mexico Press Association that CCC camp newspapers were "stepping out into the commercial field by soliciting advertising from the merchants in adjacent towns."

Publishers were "a little indignant over this invasion of their field by a mimeographed sheet that has no rightful place in the business life of the community." Press Association president Carey Holbrook wrote to Governor Tingley requesting that "steps ... be taken to keep these sheets out of the legitimate advertising [business]." Tingley agreed, stating that "the CCC camps were not organized for the purpose of giving the members an excuse to enter into ... competition with local firms." The governor's letter in support of local newspapers was sent to CCC director Fechner in August 1935. Its message hit the mark; few, if any, ads appeared in camp newspapers thereafter.[21]

At least one small businessman also objected to the competition of young entrepreneurs who sold clothing to their fellow enrollees in CCC camps. Investigating this complaint by impersonating a traveling salesman, a Silver City reporter visited two CCC camps in late 1935. At the first camp, the reporter-peddler attempted to show his sample case in a barracks, but was told "in very terse language" that only enrollees could sell men's apparel to enrollees. Receiving much the same reception in the second camp he stopped at, the reporter concluded that enrollee businessmen had gained an unfair monopoly, while "keeping the local merchants from deriving any benefit" from CCC sales.[22]

A group calling itself the 'CCC Salesmen of Company 1851' responded to these charges in a letter to the editor of the *Southwestern Bulletin*. Among other arguments in their own defense, the salesmen contended that with so little money for their personal use, enrollees needed a less expensive way to buy clothes than from high-priced stores in Silver City. Enrollees also wondered why no other businessmen had complained about other kinds of camp competition, including the camp canteen. Apparently, "it is just the clothing business (or one man) that is making all this fuss about the CCC salesman."[23]

CCC officials took merchants' complaints seriously when good relations with local communities were at stake. As J.J. McEntee, the CCC's assistant national director, put it in 1937, "there must be no competition between the camp activities of the

CCC and merchants." Camp canteens could only sell goods to camp enrollees, not to local residents. Even allowing residents to view movies in camp was curtailed if this neighborly gesture was misconstrued as a form of competition with local theaters. Camp salesmen were not shut down, but their private enterprises were never officially condoned or encouraged for fear of loosing valuable local support.[24]

Fortunately, sources of friction between camps and local communities were rare and usually short-lived. More often than not, camps and towns enjoyed a mutually advantageous, symbiotic relationship, not unlike the ties that bind small towns to military bases or college campuses. Each derived important political and economic benefits from the other and, in many cases, could not have survived without the other in the decade-long crisis of the 1930s.

## Endnotes - Chapter 10

[1] Grant County Chamber of Commerce to Franklin D. Roosevelt, Silver City, March 12, 1934, CCC, NA; *Silver City Enterprise*, March 12, 1934; List of Telegrams to Robert Fechner Asking for the Retention of the CCC Camp at Carrizozo, New Mexico, March 22, 1934, CCC File, FDRL; Clyde Tingley to Dennis Chavez, Santa Fe, February 4, 1936, and J.J. McEntee to Clyde Tingley, Washington, D.C., June 24, 1937, Governor Tingley Papers, NMSRCA; F.A. Koch to Dennis Chavez, Santa Fe, March 14, 1940, F.A. Koch Papers, NMSRCA; *Raton Range*, March 10, 1938.

[2] *Gila Monster*, October 20, 1934, and November 3 and 16, 1934; *Tip Topper*, November 1936; Collins interview.

[3] *Gila Monster*, October 26, 1934, and November 1936; Ermentrout, *Forgotten Men*, 42; Draves, *Builder*, 103-4; *New York Times*, November 4, 1936; Richardson, "Politics," 19; *Tip Topper*, November 1936; *Whirlwind*, September 1936. In an apparently isolated case, Senator Bronson Cutting objected to reports that out-of-state enrollees were registering to vote in New Mexico in 1934. Hendrickson, "CCC in the Southwest," 13.

⁴ Vega interview; Poorbaugh interview; Richardson, "Politics," 19.

⁵ *Ibid.*, 20. For cases in which enrollees were bribed to vote for one party or the other elsewhere in the U.S., see Salmond, *CCC*, 142, and the *New York Times*, December 15-17, 1936.

⁶ *Taos Valley Review*, October 8, 1936.

⁷ Robert A. Caro, *The Years of Lyndon Johnson: The Path to Power* (New York: Alfred A. Knopf, 1983): 260; Utley and Steely, *Guided With a Steady Hand*, 119-20.

⁸ Marc Simmons, *Albuquerque* (Albuquerque: University of New Mexico Press, 1982): 365; Clarence Wiggs to Clyde Tingley, El Paso, September 16, 1935, Governor Tingley Papers; F.A. Koch to Dennis Chavez, Santa Fe, March 14, 1940, and F.A. Koch to Carl Hatch, Santa Fe, March 14, 1940, F.A. Koch Papers, NMSRCA.

⁹ A.O. Steyskal to Clyde Tingley, Santa Fe, March 10, 1935, Governor Tingley Papers, and Guy Neal to Jennie M. Kirby, Washington, D.C., April 10, 1942, Governor John E. Miles Papers, NMSRCA; McEntee, *Final Report,* 110-11. The number of camps in the U.S. peaked at 1,751 in August 1935. Bryant, "Education," 5. For the number of camps each year in New Mexico from 1933 to 1942, see Appendix B.

¹⁰ *Silver City Enterprise*, September 22, 1933; Porter Memoirs, 10; Serna interview; *Albuquerque Journal*, July 16, 1936; List of LEMs Per New Mexico County, August 1, 1933, CCC, NA.

¹¹ K. Edd Teston, "Shanty on the Claim," 58.

¹² Huffman interview; Chacon interview; Forrest, *Preservation*, 116; *Silver City Enterprise*, October 12, 1934.

¹³ *Pink Pebble Periodical*, July 9, 1935; Sherraden, "Effectiveness of the Camps," 246; Kemp interview; Poorbaugh interview; Garcia interview; Coker interview; *Silver City Enterprise*, June 22, 1934; Clugston interview; John Mooney to the editor, *New Mexico Magazine,* 72 (February 1994): 5.

¹⁴ *Pink Pebble Periodical*, June 18 and July 30, 1935; *Goldbricker,* March 26, 1935.

¹⁵ *Albuquerque Journal*, August 13, 1934; *Silver City Enterprise,* August 3, 1934; Casaus interview; Dawson interview; Sanchez interview; *Gila Monster*, September 21, 1934; *Raton Range*, July 23, 1935; Salmond, *CCC*, 111.

¹⁶ Porter Memoirs, 7-8. Some companies argued that they did not get enough business from nearby camps. See, for example, E.R. Edgar (Imperial Laundry Company) to Clyde Tingley, Albuquerque, June 7, 1935, Governor Tingley Papers, NMSRCA.

¹⁷ *Silver City Enterprise*, September 1, 1937; *Carlsbad Current-Argus*, January 11, 1998. Also see *Canyon Pine Cone*, May 24, 1939.

<sup>18</sup> *Forest Pioneer,* 4th quarter, 1937, and 3rd quarter, 1938; Severns, "Tourism," 73. Rebuilt in the 1960s, the Catwalk remains the primary tourist attraction in its area of the state, drawing more than 27,000 visitors per year. *Southern New Mexico Magazine,* 2 (Winter 1998): 14-5.

<sup>19</sup> De Baca County Soil Conservation Service District, Semi-Annual Report for the Period Ending December 31, 1940, SCS Collection, CSWR, UNM.

<sup>20</sup> *Albuquerque Journal,* July 10 and 12, 1940; Camp Inspection Report, Bloomfield, September 17, 1940, CCC, NA.

<sup>21</sup> Carey Holbrook to Clyde Tingley, Albuquerque, August 19, 1935, and Clyde Tingley to Robert W. Fechner, Santa Fe, August 2, 1935, Governor Tingley Papers, NMSRCA.

<sup>22</sup> *Gila Monster*, December 1935.

<sup>23</sup> *Ibid.*

<sup>24</sup> J.J. McEntee to A.W. Stockman, Washington, D.C., October 11, 1937, CCC, NA.

Enrollees throughout the state assisted in flood control activities in the Rio Grande and Pecos River valleys. This is a Roswell street scene during the June 1, 1937, flood. Enrollees from nearby camps helped Roswell residents battle the rising water. *Courtesy: Rio Grande Historical Collection, New Mexico State University, Las Cruces, New Mexico.*

# CHAPTER 11

# To The Rescue

The CCC was much appreciated in political and economic terms. But admiration for the camps and their enrollees increased tenfold when they came to the rescue during local crises involving medical emergencies, search efforts, flood control, and fire fighting. Communities did everything in their power to thank their local CCC camps and the enrollees who often deserved to be called true heroes.

As the only physicians for miles around, camp doctors were sometimes called on in local medical emergencies. One such emergency occurred in the mid-1930s at New Mexico's famous Ghost Ranch in Rio Arriba County. A woman, employed to care for ranch children, was attacked by a buck antelope during an excursion in the wilderness. Somehow, the badly injured woman made it back to Ghost Ranch in the truck she was driving. Reaching her destination, she fainted, falling forward against the truck's horn. "Her body," wrote ranch owner Arthur Peck, "was a mass of wounds and bruises and it was easy to see that a full grown antelope had attacked her with horns and sharp feet." A ranch hand "drove frantically" to a nearby CCC camp to find the camp's doctor and rush him back to the wounded woman. Sadly, little could be done to save her. She died before morning.[1]

Doctors and camp personnel trained in first aid realized greater success in other crises. A CCC foreman, who had just taken a first aid course taught by his camp's physician, was able to treat a little girl bitten by a rattlesnake near Caballo, New Mexico, in 1936. Carefully following the procedures he had just learned, Floyd Riley treated the child so well that she recovered with no ill effects. A week later her father had a hard time "convincing anyone she was bitten by anything worse than a nice garden variety of spider." Local doctors agreed that without Riley's immediate care, the girl would have had only a twenty percent chance of surviving. The Hamilton family thanked Riley in a letter, characterizing his help as nothing short of a "miracle."[2]

On another occasion, Abe Peña, who grew up near San Mateo in today's Cibola County, recalls playing with other children on the branches of an old cottonwood tree in the summer of 1937. When Abe's brother Benito slid down a branch, it snapped, causing Benito to fall and break his leg. Benito was taken home in a wagon, but his mother knew that he needed more medical attention than either she or the local *curandera* could provide. The worried mother pleaded for her husband to go to the nearby CCC camp and ask the camp's doctor for assistance. As the first and only physician in the San Mateo area, the CCC doctor was only allowed to treat local residents in grave emergencies. Recognizing Benito's case as such an emergency, the doctor came to the Peña home, set the boy's leg, and received the heartfelt gratitude of the entire Peña family.[3]

Community residents were equally grateful for CCC efforts during dangerous rescues in the wilderness. As with medical emergencies, search and rescue operations ended with mixed results. In a dramatic success story, enrollees searched for two young boys who had wandered from their camp in the Sandia Mountains on a Monday morning in June 1938. The six- and eleven-year-olds were lost for six hours, drifting miles from their campsite after a rain and hail storm. Searchers from a nearby CCC camp combed the area and finally found the exhausted pair about 4:00 p.m. that same day.[4]

In a similar episode, nearly every enrollee in the Buckhorn camp joined in the search for Buddy Reasoner when the little boy was reported missing in the Pinos Altos Mountains. Enrollees hunted as long as they had daylight left to see. That night, searchers kept several campfires burning, "hoping the boy would see them and come in." As a result of this determination, the lost boy was "almost miraculously" discovered. CCC enrollees "received high praise from the citizens of the region for the splendid manner in which they responded to the call" for help.[5]

Robert Thomas remembers that enrollees at the Buckhorn camp also helped rescue a family of four that had accidently driven off the road and into an arroyo on a cold winter night. Enrollees rescued the victims from their car, brought them back to camp for medical care, and even drove them home to Silver City. Far to the north, enrollees joined state police, mounted patrolmen, and bloodhounds borrowed from the state penitentiary to search for Agapito Cortez, a twenty-four-year-old musician from El Macho who became lost on his way to Santa Fe. After a two-day search, Cortez was discovered alive and well. He was, in fact, found "sleeping peacefully" in a cornfield just north of Santa Fe.[6]

International travelers were also afforded CCC assistance. On a 1937 visit to New Mexico, a young French student and her two aunts from back East ventured to the Ice Caves southwest of Grants. After visiting the caves, the three women lost their way back to their car. They wandered for four days, often cutting themselves on razor-sharp volcanic rock in the lava beds they traversed. Although they had little to eat or drink, the trio "never lost hope that someone would find us." They were right. A passing rancher alerted the state police after driving by the travelers' suspiciously abandoned vehicle. State troopers, CCC enrollees, volunteers, and even Governor Tingley searched the caves and surrounding landscape. Enrollees formed a dragnet, walking twenty feet apart and swinging in a wide circle southward. Within hours rescuers found the lost vacationers "lying in the limited shade of a piñon [tree], exhausted but not at all hysterical." Relieved, Laura Piedalue reportedly "drew out her rosary, kissed it, and exclaimed, 'God bless you, boys.'"[7]

But not all searches and rescues were as successful. On the same day that Agapito Cortez was found sleeping in a field outside Santa Fe, the body of a twenty-two-year-old CCC enrollee named Lawrence Shutz was found fifteen miles from where he had fallen into a flooded arroyo. Enrollees from two camps had searched for two days before the Pottsville, Pennsylvania, native's remains were discovered. Other enrollees experienced the same disappointment following an intensive search for Sandoval County Sheriff Ramon F. Romero. Romero's nephew discovered the lawman's body three months later; he had accidently drowned while duck hunting along the Rio Grande.[8]

In another tragic drowning, a small boy was reported missing near a large irrigation canal not far from a Carlsbad CCC camp. Enrollees quickly responded to the call for help. Wearing hip boots, the searchers formed a line across the canal and "covered every foot of the bottom for a distance of several miles." The work continued late into the night. The victim's lifeless body was found on the following day. Other enrollees participated in the sad search for a young girl whose body was recovered after an eight-hour search in an irrigation ditch near Mesilla.[9]

But at least these bodies were eventually found. Former enrollee Doug Hall remembers a CCC-led search for an elderly Hispanic woman who had become lost while gathering piñon nuts east of the Sandia Mountains. The search proved futile, and the woman was never heard of again. In early 1935 four members of the High Rolls camp joined in the search for a plane that had crashed in the San Andres Mountains. Using a CCC truck, the four traveled for three days, driving 150 miles over terrain covered with "thousands of rocks, ditches, and many other hazards." The High Rolls camp newspaper reported that despite these great efforts the missing plane and its luckless passengers were never found.[10]

In the most famous rescue attempt of the 1930s, the CCC joined some three hundred other rescuers in their search for Medill 'Johnny' McCormick, the son of rich, politically powerful Ruth Hanna McCormick. On June 22, 1938, the twenty-one-year-old and his twenty-year-old friend, Richard Whitmer, had begun to climb a particularly dangerous section of the Sandia Mountains. Although few had scaled this rugged part of the mountains and the last man to try had died in the effort, the young friends were confident in their climbing skills. Despite their confidence, McCormick and Whitmer did not return home on the evening of June 22; rescuers began searching for them the following day. One-hundred-and-twenty enrollees from five camps, U.S. Forest Service personnel, National Guardsmen, state police, Albuquerque police, local Indians, and fourteen expert mountain climbers from Colorado were brought in to assist in the effort.[11]

The going was slow and perilous, with countless crevices and loose rocks. One enrollee lost his footing and fell from a high cliff, "miraculously escap[ing] injury by crashing into the top branches of a tree." Rescuers scanned the mountainous horizon with a high-powered telescope previously used to spot enemy submarines in the Atlantic Ocean during World War I. Governor Tingley lent a hand by manning this powerful telescope, but to no avail. A Soil Conservation Service plane circled overhead, taking aerial photographs with the same disappointing results. Despite exploration of "every canyon, arroyo and wooded plot" in the vicinity, little progress was made until Whitmer's "badly mangled" body was found below circling vultures. A signal of three rapidly fired shots, universally recognized in rescue efforts, relayed the sad news to those waiting below. Shortly thereafter, and eight days after the search had begun, Isleta and Sandia Pueblo Indians finally found McCormick's remains in what was described as a "nearly inaccessible spot." Efforts to remove the body from the "fortress-like cliffs" proved to be almost as dangerous as the search itself. When the youths' camera was later recovered, its film revealed photos of lightning in a storm that undoubtedly caused the climbers' fatal falls.[12]

CCC enrollees could be counted on to help rescue whole communities as well as individuals and small groups. Their labors in the so-called Grasshopper Wars of the 1930s was only one of many examples of such heroism in New Mexico. On another front, enrollees received great praise when they helped in the aftermath of a natural gas explosion in Santa Fe in early 1937. Plaza-area businessmen were impressed by the enrollees' help in searching for victims, keeping the curious at bay, and spending much of the following night guarding sewer manholes left open to allow the escape of accumulated gases. Thanks to this assistance, property damage was minimal and deaths were limited to two.[13]

But of all the emergency assistance lent to communities, none was more appreciated than during and after terrible floods. Floods had always plagued New Mexico's river valleys, causing great destruction and loss of lives. In 1929 the entire town of San Marcial was destroyed when two consecutive floods inundated that small railroad community on the Rio Grande. Floods in 1935 and 1937 threatened the future of other communities along the Rio Grande and Pecos River. Called on in these crises, CCC companies dropped whatever they were doing and rushed to provide valuable assistance. Camp commander Robert Thomas recalls receiving one such urgent call from Ft. Sumner on a summer afternoon in 1937. Preparing through the night, Thomas and his Red Canyon enrollees were ready and on the road to Ft. Sumner by seven o'clock the next morning. In a similar manner, work crews from the Española CCC camp were called in from their work sites on a Friday afternoon that same summer. Rushed to the lowlands north of Española, 250 youths toiled in two shifts, "using all available daylight," until the danger of flooding had finally passed by Sunday.[14]

Once delivered in CCC trucks at threatened spots along river valleys, enrollees worked feverishly, filling sandbags and using brush to shore up dikes. Their's was back-breaking, stressful labor, especially when so many relied on the CCC for survival. At the McMillan Dam in Eddy County over two hundred enrollees and WPA workers threw an estimated fifteen hundred sandbags into leaking dikes, knowing that any let-up in their labor could spell disaster for the residents of Carlsbad eighteen miles to the south. Enrollees from several camps worked just as feverishly near

Ft. Sumner, realizing that if the Pecos River's bank broke crop land worth up to four hundred dollars an acre could be lost. A newspaper reporter on the scene wrote that "Not a boy was hurt, despite the fact that they did hard work, and often were compelled to wade in water waste-deep." On the Rio Grande, enrollees struggled to repair dikes after "considerable damage" had been done to parts of Albuquerque in 1937. CCC volunteers worked from 8:00 p.m. to 2:00 a.m. in perilous conditions, proving that enrollees "will gladly lay down their lives for the safety of other people." Enrollees toiled with the same determination at other valley towns, including Española, Los Lunas, Hatch, Las Cruces, and Roswell.[15]

Enrollees also helped threatened flood areas in less dramatic, but no less important ways. The amateur radio station at the La Madera camp made its facilities available to anyone who needed to send urgent messages to and from flood sites. Enrollees near Roswell used every available vehicle in camp to warn locals of impending trouble caused by floods. Working in twelve-hour shifts, enrollees remained "stationed at ... danger points and at the telephone to warn and assist the general public." As flood waters rose, farm animals were pulled ashore on anything that could float; a barn door served this purpose for a group of destitute hogs and chickens in one instance. Providing these refugees with shelter, a nearby CCC camp was said to have soon "lost its neat and trim appearance and assumed the [appearance] of a barnyard."[16]

Destitute humans received special care from the CCC. Camp mess halls fed over a hundred flood victims at the height of the Roswell crisis in 1937. Forty people left stranded on or near a bridge on the Pecos River were rescued and taken to safe quarters. Once the flood waters began to recede, enrollees battled to make roads passable again. Camp members remained to help with cleanup operations in towns like Ft. Sumner, Las Cruces, and Hatch. In Las Cruces, workers were kept busy "pumping water from basements and houses, removing furniture from the flooded section of town, cleaning ... debris from the streets, and digging ditches to divert ... surplus water ... into canals and drainage ditches." Their varied chores seemed endless.[17]

Their labor completed at last, exhausted young men headed back to their respective camps in the same Army vehicles that had brought them hours and sometimes days before.

Only the grueling demands of fire fighting competed with the hard work of flood control duty in New Mexico. Although fires seldom threatened the safety of whole towns, communities appreciated CCC efforts to protect wilderness resources and scattered families living far from conventional fire fighting protection. As throughout the Southwest, the CCC's "immediate response ... to natural and man-made disasters [further] bolstered the Corps' favorable [public] image."[18]

Examples of the Corps' immediate response to local fires abound. Enrollees at the La Madera camp helped extinguish a house fire and rescue a pet cat, although at least one corpsman suffered severe leg burns while trying to remove valuables threatened by the blaze. A fire at the Gordon Ranch in southwest New Mexico brought enrollees from the Buckhorn camp on the run. Two buildings were lost and a rancher was badly burned, but much property was saved and the burn victim received essential first aid at the Buckhorn camp infirmary before being taken to Silver City for additional care. Inhabitants of remote sawmill camps were especially glad to have CCC help. Independent, strong-willed people, they were said to favor strong liquor and good fights to any other forms of entertainment in their leisure hours. But 'Si' Porter remembered that sawmill camp residents always favored CCC enrollees, particularly during fire season. "The forests were their livelihood. They could smell smoke in the air and be working on [a] forest fire before the CCC boys could get started ... . They would have someone in charge and ready to show [CCC] foremen ... what was necessary for [us] to do." After working side-by-side with enrollees, sawmill people were more inclined to share their hard liquor and less likely to pick fights with much-appreciated members of the Civilian Conservation Corps.[19]

As important as their fire fighting missions could be in saving lives and property, enrollees avoided taking themselves and their heroic roles too seriously. The Ft. Stanton camp newspaper described the reaction of three enrollees who were "plucking" apples in an orchard near camp when "the silence was broken by the shrill sound of a fire whistle." Said to have "sprung into action," the three boys spotted the flame, hurdled a fence, and ran through dense underbrush to get to the fire scene. The "brave lads dashed into the blazing inferno" and for "three solid minutes the fearless trio battled [a] blazing ironing board." Emerging triumphant, the "grinning, smoke begrimed heroes" returned to camp where they received a "rousing" hard time from their fellow enrollees. A sarcastic camp reporter told John R. Lewis, Eustachio Lillie, and Andrew Slinkosky that "The C's are proud of you boys." The "blazing" ironing board's owner displayed more sincere gratitude.[20]

Fighting forest fires in New Mexico before the CCC's arrival in New Mexico has been described as a "haphazard affair" at best. Volunteers were often "limited and undependable," if only because fires could start anywhere at any time. Most fires were caused by careless smokers or streaks of lightening, especially during dry summer months. About 43,000 acres had burned in New Mexico fires from 1928 to 1935. Members of the Mescalero Apache tribal council were among the many New Mexicans who feared this "dire peril." Using highly descriptive terms, the council reminded tribal members that when a fire was "turned loose in the woods, it becomes a terrible red wolf which runs about at a rapid pace, devouring all it sees and laying the beautiful forest waste for many years." The Mescaleros considered it their "sacred duty" to save the woodland on their reservation so that future generations could enjoy "a green forest, not one that is all black and burned."[21]

Once created, the CCC became the U.S. Forest Service's most valuable ally in its fight to control New Mexico's "terrible red wolf." When not fighting fires directly, the CCC worked hard to prevent them under Forest Service supervision. By 1941, the CCC had built 471 lookout towers in New Mexico so that rangers could spot flames and sound the alarm before blazes grew out of control. At least six new ranger stations were built in the Carson, Cibola, Gila, and Lincoln National Forests. Enrollees at forest work sites and distant side camps also served as unofficial look-outs who observed and reported countless small fires. Telephone lines were strung on forest land to help communicate the location of potentially dangerous new fires. In addition, CCC workers built nearly five thousand miles of forest roads in New Mexico to facilitate transportation of workers and equipment to fire sites in the wilderness. Others removed dead trees and other inflammable materials from forest floors. Fire breaks were constructed by clear-ing long strips of land. Whole camps assigned to the National Forest Service spent thousands of man-hours accomplishing these essential tasks.[22]

Beyond working to prevent or contain forest fires, enrollees received training in fire fighting techniques. While few enrollees received such training in the CCC's early years, more emphasis was placed on instruction after several tragedies occurred else-where in the country. In 1938 eight enrollees died while attempt-ing to extinguish a blaze in Cameron County, Pennsylvania. An inquest revealed that the dead youths "had no formal fire-fighting instruction, ... were poorly equipped for the task, and ... were inadequately supervised." As a result of this and similar disasters, fire fighting training became a high priority in CCC camps across the nation, including New Mexico.[23]

Training was conducted in a number of venues. Forest Ser-vice officers lectured to enrollees in camps like Mountainair. Films were also shown; the script in one such film in 1938 declared that "He who burns a forest is a greater enemy than a dozen foreign dictators." At the Bosque del Apache camp a fire was intention-ally set in an open area of grass and brush so that enrollees could practice fire fighting methods under the watchful eye of camp supervisors. Each new group of enrollees underwent similar instruction shortly after arriving in the bosque, according to camp superintendent Oliver C. Payne.[24]

Other drills were conducted to see how fast enrollees could respond to emergency calls. In one instance, a visitor to the Mayhill camp foolishly offered a wager on the company's "get-away time." Taking the bet, a camp leader "turned loose a series of shrill blasts on his whistle." Enrollees responded from all directions, "some hatless, others' shirt-tails flapping but all with one objective—to get up ... into [their] fire truck." Within thirty seconds, the truck driver was in his seat with the motor running. In thirty more seconds, the truck's tail gate was closed with its trained fire crew, fire fighting tools, and rations for up to twenty men safely inside. Red flags flew from all four corners of the Dodge truck, "warning road traffic that the Mayhill [camp's] fire truck was on its way to keep another Sacramento Mountains fire in Class A," or minor fire status. The company leader had won his bet, but, more importantly, CCC fire fighters were even better prepared for a real fire that broke out the next morning. With good training and practice, the camp's fire fighting team "hit the camp exit ... [in] about fifty-five seconds" after hearing a series of shrill whistle blasts, much as the group had responded the day before.[25]

Enrollees who responded quickly and efficiently to fire alarms at Mayhill and other camps were members of special crews known as CCC 'hot shots.' Hot shots received special training in fire fighting methods, the use of fire equipment, and the need for strict discipline on fire lines. As well-trained, experienced workers in a risky field, hot shots "took pride in this distinction," much like an elite squad of soldiers assigned to special missions in combat. Other enrollees were called in only if fires could not be contained and backup troops were clearly needed. The worst fires required help from as many as five camps; enrollees from the Ft. Stanton, Ruidoso, Tularosa, High Rolls, and Roswell camps converged on one such blaze near Altos in May 1940.[26]

CCC trucks sped to fires as quickly as rough roads and safety precautions allowed. While some fires were relatively close, others broke out at considerable distances; Ft. Stanton enrollees drove seventy miles to a fire on the Mescalero Reservation in April 1940. Once near a blaze, enrollees left their trucks and began long hikes through dense underbrush to the fire's front lines. Everything, from axes and shovels to first aid kits and food rations, had to be carried to a fire's location in the wilderness. Problems often arose en route. Jim Johnson recalled walking in the direction of a reported fire only to find that the elevation map that he and his fellow enrollees were using inaccurately described the steep hills they had to cross. What had looked like the easiest route became the hardest, especially as the enrollees' water supply ran low. Luckily, the fire fighters found a local resident who knew the land well and gladly led the crew to the fire site, riding ahead on his burro.[27]

XEach fire presented its own set of problems and complications. A May 1937 blaze in the badlands region south of Grants was difficult not only because it spread over four sections of land, but also because what started as a timber fire soon ignited dry brush and grass; the resulting flames caused a "haze of smut and smoke" that hindered progress "and made the work most unpleasant." A fire in the same area burned more than a thousand acres of Cibola National Forest land in 1936, requiring CCC crews to haul water from as far as fifteen miles away. Spring winds could cause flames to spread faster and wider than fire lanes could be dug or dirt could be thrown on hot embers. In May 1937 a strong wind blew a fire along at such a rapid pace near the Bandelier National Monument that soon "both sides of [the] steep canyon [were] in flames." Fortunately, the wind subsided about 5:30 p.m., and the danger to the monument passed. Nature also took pity on enrollees at the 1937 Malpais fire. After three days of "tedious fighting," the fire was almost extinguished when "From the heavens ... came a blessing in the form of rain drops." Moments later, "all that remained was a ghastly black gummy smudge on the ground from which faint spirals of smoke issued forth."[28]

Keith Humphries of Grant County wrote one of the most graphic descriptions of a typical fire in the wilderness:

> When you have stood on a high ridge and heard the crackling and popping of burning pine and watched the smoke come bellowing up through the treetops; when you have heard the deer running through the underbrush and seen the mother doe butting her fawns along;

when you have ... seen a black bear come cuffing her cubs through the saddle ... so close you can hear her breathe and see her bloodshot eyes; ... when you have seen the Piñon jays come screaming out of the trees saturated with heat and smoke; ... [when you have seen men] hurry past you, their faces taut and smeared with dust and soot; ... [when you have seen] fresh CCC boys hurrying along [showing] eagerness in their excitement to attack ... . And ... when you later look back across the canyon where yesterday beautiful pine and stately spruce once stood, you see only charred logs and trees —ghost-like—standing back without arms. Then—and only then—will you know the ravages of a forest fire.

Eight hundred CCC enrollees and other volunteers helped to finally extinguish this terrible Black Range fire following a week-long test of strength and endurance in June 1938.[29]

Fires were extinguished in as little as a few hours or as long as a week, including mop-up operations and patrol duty to make sure all sparks were dead. After hours of tiring, backbreaking labor, enrollees were relieved when fires were finally out, all danger had passed, and it was time to head home to camp. Witnessing the return of fire fighters from a Black Range blaze, Ross Calvin wrote succinctly of "Clouds of smoke drifting. Rangers on horses. C.C.C. enrollees at 9:00 a.m. coming in after night on duty—Dirty, sooty, dusty." Exhausted, most enrollees were given a day or more to recover before heading back to their regularly assigned duties. Some became ill, as in the case of Jim Johnson and his fellow fire fighters who complained of a strange tightness in their stomachs after hours of forest fire combat; they experienced difficulty in drinking and eating for several days.[30]

Worse, some enrollees were injured and at least three were killed while battling flames in New Mexico's wilderness. Ray Dawson remembered an enrollee who panicked and ran in a fire near Ruidoso. Tripping over a log, the youth was injured so badly that he was unable to escape the fire's deadly smoke. A fire near Alto left an enrollee dead when he was trapped in flames and burned to death. A third victim died as he attempted to lead his crew of fourteen enrollees to safety after three hours of dangerous labor on a fire west of Bandelier in 1934. Although the flames had diminished, Santos Martinez realized that "scattered throughout the canyon were large tombstones of trees, still smoldering, still standing erect." The cautious leader knew that at "any moment and without warning [these trees could] come crashing down, raining death from above." Martinez worked feverishly, "felling trees and burying charred logs with dirt" to insure the safety of his fellow enrollees. Tragedy struck nevertheless. "It was doubtful if he heard the tree fall. No one else did until it had shattered his young body. It was a large tree, at least three feet in diameter, and he was directly under it." It killed him almost instantly. A hero, Martinez posthumously received an award for courage and meritorious service from CCC director Robert Fechner on May 28, 1934. Years later, former enrollees still talk of erecting a memorial to this little-known, but much admired young man.[31]

With yeomen service by brave youths like Martinez, it is not surprising that while the CCC existed the acreage lost to fires in the United States fell to the lowest level since records were first kept on such destruction. As one observer wrote in 1943, "wherever there were great disasters or emergencies, the CCC was always called on—and they always answered, with supplies, food, and ready and willing hands, arms, and backs."[32]

New Mexican communities expressed their appreciation for the CCC in large and small acts of kindness. Letters arrived from state and local leaders in the aftermath of dangerous floods. The mayors of Hatch and Las Cruces were quick to thank camps for coming to their towns' rescue in 1935. Governor Tingley wrote a special note of thanks, commending enrollees and their officers for their "excellent cooperation" and selfless willingness to work day and night until all danger had passed. Elsewhere, the editor of the *Roswell Daily Record* reported "hearing comments ... on the fine work done by the CCC" during Roswell's 1937 flood. The impressed newsman asked camp commander Ross O. Sare to summarize his company's efforts in a front page article that appeared in June 1937. Robert Thomas recalls the attention his company received from the citizens, and especially the young ladies, of Ft. Sumner when enrollees appeared in town in their dress uniforms soon after their rescue efforts were completed. Las Cruces showed its appreciation by paying fifteen cents toward each enrollee's ticket to a traveling circus that had come to town in September 1935.[33]

In gestures reminiscent of the treatment of soldiers in training camps during World War I, enrollees were often invited into homes and businesses to be fed, cared for, and showered with praise for all their labors. Early fears of young male enrollees were soon overcome in most of the state. Even in 'Si' Porter's Corona relations changed so drastically that "quite a few of the boys learned what time of the day [local] bean farmers had a few groceries on the table and [often] got an invitation to stay and eat." Bean farmers didn't eat "anything fancy," according to Porter, but the food was fresh and the cooking was homemade. More affluent farmers and ranchers donated food to whole camps, as when the Circle Cross Ranch gave bushels of apples to the High Rolls camp or when Steve Villareal contributed fifty fruit trees to the Gila camp. John Mooney recalls that a grateful Las Cruces bakery cooked camp BR-39-N's Thanksgiving turkey at no charge to the CCC or its hungry enrollees.[34]

Free or reduced fares were also offered for movies, dances, sporting events, and attractions like Carlsbad Caverns. Enrollees from nearby camps were invited to the big football game between the Deming High School Wildcats and the State Teachers College High School Colts for only twenty-five cents, according to a newspaper ad promoting the contest in October 1933. Businesses were equally generous. The movie theater in Mountainair gave a twenty percent discount to enrollees in August 1937 and distributed free tickets to a movie show later that same year. James A. Rivers fondly remembers that Carlsbad merchants were so kind to enrollees that boys often returned to camp from a visit to town with the same few dollars they had left with earlier that day.[35]

Fittingly, local residents came to the aid of distressed enrollees just as enrollees had often helped individuals and whole towns in distress. Martin Serna tells of a truckload of CCC athletes who were caught in a terrific rain storm. The team found help in the form of food and lodging in a small village ironically named Punta de Agua (Point of Water). Even local jailers could be helpful to enrollees in distress. Roy Huffman remembers going to Santa Fe with two fellow enrollees to see a movie. The threesome had planned to stay in town overnight, but, when unable to find a place to sleep, they resorted to asking for shelter at the city jail. With room to spare that night, the jailer agreed. It was the only night Huffman ever spent in jail and probably the only occasion in which CCC enrollees ever volunteered to be incarcerated in New Mexico. Returning to camp, enrollees like Robert Michaeli were often given rides by townspeople on rural roads. Neighbors closer to camps, like innkeepers George and Evelyn Frey near Bandelier, were consistently kind and supportive. With so many good neighbors, it was not unusual to hear enrollees describe local residents as "just like the folks of your old hometown."[36]

Public and private institutions proved equally helpful. Local colleges and schools let camps use everything from gym floors for basketball games to training equipment for vocational instruction. Schools were often available for CCC dances, plays, and graduations. Armories were opened for sporting events, including boxing in Silver City and basketball in Socorro and Las Cruces. Businesses, like the Oldsmobile car dealership in Las Cruces, sponsored CCC teams, contributing funds for uniforms and equipment.[37]

To help facilitate communication, the Lordsburg High School printed early editions of the local camp newspaper. Radio stations KVSF in Santa Fe and KOB in Albuquerque aired interviews with camp commander Arthur Marshall so that Marshall could describe the CCC's history and goals to New Mexican listeners. In perhaps the most unusual contribution to improve communication in camps, the Carlsbad city fire department gave its bell to camp BR-82-N so it could be used as a dinner bell to signal meals. Grateful enrollees were reminded of the fire department's generosity each time they heard the fire bell toll, calling them to breakfast, lunch, and dinner.[38]

As a further sign of appreciation, communities often invited enrollees to holiday celebrations and local cultural events. Few measures drew town residents and camp enrollees closer. As early as August 1933, two hundred enrollees marched side-by-side with the American Legion, Masons, womens clubs, and La Orden Commercial de Nueva Mexico in an Albuquerque parade in support of President Roosevelt's new National Recovery Administration (NRA). With hundreds of participants, the parade was said to be the largest held in Albuquerque since the end of World War I.[39]

Elsewhere, a thirty-man drum and bugle corps from camp BR-82-N was invited to perform at various local gatherings, including parades, high school pep rallies, and college football games. Echoing the opinion of many appreciative civic organizations, the Carlsbad Chamber of Commerce wrote to CCC director Robert Fechner to praise this musical group and its drum major, whose "baton trickery" was nothing less than "outstanding." Chamber secretary Victor L. Mintor concluded that Carlsbad was "one city that is deeply appreciative of the CCC enrollees whom we have had with us and of the very excellent work which they have performed." Much the same reaction was recorded in Glenwood after the Buckhorn camp's dance band performed at a school benefit. According to SCS-18-N's camp newspaper, "The people of Glenwood were lavish in their praise of what a fine bunch of boys [live and labor at] the Buckhorn CCC camp." Pleased, *Save Our Soil's* editor asserted that such cordial relations were exactly "how it should be ... between the boys of our camp and [residents] in the vicinity."[40]

Local communities also invited CCC companies to be "big parts" of patriotic celebrations. In the most important of these holidays, enrollees joined New Mexicans in Fourth of July festivities in towns like Artesia, Carlsbad, Loving, Magdelena, and Silver City. Independence Day events usually included cowboy rodeos in these scattered ranching communities. Arriving in

Silver City on July 4, 1938, enrollees encountered locals "decked out in rodeo shirts, big hats and boots." Three days and nights of roping, riding, and ceremonial dancing by Pueblo Indians followed.[41]

But of all the holidays that drew enrollees and their adopted home towns closer, none was more fondly remembered than Christmas. While many enrollees went home for Christmas, those who remained were often welcomed in nearby churches and towns. Jim Duffy from far-off Pennsylvania was one such enrollee on Christmas Eve in 1938. Assigned to the CCC camp near Apache Creek, Duffy and his fellow enrollees were spending a quiet Christmas Eve in camp when camp bugler 'Duckey' Crane sounded church call at about 11:00 pm. CCC trucks rolled out to take Protestant boys to services in Reserve and Catholic boys, including Duffy, to a small Spanish chapel in nearby Aragon.[42]

Once in Aragon, Catholic enrollees discovered that parishioners had built a large bonfire that cast a red glow on the faithful who stood near it for warmth. Men smoked hand-rolled cigarettes and spoke Spanish in respectfully low voices. Women offered coffee and homemade pies. As midnight approached, several nuns led school children to a landing near the church door. The children, dressed in their best Communion clothes, sang "Silent Night" in Spanish. Everyone applauded. Then, as if on cue, the CCC truck driver, an enrollee named Frattini, jumped on the tailgate of his parked truck and "clapped his hands like a conductor tapping his baton." Duffy and his fellow enrollees responded, singing "Silent Night" with such feeling that Duffy declared that "If I live to be a thousand I do not think I will ever hear [that song] sung with such reverence and so much heart." Years later, Duffy could still see Frattini

> with his hands weaving a magical musical spell. His black mustache and curly black hair shone in the fire light. His mouth formed the words [while his] hands directed us to sing softly, now gently, now strongly ... . There was not a dry eye in the crowd. Not a sound but the a cappella male choir ... and the ... popping log fire.

Duffy recalls that "when we finished the carol the applause was thunderous." Afterwards, Duffy and another enrollee helped serve Mass, and all enrollees joined the grand procession around the church. Enrollees and residents were spiritually united to the benefit of all.[43]

Thankful for the hospitality shown in communities like Aragon, CCC companies reciprocated by inviting local residents to their camps throughout the year. Each visit helped to cement and improve camp-town relations. Camp dances and movie nights were especially appreciated by New Mexicans in isolated regions where social events were rare. Educational experiences were also appreciated, as when students from the San Juan Pueblo day school, the Santa Fe Indian School, and the State Teachers College visited CCC camps to study soil conservation methods. The public was invited to the camp at Ft. Stanton to view similar methods with proud enrollees as their guides in 1938.[44]

Other locals arrived in camps to perform in bands and choruses. The Lordsburg High School band played a concert of twelve songs at the Redrock camp, ending with the New Mexico state song, "O, Fair New Mexico." The State Teachers College's twenty-five piece band "fairly shot the rafters" with their "sterling quick-timed marches" when they visited the Gila camp in early 1936. Mescalero Apaches appeared at the Ft. Stanton camp later that same year. Dressed in their native costumes, the Indians performed three traditional dances: the Buffalo Dance, the War Dance, and the Hoop Dance. Although this was "the first time in the lives of most [enrollees] that we ever witnessed a real Indian dance," they soon overcame their initial apprehension of the "savage looking" Apaches and responded to the performance with "deafening applause." The dancers were called back for many encores.[45]

CCC camps hosted occasional social outings for local civic organizations. The Española Chamber of Commerce held its April 1937 meeting at camp SCS-5-N. Enrollees served a special dinner in their mess hall, and the camp orchestra played Spanish music following the meal. Hispanic enrollees showed "much amusement" when Anglo couples attempted to dance the *varseliana*, an

Hispanic folk dance with rather tricky steps. At camp DG-38-N forty members of the Las Cruces Chamber of Commerce enjoyed a similar meal as well as a tour of the camp and a stirring rendition of "America." In early 1938 nearly a thousand visitors gathered at a barbecue in the Pecos wilderness hosted by camp F-53-N and the Pecos River Sportsmen Club. The barbecue was served by enrollees "dressed for the occasion in white jackets and white caps." Music by a Spanish string orchestra and a calf roping contest followed. Impressed by all this attention, a prominent merchant declared that "our entire community is one hundred percent for the CCC camp and the work they are doing."[46]

But the largest gatherings hosted by camps were usually reserved for anniversaries of particular camps or the CCC as a whole. For example, enrollees at the Jemez camp celebrated the CCC's fourth anniversary with a gala event that drew three hundred visitors, despite a heavy late winter storm in 1937. Those in attendance included Archbishop Rudolph Gerken, a twenty-two piece band from St. Michael's College in Santa Fe, and pueblo Indians who reportedly "staged some of the most inspired and colorful Indian dances ever witnessed by whites." Four months later, camp F-41-N near Corona celebrated its second anniversary in far better summer weather. With the help of the local American Legion, the camp staged an elaborate evening, featuring a dinner, tours of the camp and its work sites, a large bonfire, and a dance for residents of the surrounding area. Despite their early fear of the CCC, the citizens of Corona displayed "splendid cooperation" and "expressed their appreciation for the work done by the Civilian Conservation Corps." Similar goodwill was shown at anniversaries held in camps near Carlsbad, Ft. Stanton, Bosque del Apache, La Madera, and elsewhere across New Mexico.[47]

Visitors returned home with a favorable impression of most CCC camps. With few exceptions, locals counted the ways the CCC had benefitted and improved the life of their communities. Yes, votes could be tallied and profits could be made with the help of whole camps and individual enrollees. But the goodwill created by CCC activities, especially in the heat of crises and the warmth of special events, could never be calculated with pen and paper. The praise of local residents helped swell enrollee pride and individual self-esteem. Young men realized the satisfaction of contributing their skills and becoming valued members of larger communities beyond their barracks and camps. Another important rite of passage had been experienced in the CCC.

## Endnotes - Chapter 11

[1] Pack, *Ghost Ranch*, 49-50.

[2] *Mirager,* June 1936.

[3] Abe Peña, *Memories of Cibola: Stories from New Mexico Villages* (Albuquerque: University of New Mexico Press, 1997): 46.

[4] *Albuquerque Journal*, June 14, 1938.

[5] *Buckhorn Buzzer*, July 15, 1937.

[6] Thomas interview; *Albuquerque Journal*, August 4, 1939.

[7] Haniel Long, *Piñon Country* (New York: Duell, Sloan and Pearce, 1941): 206-8.

[8] *Albuquerque Journal*, August 4, 1939, and February 22, 1942.

[9] *Camp Chatter*, April 1937; *Organ Echoes*, June 30, 1937.

[10] Hall interview; *Fresnal Ranger,* February 15, 1935.

[11] Kristie Miller, *Ruth Hanna McCormick: A Life in Politics, 1880-1944* (Albuquerque: University of New Mexico Press, 1992): 250-1; *Albuquerque Journal,* June 24-27, 1938; Churches, "History of the CCC, Cibola National Forest," 30-1.

[12] Miller, *McCormick*, 251-55; *Albuquerque Journal*, June 24-30, and July 1-3, and 6, 1938; *Raton Range*, July 1, 1938.

[13] *Santa Fe New Mexican,* January 20, 1937.

[14] Scurlock, *From the Rio to the Sierra,* 32-9; Richard Melzer, "Floods Haven't Washed Away Memories of Railroad Town," *New Mexico Magazine*, 68 (July 1990): 86-92; Thomas interview; *El Campo*, April 1937; H.W. Hurd, "A Report on Soil Conservation Service Activities in the Ft. Sumner Flood Area, June 7-25, 1937," SCS Papers, CSWR, UNM.

[15] Gibson interview; Kemp interview; Harrison *et al.*, *Bandelier,* 27; *Albuquerque Journal,* May 20 and June 4, 11, and 29, 1937; *El Campo*, April 1937; *Wasp,* April 1937; *Mal Pais*, June 1937; *Dark Canyon Avalanche*, June 15, 1937.

[16] *Santa Fe New Mexican*, January 28, 1937; William H. Pickens, "The New Deal in New Mexico" (Unpublished Ph.D. dissertation,

University of New Mexico, 1971): 149; *CCC Annual, 1936, Ft. Bliss District*, 57, 69.

[17] *Ibid.*, 57.

[18] Parham, "CCC in Colorado," 129; Booth, "CCC in Arizona," 70n. On the history of forest fires in New Mexico, see Scurlock, *From the Rio to the Sierra*, 266-69.

[19] *Kangarowl*, May 17, 1935; *Buckhorn Buzzer*, September 15, 1937; Porter Memoirs, 26.

[20] *Lonely Pennsylvanian*, September 1939.

[21] Rothman, *Rims and Ridges*, 182; Stephen J. Pyne, *Fire in America: A Cultural History of Wildland and Rural Fire* (Princeton: Princeton University Press, 1982): 362; *Albuquerque Journal*, June 10, 1935; *Santa Fe New Mexican*, April 17, 1926.

[22] *Albuquerque Tribune*, May 8, 1939; *New Mexico Magazine*, 73 (June 1995): 42; Riesch, "Conservation Under FDR," 231-5; Paige, *CCC and the Park Service*, 73; Salmond, *CCC*, 122-4; *La Poliza*, December 1937; Rothman, *Rims and Ridges*, 254; Harrison *et al.*, *Bandelier*, 23, 189; *Forest Pioneer*, 4th quarter, 1938; Cox *et al.*, *Well-Wooded Land*, 219; Otis *et al.*, *Forest Service and the CCC*, 32; A Brief Summary of Certain Phases of the CCC Program in New Mexico, April 1933 to June 30, 1941, Governor Miles Papers, NMSRSA; Propper, "A Job at Honest Pay," 34.

[23] Lucero and Roybal interviews, OHPB; Kenneth E. Hendrickson, Jr., "The Civilian Conservation Corps in Pennsylvania," *Pennsylvania Magazine of History and Biography*, 100 (January 1976): 81; Erle Kauffman, "Death in Blackwater Canyon," *American Forests*, 43 (November 1937): 534-40, 558; Paige, *CCC and the Park Service*, 101. In all, forty-seven CCC workers died in fires across the United States. Pyne, *Fire*, 367.

[24] *Tip Topper*, May 1937; *Yucca*, June 1938; Oliver C. Payne, Camp Report, Bosque del Apache, October-November-December 1940, BANWR. Small fires sometimes broke out in camp, but were usually quickly extinguished. See, for example, Harrison *et al.*, *Bandelier*, 110; *Carson Pine Cone*, January 31, 1939.

[25] *Forest Pioneer*, 2nd quarter, 1939.

[26] Benito Montoya interview, OHPB; Chavez interview; Rothman, *Rims and Ridges*, 183; *Lonely Pennsylvanian*, May-June 1940. CCC regulations regarding fire fighting are included in Draves, *Builder*, 168-9.

[27] *Lonely Pennsylvanian*, April 1940; *Kangarowl*, April 19, 1935; Johnson interview.

[28] *El Conejo*, May 1937; *Albuquerque Journal*, June 20, 1936; *Los Frijoles*, May 1937.

[29] *Albuquerque Journal*, June 23, 1938, and Keith Humphries to the Editor, *Albuquerque Journal*, Silver City, June 28, 1938.

[30] Blake interview by Foote; *El Conejo*, May 1937; Ross Calvin Log Book, entry of June 16, 1938, Ross Calvin Papers, CSWR, UNM.

[31] Dawson interview; *Lonely Pennsylvanian*, May-June 1939 and May-June 1940; Erle Kauffman, "Heroes of the C.C.C.," *American Forests*, 40 (July 1934): 303-4; *Albuquerque Journal*, June 17, 1938; Salmond, *CCC*, 121; Cox *et al.*, *Well-Wooded Land*, 219.

[32] Sellars, *Preserving Nature*, 126; Guthrie, "CCC and American Conservation," 412.

[33] Radium Springs camp newspaper (unnamed), September 29, 1935; *CCC Annual, 1936, Ft. Bliss District*, 36; Clyde Tingley to Lt. Wharton, Santa Fe, September 3, 1935, Governor Tingley Papers, NMSRCA; *Roswell Daily Record*, June 5, 1937; Thomas interview.

[34] *Ibid.*; Blake interview by Foote; Porter Memoirs, 8; *Fresnal Ranger*, October 5, 1934; *Gila Monster*, January 15, 1935; Mooney interview.

[35] *Gila Monster*, November 16, 1934; *Pink Pebble Periodical*, February 12 and May 21, 1935; *Dark Canyon Avalanche*, July 25, 1937; *Tumbleweed*, December 1938; *Ft. Sumner Bugler*, January 1941; Camp Inspection Report, Mangas, August 20, 1937, CCC, NA; *Silver City Enterprise*, October 13, 1933; Rivers interview.

[36] Serna interview; Huffman interview; *Carlsbad Current-Argus*, January 11, 1998; B. Montoya and Frey interviews, OHPB; *Kangarowl*, August 12, 1935.

[37] *Pink Pebble Periodical*, March 12, 1935; *Wasp*, January 1937; *Organ Echoes*, October 1936 and February 1937; *Yucca*, December 1937; *Tumbleweed*, May 1939 and June 1939; *Lonely Pennsylvanian*, May-June 1939; *Ft. Sumner Bugler*, April 1941; Smith interview; Gibson interview; Mooney interview; Educational Advisor's Report, Las Cruces, January 22, 1940, CCC, NA; Oliver C. Payne, Camp Report, Bosque del Apache, October-November-December 1940, BANWR; *Silver City Enterprise*, August 18, 1937.

[38] *Pink Pebble Periodical*, February 12, 1935; *Tumbleweed*, October 1938; *Santa Fe New Mexican*, June 23, 1940; *Cactus Courier*, March 1940.

[39] *Albuquerque Journal*, August 13, 1933.

[40] *Camp Cactus Carrier*, October 1939; *Save Our Soil*, April 1936.

[41] *Gila Monster*, June 1936; *Yucca*, June 1938; *Camp Cactus Carrier*, October 1939 and March 1940; *Socorro Chieftain*, July 15, 1933; Thomas interview.

[42] Casaus interview; J.T. Duffy to the author, Philadelphia, Pennsylvania, October 3, 1991.

[43] *Ibid.* CCC conservation efforts had helped to produce an abundance of Christmas trees for New Mexico communities, including Albuquerque, by 1937. *Forest Pioneer*, October 1937; Churches, "History of the CCC, Cibola National Forest," 34.

[44] *Silver City Enterprise*, September 1, 1933; *El Campo*, January 1937; *Yucca*, June 1938; *Happy Days*, April 2, 1938.

[45] *Pink Pebble Periodical*, March 26, 1935; *Gila Monster*, January 1936; *Peñasco Pennant*, April 9, 1936; *Wasp*, December 31, 1936; *Mal Pais*, February 1937; *Ghost Talks*, February 1937; *Stanton Static*, April 1937; *Lonely Pennsylvanian*, September 1940.

[46] *El Campo*, April 1937; *Organ View Optic*, April 10, 1936; *Forest Pioneer*, 4th quarter, 1938.

[47] *La Poliza*, April 1937; *Lincoln Lookout*, August 1937; *Dark Canyon Avalanche*, September 27, 1936, and July 25, 1937; *Lonely Pennsylvanian*, March 1940; Oliver C. Payne, Camp Report, Bosque del Apache, April-May-June 1940, BANWR; *Carson Pine Cone*, May 5, 1939.

# CHAPTER 12
## Hardly Utopia

The vast majority of enrollees grew and matured during their months in the Civilian Conservation Corps. Most gained weight from nutritious food, developed muscles from hard labor, and enjoyed good health in a wholesome environment. Many also learned job skills at work, mental skills in the classroom, and life skills throughout their busy days. All helped their families financially, and some even managed to earn extra cash as enrollee entrepreneurs. Few complained, no less protested, about conditions in the CCC. Fewer still caused serious trouble.

But New Mexico's CCC camps were hardly utopias in the wilderness. Real or imagined problems surfaced at one time or another in most camps. The CCC's ability to deal with problems in a timely, effective manner served as another measure of the organization's ultimate success in the Southwest.

Some of the most frequently heard enrollee complaints involved a condition that no mortal could hope to alter: New Mexico's weather. As difficult as it was for native-born enrollees to deal with inclement weather in New Mexico, it was often more difficult for out-of-state enrollees to handle the extreme seasonal conditions that often plagued the region.

New Mexico's powerful winds topped most complaint lists regarding weather. When 192 enrollees arrived at Glenwood's camp F-25-N in 1936, the "daily battle with the elements soon began." Terrible winds "blew tons of sand ... throughout the barracks, in the beds, in the food, [and] even in ones [sic] hair." Spring winds were the worst. A rookie enrollee at the Carrizozo camp wrote in his diary—with only slight exaggeration—that the wind was so brutal in March 1937 that every stone in the vicinity had been blown away and he fully expected a nearby boulder to go next. Dust storms disrupted athletic events and, less upsettingly, even work, as happened at Bosque del Apache on a spring day in 1942. Wind and sand storms were so prevalent that five of New Mexico's eighty-five camp newspapers referred to them in their titles: *The Whirlwind* at Animas, *Winds* at Elephant Butte, *Sand Blast* at Las Cruces, *Sandman* at Radium Springs, and the *Dust Bowl* near Tucumcari.[1]

Summer heat caused additional discomfort. Temperatures soared to triple-digit levels in summers like 1936, said to be the hottest in New Mexico since the mid-1920s. Enrollees at the Gila camp were convinced that "old man sun" was "working overtime" in 1936, causing furnace-like conditions, especially during working hours. Parts of the desert Southwest were factiously said to be so hot and dry that it "requires five hundred acres to support one lizard." Writers for the *Gila Monster* reworded a common Depression-era question by asking, "Brother, can you spare a little shade." To create some shade, enrollees requested more trees at their Whitewater camp to "make our camp much cooler and less like a dust-bowl relief headquarters."[2]

To the surprise and dismay of many out-of-state enrollees, New Mexico's winters were sometimes as cold as its summers were hot. Andres Hernandez recalls working in such frigid conditions at the La Madera camp that he and his fellow enrollees had to build fires from sagebrush to stay warm at their work sites. Bennie Casaus remembers being snowbound for thirty days in his camp near Mountainair. E.L. Partridge joined other enrollees at Bandelier in getting up at night to shovel snow off the roof of their barracks before the snow got too heavy and caused a cave-in. Pipes froze in several camps, including one near Abiquiu in early 1937. Winter nights in New Mexico's higher elevations were especially cold. One of the most important jobs in camp was performed by the enrollee who kept barracks' stoves well fueled through the long hours to daylight.[3]

New enrollees often found the most to object to if only because they had the most to adjust to in camp. Rookies—and some veterans—complained of being bored in camps with few recreational facilities, especially on winter nights when "we had nothing to do [but] look at each other." The first question that many newcomers asked on arrival was "How far is it to town and how often do you get to go there?" But some camps were so far from the nearest town that weekend liberty parties were infrequent. Morale suffered at the Conchas Dam camp, for example, when enrollees were driven the three hours to Tucumcari only once a month. The return trip from Tucumcari was so long that CCC trucks that arrived on Saturdays didn't leave until Sundays, forcing enrollees to stay overnight in town at their own expense. Elsewhere, enrollees complained that not enough trucks were available for all those who chose to go to town on weekends. To make matters worse, enrollees were sometimes charged for the gasoline used in CCC trucks on recreational trips.[4]

Once in town, some enrollees were disappointed by a lack of activities and diversions. An enrollee from camp SCS-10-N reported that night life in Grants "consists of a stuffy dance hall situated between two saloons." A half factious joke in the Ft. Stanton camp newspaper told of an enrollee who was ticketed for speeding on his first visit to the small town of Capitan. When the boy's foreman asked if he hadn't seen the sign "Dead Slow," the enrollee replied, "Of course I did. But I thought that meant the name of the town."[5]

Back in camp, enrollees found fault with a wide range of objectionable circumstances. Some complaints focused on housing: prefab buildings moved from West Virginia to a camp near Roswell were literally in bad shape with warped walls and doors and windows that never quite fit. At Mountainair, the rec room was described as "bare" with only one football, ten baseball gloves, and one pair of boxing gloves, allowing for shadow boxing at best. Shoes and clothing were also said to be inadequate in certain camps. Shoes at the Sandia Peak camp were in such bad need of repair in 1940 that when an enrollee sent one of his two pairs out to be fixed, the second pair was usually "beyond repairs" by the time the first pair returned. Sleeping was impaired by an infestation of bed bugs at some camps, including the Redrock camp in 1935. Poor manners irritated other enrollees. One youth asked that magazines read in the latrine at Radium Springs be returned to the camp's regular library when completed. An editorial writer for the Hillsboro camp newspaper took exception to enrollees with bad table manners. The greatest criticism went to those who practiced their "boarding house reach," ate excessive portions, or made a "conglomeration of noises" heard from one end of the mess hall to the other.[6]

More serious complaints surfaced as well. In 1935 the CCC began requiring that fingerprints be taken of every enrollee as part of an FBI campaign to eventually fingerprint every citizen of the United States. Some enrollees objected, associating fingerprinting as a procedure required of criminals only. Did the FBI think that enrollees were established or potential criminals hiding out in CCC camps? Defenders of the new requirement responded that more good than harm would come from the fingerprinting. Remembering the fingerprinting of soldiers during World War I, one camp author claimed that such evidence could be used to help enrollees for the rest of their lives. Fingerprints could help authorities identify unclaimed corpses, victims of amnesia, and, yes, innocent defendants wrongly accused of nefarious crimes. After all, "Who knows when fate might resort to some trick [at which time] CCC identification [could] be referred to to insure that the right person is getting his just dues."[7]

Other enrollees focused their complaints on camp leaders. A number commented on the frequent changes of educational advisors, chaplains, and qualified camp doctors and dentists. Doctors and dentists were recognized as especially important to a camp's fitness and vitality. The camp at Apache Creek was served by as many as three different doctors in a ten-month period from 1933 to 1934. Camp SCS-4-N near Española suffered the same rate of change from August 1935 to July 1936. Kept busy in other camps or in private practice, doctors were often away from camp as often as they were present. Enrollees at Ft. Stanton noted that they hadn't seen their camp physician in three weeks because he was so busy at other camps in the district; the Ft. Stanton camp newspaper sarcastically expressed the hope that the missing doctor might return "in time to say goodbye." Observers at the Redrock camp noticed that their camp doctor had only spent five nights in camp during his first month of duty, preferring to stay at home in distant Silver City. When present, most doctors were praised for their work, but some had personal problems that hindered the medical treatment they might otherwise provide. A doctor at Bandelier was known to spend much of his time drinking in Santa Fe bars, while a physician at Columbus was accused of stealing and presumably using drugs he had ordered for camp supplies.[8]

Other doctors and dentists were criticized for their uninspired treatment of most ailments. The "old army Doc" at a Las Cruces camp was said to have one standard treatment for all ills: APC pills followed by lots of Castor Oil. A dentist at Bandelier pulled two of E.L. Partridge's teeth, but even before he completed the extractions admitted that the targeted teeth were not as rotten as he had originally thought. Roy Robertson had all of his teeth removed in February 1937, but was still "patiently waiting" for their replacements in June of that year. "It's a good thing we were all strong, healthy boys," wrote former enrollee Lee F. Sanders. "Somehow we all survived."[9]

One historian has claimed that "a number of camps [across the United States] became laboratories for federal and army scientists who wanted human guinea pigs on which to try out vaccinations and medications." Fifty-four enrollees volunteered to take one such new serum at camp SCS-4-N near Española in 1937; another seventy were said to be ready to test this anti-pneumonia serum if called upon. The federal government admitted using enrollees to test new vaccines, but vehemently denied exploiting enrollees in dangerous secret experiments of any kind.[10]

Like camp medical personnel, most camp officers were praised as fair and understanding. Many became role models for the impressionable youths in their command. Only a handful of officers were considered too arbitrary and strict. Some enrollees objected, for example, when officers assigned extra work details on Saturdays after long forty-hour work weeks. Others claimed that punishments were sometimes unjust and excessive. Enrollees at the Columbus camp complained when their commander punished them with one week's confinement in camp for being late for breakfast, two hours of extra duty for wearing poorly shined shoes, and one week's confinement, sixteen hours of extra duty, and a fine of one day's wages for missing camp meetings. Although many may have resented such treatment, most enrollees in New Mexico kept their opinions to themselves, if only because they hoped not to draw attention—and official wrath—to themselves.[11]

While individual complaints were rare, group complaints were more common, especially when the topic was food. A majority of enrollees appreciated the quality and quantity of food served in camp mess halls. However, a vocal minority expressed objections. Some complained of being served too much of the same foods. Lunch at work sites was often monotonous, consisting of cold bologna or peanut butter and jelly sandwiches week after week. The best enrollees at the Redrock camp could say about their noontime meals was that they were "repetitious, unappetizing, inedible and insufficient." Beans were served so often at evening meals at the Abiquiu camp that enrollees feigned amazement on the day beans did not appear on their plates. "Long after we are gone from the CCC camps," wrote one enrollee, "we shall tell [our grandchildren] of this hysteric event while their little eyes grow wide in disbelief." Elsewhere, too few fruits and vegetables were served in isolated camps, while milk was often in short supply at remote side camps.[12]

Some complained of small portions or a lack of enough food for seconds. At Bandelier, enrollees complained that their breakfasts of two hotcakes and a cup of coffee were not nearly enough. Their complaints only subsided when their camp commander declared, "Forget the grub complaints and I will bring in twenty cases of beer and a hundred women." The commander fulfilled his promises at a camp dance, although he was soon dismissed by CCC officials who disagreed with his tactics in handling food-related problems. Attempting to inject humor into complaints about not enough food, a 1934 *Happy Days* joke told of a cook who supposedly asked his commanding officer, "How did you find the beef, Sir?" to which the officer replied, "Oh, I just moved a bean —and there it was!" More seriously, enrollees at the Columbus camp complained that they were not served evening meals on Sundays, leaving them unfed for as long as sixteen hours, from Sunday lunch to Monday breakfast. But food shortages were due to poor planning rather than CCC policy: shortages occurred when cooks were too frugal or spent their budget unwisely, especially near the end of each month.[13]

Although rare, some enrollees complained about the quality as well as the quantity of food in camp. Leo Murphy wrote home to his mother in Philadelphia, saying that the milk was sour and the biscuits were "as hard as cement" at Conchas Dam in July 1940. Another enrollee waxed poetic on the subject of poor food, writing several pointed verses for his camp newspaper. 'Doc' Ewing, the poet, wrote of a fictional mule that had dutifully pulled a plow for forty years. Upon its death, the animal's straggly meat was stripped from his bones, ground up, salted, and put in cans for sale "to Uncle Sammy ... to feed his CCC."[14]

But there is no evidence of mule meat being served in New Mexico's camps. On the contrary, reports on food and drink in New Mexico were usually favorable compared to states like Virginia, where roaches were found in bowls of beans, or North Dakota, where the water was said to be less than pure. Asked about the water in his North Dakota camp, a sarcastic enrollee replied, "It's absolutely perfect, couldn't be better. Twenty million tadpoles and lizards can't be wrong." With purer water and better food than many states, a New Mexico camp newspaper editor urged his fellow enrollees to try to "stop griping and howling about the food. There is absolutely no record of anybody being undernourished in a CCC camp." After all, the editor reminded his readers, everyone ate more than "enough to keep him warm and fat," especially compared to the enrollees' collective condition prior to their enrollment.[15]

Enrollee morale and camp unity were periodically endangered by an issue that became more difficult to resolve than any other in camp life. Unfortunate friction existed in almost every camp where native-born and out-of-state enrollees lived and worked side-by-side. While thousands of out-of-state enrollees adjusted to their new surroundings well, many found it hard to adjust not only to the weather and terrain, but also to the people and cultures of the Southwest. A clash of cultures was perhaps inevitable.

With more conservation work than native youths to fill its camps, New Mexico drew 21,800 out-of-state enrollees to its borders. A majority came from three states in particular: Texas, Oklahoma, and Pennsylvania. Smaller contingents arrived from Colorado and Wyoming, especially during bad winters in their home states.[16]

Enrollees arrived from the San Antonio area of Texas as early as May 1933. Traveling in a special Santa Fe Railroad train, over 350 Texan recruits helped fill New Mexico's first camps. Thousands followed in the ensuing years. Departing from large cities like El Paso, Ft. Worth, and Austin as well as from small towns like Mt. Pleasant, Kennvilve, and Belton, nearly every region of Texas was represented in New Mexico's camps. In fact, so many Texans arrived that they often outnumbered all other enrollees in camps like F-31-N near Jemez. By mid 1934, seventy-two percent of F-31-N's enrollees came from Texas, twenty-six percent came from New Mexico, and two percent came from Colorado and Oklahoma. A year later, ninety-five percent of the enrollees who opened the new Dark Canyon camp near Carlsbad hailed from the Lone Star State.[17]

While most Texans were said to be "good fellows" who got along well with others, some were said to "look and act like some of Pancho Villa's army." Texans were especially hostile if they had enrolled in the CCC thinking they'd be assigned to camps closer to home. Typically, E.L. Partridge objected when he was shipped to distant New Mexico rather than to the camp in his hometown of Bayfield, Texas. Partridge felt particularly jilted because three enrollees from the Bayfield CCC camp had recruited him and other members of his high school graduating class by offering them a chance to earn money and "be there close to home." Once in New Mexico, Partridge and others from his Southern state had to adjust to the cold, mountainous country near Bandelier after spending most of their lives in the low hills and milder climate of Texas. Pining for home, some wrote poems to reflect their somber moods. In the words of a homesick enrollee in 1935, when he and his fellow Texans left home they had no idea they were headed for Hatch, New Mexico.

> When we boys reached this place
> Our hearts began to freeze.
> There was nothing round about us,
> But mountains, rocks, and trees.

Other poems, with titles like "Texas and Home" and "The Sad Texas Buckaroo," expressed similar remorse.[18]

Enrollees from Oklahoma felt much the same distress when they first arrived in New Mexico. Ecological and economic crises had wreaked havoc on farms and ranches throughout their home state. Wheat that had sold at $1.25 per bushel in 1928 brought only thirty-two cents per bushel in 1932. The price of corn also plummeted, from eight-one cents a bushel in 1929 to twenty-three cents a bushel three years later. Ranchers fared no better. Cattle that sold for $8.40 per hundred pounds in 1928 sold for only three dollars per hundred pounds in 1933. Drought and dust storms added to the 'Okies'' plight. Often arriving from Dust Bowl regions of their state, Oklahomans said they missed home so much because they saw so much of it blow by in dust storms. Some kiddingly said they needed to go home to help hold down what remained of Oklahoma before it all blew away.[19]

Like Texans, enrollees from Oklahoma soon outnumbered New Mexicans on many camp rosters. And, like many Texans, many from Oklahoma missed home and criticized New Mexico because it was so different from what they were used to. Commenting on New Mexico's landscape, an Oklahoma enrollee told his foreman that he had never been to a place where he could see so far and see so little. Others found fault with conditions in specific camps. In the spring of 1936 Oklahoma enrollees described their camp near Grants as a "miserable hole." Food served in the mess hall was so sour, moldy, or spoiled that it reportedly made most of them ill. Working conditions were equally bad, especially when they were assigned work on private land owned by Democrats with "big political pull."[20]

More seriously, many Anglo enrollees from Oklahoma objected to working with, no less under, Hispanic enrollees from New Mexico. Coming from a segregated state, many Oklahomans did not believe it was "right to associate with a negro [sic] or Mexican, or have a negro [sic] or Mexican in authority over [them]." As a judge from Oklahoma put it in defending disgruntled enrollees from his state, not even the CCC could force integration or other "acts of equality." Over half of the seventy-three new enrollees who arrived from Oklahoma to a camp near Española objected to working with "Mexicans" in the spring of 1936. This same group complained that their commanding officer was often drunk and had had "a grudge in for the Oklahoma boys" ever since their arrival in New Mexico.[21]

Oklahoma enrollees were even more upset by conditions they found and the commanders they served under at their camp near Roswell. In December 1938 complaints focused on poor food, few liberty parties, and a camp doctor who forced boys "to work when they were really sick." Conditions hardly improved in 1939 when a shortage of water prevented enrollees from showering for many days, despite long hours of labor under the summer sun. The camp commander was said to be too lax, allowing as many as ten enrollees to be listed as AWOL without punishment.[22]

The enforcement of camp rules changed dramatically when a new commander was assigned to BR-1-N in November 1939. While their previous officer was supposedly too lenient, their new one was bitterly criticized for being too strict. By January 1940 the new commander was blamed for cursing, charging excessive fines (including three dollars for going AWOL), kicking two boys, and making enrollees work in bad weather. When sixty-two enrollees refused to work on a cold January morning, the commander displayed his "violent temper" by discharging fourteen and vowing to call the Lea County sheriff if they were not gone from camp in an hour. Enrollee Leon Boyd claimed that the discharge of fourteen enrollees and the threat to have them all arrested was "only the climax to [a] long continuance of mistreatment." Faced with what he perceived to be terrible living and working conditions, Boyd may well have agreed with a fellow Oklahoman who declared that "I'd rather do the rest of my [CCC] time in the Oklahoma State Prison than do it here and I think a lot of the boys feel the same way about it. At least we would be in civilized country" and closer to families and friends.[23]

While enrollees from Texas and Oklahoma came from predominantly rural backgrounds, those from Pennsylvania had had more urban, industrial experiences prior to serving in New Mexico. Thousands poured into New Mexico's camps, soon outnumbering natives, just as Texans and Oklahomans had done at other Southwestern sites. Most knew extreme poverty back East. By 1930 Pennsylvania was third only to New York and Illinois in unemployment. Two years later Pennsylvania "bore the nation's heaviest welfare burden." Eleven percent of all families in Philadelphia and eighteen percent of all families in Pittsburgh were on relief in 1933. As late as 1940 Pittsburgh's unemployment rate equaled twenty-two percent of its work force, largely because its main industry, steel, suffered so badly through the 1930s. In 1933, with steel factories working at only fourteen percent of capacity, fifty-six percent of all steel workers were unemployed. U.S. Steel "declared that it had *no* full-time workers on its payroll."[24]

Youths in Pennsylvania had a particularly hard time finding employment in such an economy. The New Castle, Pennsylvania, high school graduating class of 1938 listed sixty percent of its graduates as unemployed. The class of 1939 was no better off; only one class officer landed a full-time job, as a bellhop, when a local hotel's regular bellhop joined other hotel employees out on strike. The 1939 class president worked part-time as a movie theater usher until he "was lucky" enough to enroll in the CCC. As a school official said, "The 1939 graduates are not competing for private [sector jobs because] there are none to compete for." They were, instead, "fighting to get into the CCC."[25]

Most Pennsylvania enrollees assigned to New Mexico adjusted to the Southwest well. In fact, many volunteered for service in the Southwest for better opportunities, for improved health, or to simply "see some of our beautiful country." Like J.T. Duffy, many were awed by New Mexico's "majestic" ponderosa pines, pure streams, "overwhelming" quiet, and intriguing local cultures. Like John Mooney of New Castle and Tom Mikolay of the coal camps of central Pennsylvania, a majority considered their CCC experience in New Mexico the "best thing that ever happened" in their lives.[26]

Despite such praise, some Pennsylvania enrollees found fault with much of what they found in New Mexico. Thousands of miles from home, many were at least initially homesick. Ft. Stanton's camp newspaper was appropriately named *The Lonely Pennsylvanian*. The cover of *The Lonely Pennsylvanian's* May/June 1940 edition pictured two forlorn enrollees sitting on their trunks by a railroad station; one boy dreamed for a girl near camp, but the other dreamt of his mother and father back East. In addition to homesickness, many Easterners needed time to adjust to New Mexico's high altitude and heat. Steve Bubernak recalls that at the Española camp three of his fellow enrollees from Pennsylvania fainted on the their first day of work, two fainted on the second day, but only one fainted by the third.[27]

Unfortunately, many urban enrollees never adjusted to rural life in the CCC. Using dishonorable discharges as a measure of poor adjustment, a 1938 study found that enrollees from states located east of the Mississippi River had above-average dishonorable discharge rates, while those from states west of the Mississippi had below average rates. A 1939 study of ten cities, including Pittsburgh and Philadelphia, showed a 27.3 percent dishonorable discharge rate compared to a 17.5 percent for the nation as a whole.[28]

Statistics for Eastern enrollees reflected their often poor adjustment records in New Mexico. In December 1938 camp inspector A.W. Stockman reported that "unruly boys" and "agitators" from Scranton, Pennsylvania, had been assigned to a CCC camp near Las Cruces. The group became "increasingly intractable," hurling "profanity and obscene language" at their officers and foremen. Many refused to labor, telling more diligent enrollees "they were fools to work as they would get their dollar a day anyway." The situation grew worse until camp leaders finally listed twenty-five of the worst offenders as unworthy for reenlistment. Camp commander Fred Poorbaugh didn't wait until the end of an enlistment period to deal with Pennsylvania boys who arrived at his Bosque del Apache camp. Spotting five potential troublemakers on their first day in camp, Poorbaugh discharged them one by one "and things settled down after that."[29]

Regardless of their state of origin, enrollees usually expressed their grievances in spontaneous acts of complaint and protest. For example, enrollees were known to engage in spontaneous griping sessions held in their barracks, mess halls, or rec halls. A certain amount of griping was natural and no doubt therapeutic for any group of youths living far from home. But some griping was considered excessive. As early as July 1933 the editor of a camp newspaper proposed the abolition of all griping at his CCC camp in the San Mateo Mountains. Jesse F. Tunnell, editor of the *Kangarowl* at camp F-43-N near La Madera, agreed. "Griping is a habit," wrote Tunnell, and, like most habits, it "can be carried to an extreme." The editor's best advice was for enrollees to "quit some of our griping; be pleasant in all our talk and actions, whether we are giving orders or receiving them." After all, as a *Gila Monster* writer reminded his fellow enrollees in 1934, if "You say that there are hardships in camp ... consider [how] being without work at home would be a larger hardship" to enrollees and their families alike.[30]

In an effort to deal with complaints before they escalated, some camp officers urged enrollees to bring up matters of concern at regular camp meetings. For those who preferred to remain anonymous, suggestion boxes were installed in some camps, including those near Carrizozo and Española in 1937. More assertive enrollees could, of course, go directly to their officers, foremen, or camp inspectors. Many supervisors were receptive to reasonable grievances, but others were not. The Roswell camp commander was clearly unreceptive when he summarily discharged protesting enrollees and vowed to have them all arrested if they remained in camp longer than an hour. As an enrollee later explained when asked why he had not spoken up about this harsh officer, "I did not complain at the time as I knew it [might cause] a discharge, and my parents need the Twenty-two Dollars [sic] each month." Most boys were "just grateful to have a good meal and a little money" and would do nothing to threaten their enrollment status by alienating those in charge.[31]

When formal channels did not exist or when commanders were unresponsive to their complaints, enrollees sometimes resorted to letter writing to vent their anger over issues. Most of this correspondence went to friends and relatives back home. An unknown percentage of letter writers hoped, and sometimes directly asked, that their families take action in their behalf. After receiving a letter from her son in New Mexico, one mother went so far as to write to Eleanor Roosevelt about the poor food her son said he was served at the Jemez camp in early 1934.[32]

More aggressive enrollees took matters into their own hands by appealing directly to higher authorities. As a popular grassroots leader, Senator Dennis Chavez received several complaints of this nature, especially from Hispanic enrollees who felt they had been treated unfairly based on their ethnicity. In October 1938, for example, Charles Romero wrote to Senator Chavez to complain about the commanding officer at his camp near Mountainair. According to Romero, Lt. R.R. Greiner showed his prejudice against Hispanics by using profane language when giving orders and by generally treating them "like dogs." More typically, large groups signed petitions and expressed their concerns in letters addressed to political leaders in the enrollees' home states. Oklahoma enrollees at camp SCS-10-N who protested against working with Hispanics signed a petition with fifty-seven signatures and sent it to a Pittsburg County judge, William Jones, Jr., and U.S. Senator Elmer Thomas in 1936.[33]

The majority of complaints filed by disgruntled enrollees, parents, and political leaders received quick, thorough action by CCC officials. Most complaints were forwarded to CCC director Robert Fechner and his staff in Washington, D.C., who routinely launched investigations. In each case, camp inspectors were dispatched to the affected camp where they searched for the root problems that often lay behind general complaints. Inspector Matthew J. Bowen's experience at camp BS-1-N was typical. When Bowen arrived at BS-1-N near Roswell to check on complaints by Oklahoma enrollees who refused to work in the cold on January 5, 1940, he uncovered a long list of deeper concerns that had plagued the camp for months. Action was taken, starting with the removal of the camp commander in question. In other cases, inspectors discovered that enrollee complaints had less validity, having often been made in the heat of anger or frustration. While enrollee Charles Romero complained about discriminatory remarks made by his camp commander in late 1938, he later admitted that he made his charges when he was angry with the officer for criticizing his work. Romero admitted that he "could not be sure of any [harmful] remarks" uttered by his commander at the time of the alleged incidents.[34]

Investigations or simple requests could also lead to enrollee transfers to their home states. Twelve of the 124 enrollees who left Ft. Stanton for Pennsylvania in June 1940 did so to serve in camps nearer to home. While their camp newspaper editor heard some disparaging remarks about New Mexico, he hoped that each enrollee had "learned something that made him a better person" for having served in the Southwest.[35]

But some enrollees grew impatient with regular channels of protest and appeal. Seeing thousands of workers of their parents' generation organize and strike against employers in the 1930s, enrollees sometimes emulated this more extreme form of protest in camps across the United States. New Mexico was no exception. New Mexico's CCC strikes shared five main characteristics with CCC strikes launched elsewhere in the nation.

First, most strikes were led by out-of-state enrollees, especially those from parts of the country where labor protests were seen as a normal means of achieving redress. As Ray Dawson put it, enrollees from Pennsylvania knew how to strike in New Mexico from watching their fathers strike in the coal mines and factories back East. Second, all strikes were wildcat strikes, organized on the spur of the moment without formal union organization or leadership. In fact, union membership was cause for immediate dismissal from the CCC, despite CCC director Fechner's long career as a powerful union official prior to 1933.[36]

Next, concrete issues, rather than abstract principles, galvanized enrollee unity and action. As in other camps in the United States, these concrete issues usually involved one of two basic concerns: inadequate food or poor working conditions. On January 3, 1939, for example, ten enrollees at DG-36-N near Deming refused to work their afternoon hours because they complained that their noon meal, consisting of two sandwiches and two oranges, was inadequate. Back in camp that evening, the strike's ringleaders did "considerable boasting and loud talking about what [more] they were going to do." Learning that they had caused similar friction at their last camp, Deming's company commander acted quickly by having six of the protesters confined to the Luna County jail. Martin Serna recalls another threatened strike by enrollees who found fault with lunches served at work sites. In this instance, protesters returning to camp were informed by their commanding officer that they would be limited to a diet of bread and water until they got back to work. Work soon resumed.[37]

Work-related issues caused strikes elsewhere in New Mexico. Serious trouble surfaced when twenty-five Hispanic enrollees were transferred from Bandelier to help open a new CCC camp in Chaco Canyon. Former enrollee Alex Salazar recalls that tension mounted when Anglo enrollees in the new camp outnumbered Hispanics and "were pretty mean ... [b]ecause there were few of us." To make matters worse, camp supervisors insisted that Hispanic enrollees work digging trenches not only five days a week, but also on Saturdays. On one particular Saturday they were told that if they worked hard enough that day they would only have to work until noon on Sunday. Hearing that they might now be required to labor seven days a week, the Hispanic enrollees refused to return to work when the whistle blew ending their Saturday lunch break. Angered, their commander told the strikers that they would not be fed until they worked again. True to his word, the lieutenant did not allow them to eat dinner that evening. Salazar and his fellow protesters responded by threatening to write to their Congressman. They later broke into the supply tent and foraged for whatever food they could find. By Sunday the strike was settled when the Hispanic enrollees were not forced to work and were, in fact, called to a hardy breakfast. They returned to Bandelier within a week.[38]

As at Chaco Canyon, most CCC strikes in New Mexico were non-violent. While some strikes were marred by serious injuries and the destruction of camp property elsewhere in the country, the vast majority of strikes in the United States, including New Mexico, did not involve violence by either labor (enrollees) or management (military or civilian supervisors). Finally, most strikes were short in duration. Few lasted more than a day and most were resolved within hours, to the credit of both enrollees and their officers. Fortunately, the image of enrollees picketing at camp gates or supervisors transferring scab enrollees to break up strikes was completely alien in the CCC camps of New Mexico and the country as a whole. In most cases, the CCC helped defuse labor conflict rather than cause it.

In another form of protest against conditions in the CCC, some enrollees resorted to deserting their assigned camps on either a temporary or permanent basis. Going AWOL did not necessarily mean dissatisfaction with the CCC. Returning late from holidays, when most AWOLs occurred, or encountering problems on return trips from long distances like Juárez were hardly planned acts of protest. However, frequent AWOLs for extended periods of time could be interpreted as danger signals reflecting larger problems in camps. Efforts were therefore made to discourage unapproved extended leaves. Enrollees were reminded that the normal fine for going AWOL was a dollar a day. The Corona camp even created a tag board to help keep track of enrollees through the week and on weekends. Much like a system used by coal miners, each enrollee's tag was hung on an appropriate nail to signify his whereabouts. Elsewhere, great praise was given when weekends and holidays passed with few if any AWOLs. The *Kangarowl* reported only three AWOLs at the Glenwood camp in April 1935, the lowest number of any camp in the district that month. Not satisfied, the *Kangarowl's* editor called for a zero percent AWOL record in May.[39]

Enrollees nevertheless continued to go AWOL individually or in small groups. If still missing after eight days, they were officially classified as deserters. Lacking time and resources, camp officers seldom pursued deserters. Instead, public welfare officials near deserters' homes were routinely notified so that efforts could be made to convince missing enrollees to return to camp. However, welfare officials complained that such efforts were costly, distracting from their regular duties, and usually unsuccessful. Unresponsive deserters were sent letters formally notifying them that they had been dishonorably discharged. Similar notices were mailed to beneficiaries who would, of course, no longer be receiving twenty-five dollars a month in aid.[40]

Enrollees took the radical step of deserting for many reasons. Homesickness was clearly the number one reason for newcomers far from home and family. Girl friends, or the fear of losing girls to male competitors back home, caused others to return home prematurely. Simple spring fever was enough to tempt enrollees who enjoyed the thrill of travel to new places. The *Peñasco Pennant* at Mayhill quoted an enrollee who said that "warm days give him a hankerin' to hear a freight train whistle, and if he could just hear one he would run ten miles to catch it."[41]

Increasing numbers also deserted for work-related reasons either in the CCC or in the economy as a whole. Some left because they were angered by working conditions in camp. More often, they left to seek work in the private sector when the U.S. economy showed signs of recovery by the early 1940s. In case after case, enrollees took outside jobs but never bothered to apply for honorable discharges if only because the process of applying for discharges was often inconvenient and rushed. To qualify for an honorable discharge for work-related reasons, an enrollee had to have his employer send a letter (certified by a notary public) verifying the former enrollee's new employment status. The whole process had to be completed within a short period before the enrollee's AWOL status had expired and he was officially declared a deserter.[42]

Eager to get on with their lives and busy with new challenges, many former enrollees neglected to apply for honorable discharges by the specified deadline. Others simply took off in search of work without permission, although the CCC encouraged and allowed job-search leaves of absence. Nationally, desertion rates ranged from as low as eight percent in 1933 to an average of twenty percent by 1939 and slightly higher by the early 1940s. In New Mexico, desertion rates rose to twenty-seven percent of all New Mexican enrollees leaving the CCC in the period 1938 to 1942. It rose to as high as forty-five percent of all state enrollees leaving the CCC in the first six months of World War II.

Unfortunately, less than one percent of all discharged New Mexican enrollees were officially discharged to accept outside employment from December 1941 to June 1942.[43]

In the most dangerous, least acceptable form of protest, a faction of enrollees resorted to violence in their camps. Disagreements and fights were perhaps inevitable among young males confined in small quarters for extended periods of time. As former enrollee Martin Serna put it, "if you have a bunch of young men who don't fight, you're probably in a monastery."[44]

Most fights involved personal issues. This was especially true when too much liquor had been consumed by rivals for the attention of local girls. A 1936 cartoon in the Deming camp newspaper showed two roughed-up fighters, a bottle of liquor, and the caption, "It appears to be an epidemic!" Fights were usually broken up quickly or postponed until contentious enrollees could resolve their differences with boxing gloves and a semblance of order in their camp's boxing ring. Wearing heavy sixteen ounce gloves, combatants fought until one or the other conceded defeat from exhaustion or, less often, from injury.[45]

More serious fights broke out between racial and ethnic groups who fought to protest living and working together in camps. Fights typically occurred between Anglos from out-of-state and native-born Hispanics shortly after new groups arrived in New Mexico and before cultural adjustments could be made. Brawls often began in mess halls, as when Anglos and Hispanics fought with knives and forks as weapons at the camp near Mountainair. Elsewhere, Hilario Baca described a fight that started in a mess hall and ended in his camp's latrine. Enrollees from El Paso stood guard with knives so that combatants in the latrine would not be disturbed. Only the intervention of an armed officer, who fired a warning shot into the air, ended the brouhaha. Another fight became so violent that witnesses rang the camp's fire alarm to get help and extinguish the "flames" of anger.[46]

In addition to knives and forks from the mess hall, enrollees with "a taste for roughness" battled each other with knives made from saw blades and rolling pins made on lathes in camp wood shops. Baseball bats were also employed with predictable results. Knives and pick handles were the weapons of choice during an inter-racial struggle at a lunch break in Lee Sander's Soil Conservation Service camp, SCS-16-N. Ray Dawson recalled so much friction between Anglos and Hispanics at his Elephant Butte camp that each side identified its best fighter and let fists resolve all differences. Meeting outside their mess hall, the Anglo Texan beat his Hispanic opponent after several rounds. A.B. Barela recalls similar combat when a large Texan tried to cut in front of a smaller Hispanic in the Montebello camp's mess hall. The Texan was apparently unaware that he had challenged an accomplished amateur boxer; he had time to bemoan his poor choice of opponents while later recovering in the Army hospital at Ft. Bliss. Another mess hall riot ended with boxing competition involving not one, but several bouts at the San Ysidro camp. In the most tragic violence of this kind, enrollee Ray C. Densmore was beaten to death when a recreational boxing match deteriorated into a riot at a CCC camp in southern New Mexico. A later investigation traced the cause of this riot "directly to race and language difficulties." Fortunately, no deaths occurred in a gang fight between Anglo enrollees from Oklahoma and Hispanics from New Mexico at the camp near Grants in 1936 or in a "rough house" in the barracks at Española later that same year. However, ethnic relations grew so strained at some camps that at least one CCC official suggested that Hispanics and Anglos be segregated in separate camps in the interest of peace and order.[47]

Ethnic tension may have been far worse if not for alleviating circumstances in New Mexico. First, Hispanic enrollees outnumbered Anglo enrollees in many camps and in New Mexico overall. This presented a "different situation" for out-of-state Anglos who, after "a few forceful events and constant advice by officers," soon learned "the impropriety and hazard of being too aggressive in a predominantly Spanish speaking ... area." With "forceful events" usually occurring during the first weeks of service in New Mexico, a process of natural selection took place: most out-of-state enrollees adjusted, some deserted, and a few were discharged by strong-willed commanders. Peace prevailed until the next shipment of rookies arrived in camp. Hardly unique to the CCC, this pattern of friction and violence was typical of young males in isolated environments, including boys schools, youth camps, and, often, military bases.[48]

Ethnic differences no doubt increased friction in New Mexico's CCC camps, but friction would have occurred in any case, as proven in camps across the United States. In New Hampshire, tension existed between Anglo enrollees and those of French descent. In Arizona, Anglo enrollees from Oklahoma and Texas "frequently hated each other," while Pennsylvanians from the North and Texans from the South "almost re-fought the Civil War on several occasions." In Utah, Anglos from Kentucky and Ohio were so sharply divided in one camp that they barricaded themselves in separate barracks, announced they were armed, and vowed to fight to the finish against their regional rivals. Only a mutually trusted foreman negotiated a truce after confiscating a pistol from one barracks and a blackjack from the other. In St. George, Utah, liberty parties had to be scheduled on different nights of the week so that enrollees from different states "would not be in town at the same time." Separate liberty parties were also required in Douglas, Arizona, where 'lumberjacks' (enrollees serving in Forest Service camps) could not be in town with 'sod busters' (enrollees serving in Soil Conservation Service camps) for fear of fights and bloodshed.[49]

Even racial and ethnic minorities were known to fight among themselves. In Ysleta, Texas, black enrollees from Colorado faced "hazing and ill treatment" by black enrollees from Texas when "differences in regional outlook" became apparent. Back in New Mexico, intra-ethnic strife broke out when Hispanics from Texas (called *pachucos*) clashed with Hispanics from New Mexico (called *manitos*); dialect, clothing, and customs often divided the groups and led to friction. Clashing cultures, as much as clashing ethnic identities, help explain group violence, almost regardless of time or place in the CCC.[50]

\* \* \*

$X$ But what of CCC policy regarding the treatment of Hispanics in general? Did this federal program discriminate against Hispanics in New Mexico as it so blatantly discriminated against other ethnic and racial groups across the United States? Officially, discrimination was never tolerated. The March 1933 bill that created the CCC specifically declared that the new federal program would not allow discrimination "on account of race, color, or creed." But reality often varied from the ideal. Historians have noted four main ways in which the CCC violated its promise not to discriminate against minorities in general, and Southern blacks in particular. A comparison of CCC treatment of blacks in the South to CCC treatment of Hispanics in New Mexico can serve as a measure of just how much—or how little—the CCC deviated from its anti-discrimination policy in at least one Southwestern state.[51]

CCC discrimination against African-Americans began as early as the selection process. Although black unemployment rates were twice the national average in 1933, CCC officials consistently limited black enrollment. In Mississippi, for example, blacks represented fifty percent of the state's population, but only two percent of all state enrollees in 1933. While the National Association for the Advancement of Colored People (NAACP) objected and the CCC in Washington, D.C., officially demanded increased black enrollment, many local CCC leaders harbored racist attitudes and never intended to press this sensitive issue.[52]

In sharp contrast, Hispanics in New Mexico were never discriminated against in the CCC's selection process. Indeed, while Hispanics equaled about fifty percent of New Mexico's population in 1930, Hispanics enrollees represented eighty-one percent of all members of the CCC drawn from within the state by the period 1938 to 1942. Rather than discriminating against Hispanics, CCC officials took recruiting trips through New Mexico, visiting Hispanic homes accompanied by Spanish-speaking enrollees who could translate and help describe the advantages of joining the CCC to potential enrollees and their families. Once enrolled in the CCC, the average Hispanic enrollee served two enrollment periods, compared to one for non-Hispanics, proving that Hispanics faced no more discrimination in "reenlisting" than they had in first enrolling in New Mexico.[53]

If allowed to enroll in the CCC, blacks were usually segregated in all-black camps not only in the South, but across most of the United States after July 1935. In California, for example, blacks were assigned to segregated facilities in some of the oldest, most dilapidated camps of the state. Even New Mexico, with its small black population (.7 percent in 1930), had a separate camp for black enrollees in Berino, New Mexico.[54]

Hispanics never faced such discrimination. While many camps had large Hispanic majorities and friction sometimes existed with recently-arrived out-of-state enrollees, there were no separate camps for Hispanic enrollees in New Mexico and no separate facilities for Hispanics within each camp. Camp barracks, mess halls, rec halls, and other facilities were open to all. However, as often happens in settings populated by different cultural groups, Hispanics tended to socialize with Hispanics, while non-Hispanics tended to socialize with non-Hispanics. But such self-segregation within camps was purely voluntary and never officially mandated. The CCC never used the letter 'H' to designate all-Hispanic companies as it used the letter 'I' to designate all-Indian companies and the letter 'C' to designate all- "colored" companies in the nation.[55]

In a third form of discrimination against blacks, black enrollees faced Jim Crow regulations in the CCC similar to the racist customs they encountered in their everyday "civilian" lives. This was especially true in leadership roles. With only two exceptions in the entire nation, white officers commanded black camps. Whites also dominated all other leadership roles in black camps, from work supervisors to educational advisors. Protesting this discrimination, one black leader wrote to President Roosevelt, asserting that "We shall learn to lead only by leading." Blacks seldom got the opportunity to learn, much less lead in the CCC.[56]

Did Hispanics receive promotions into leadership roles or did they suffer the same fate as most blacks in the Civilian

Conservation Corps? The record in New Mexico was mixed. Initially, Hispanics could not rise to the rank of camp commander if only because commanders were originally drawn from the ranks of the regular Army and the Army Reserve where few Hispanics served in the 1930s. However, with the nation's war preparedness of the early 1940s, officers were in short supply and civilians were called on to command CCC camps in New Mexico. A handful of Hispanics rose to leadership roles in this period, and at least one, Bennie Casaus, became a camp commander. But Casaus was the exception, rather than the rule. Of the 205 camp commanders, project supervisors, educational advisors, doctors, dentists, and chaplains listed in New Mexico's forty-one camps of early 1941, not a single Spanish surname appeared.[57]

More typically, Hispanics were promoted to responsible leadership roles below the officer class. Many served as respected—and sometimes feared—enrollee Leaders, an official rank roughly equivalent to a non-commissioned officer in the Army. Rupert Lopez rose through the ranks until he was chosen as the Leader in charge of his company's side camp in Cerrillos for about two years. Other Hispanic enrollees, like Candelario Chavez, became head cooks, a position second only to camp commander in importance to camp health and high morale. Some Hispanics were promoted to supply clerk; Henry Arellanes's commander allowed him to purchase everything needed in camp, with the authority to sign his commander's name for all transactions. Hispanics became highly valued camp clerks, and one, Sammy Saez, was promoted to district clerk in 1936. Less officially, Hispanics became trusted leaders of athletic teams and stars on many camp baseball, basketball, and boxing teams. They also served as leaders on newspaper staffs, on debate teams, and in musical groups.[58]

Only a general lack of higher education, rather than ethnic discrimination, prevented Hispanics from assuming a greater number of leadership roles in camp. "We were all treated pretty good—the same," said Alex Salazar of Española, New Mexico. "When they treat someone better than you and they bypass you on a lot of breaks, that's when you get discouraged. But over there [in the

CCC] we were all treated the same." A.B. Barela agreed. According to Barela, job opportunities were always posted in camp and were available to all. How far you went depended more on individual ambition and skill than on race or ethnicity in New Mexico.[59]

Conditions were never as good for most black enrollees. Sadly, even camp entertainment discriminated against blacks. Minstrel shows mocking black speech and culture were among the most popular forms of amusement in white camps. At one Southwestern camp, a "black faced debate comedy" considered the racist question, "Resolved: That it ain't no crime to steal chickens." Racist jokes also appeared in camp newspapers, employing cruel stereotypes and racist slurs, including the hated 'n' word. In June 1935 a race riot broke out in a CCC camp in Idaho when black enrollees complained about derogatory name-calling by white enrollees. Although the black youths "had to stay on guard all night to keep white fellows from coming in[to their quarters], the black enrollees, rather than the whites, were all discharged from the Corps." Little wonder that while President Roosevelt remained popular among blacks and many benefitted from his federal programs, others, including a good many in the CCC, claimed that FDR's New Deal was nothing more than a raw deal for African-Americans.[60]

Were Hispanics in New Mexico made the brunt of similar derision? With few exceptions, the answer was no. On the contrary, Hispanic language and culture were generally respected and intentionally preserved in New Mexico's camps. Early camps were named after Spanish heroes like Francisco Coronado, Juan de Oñate, and Diego de Vargas. Enrollees who spoke Spanish in camp were not reprimanded (as they often had been in public schools), although camp leaders urged them to learn English in order to improve their chances of getting jobs after leaving the CCC. Rather than be discouraged, Spanish was often taught in class and used in religious sermons, in safety lectures, in special sections of camp newspapers, and in the newspapers' titles themselves. Henry Arellanes recalls that all but one of his Anglo officers spoke Spanish, including his fluent commander, Lt. E.L. Kelly of Las Vegas, New Mexico.[61]

Culturally, Hispanic arts and crafts, from wood carving to adobe making, were taught, encouraged, and conserved almost as if they were endangered natural resources. Spanish food could sometimes be found on camp menus. Work projects, such as archeological digs at Spanish mission ruins, honored the Hispanic past and helped preserve much of what might otherwise have been lost. Nina Otero-Warren's *Old Spain in Our Southwest* was respected not only as a fine teaching tool for its day, but also as an ideal resource to help reenforce traditional Hispanic values and customs. Spanish music was also popular, with performances at dances, on talent nights, after camp meetings, and at special events. Informal concerts in barracks could be heard all over camps, "irresistibly" drawing enrollees of different backgrounds together. According to one educational advisor, "enemies were transformed into friends and a fine feeling of comradeship developed" during these therapeutic musical sessions. Usually assigned to camps in their home state, rather than to sites across the nation (as happened to thousands of other enrollees), New Mexicans remained geographically, and hence culturally, close to their homeland. What historian Suzanne Forrest has said of the New Deal as a whole in New Mexico was specifically true of the CCC: in sundry ways it "helped preserve, and even foster, [a strong] sense of ethnic identity ... that may [well] be its most enduring legacy."[62]

Fortunately, with fair access to enrollment in the CCC, integrated camps, at least some opportunities for advancement, and general respect for their language and culture, Hispanic enrollees never faced the blatant discrimination experienced by black enrollees in camps across the country. Sadly, the same could not be said of Hispanic enrollees and their treatment in several New Mexico communities and in CCC camps in neighboring states, including Arizona, Texas, Colorado, and Utah. Only a fortuitous set of circumstances made camp life better, if hardly utopia, in New Mexico.[63]

## Endnotes - Chapter 12

[1]    *Glenwood News*, August 1936; *Mal Pais*, April 1937; *Tip Topper*, May 1937; P.A. Campredon, Camp Report, Bosque del Apache, April-May-June 1942, BANWR. On weather conditions in New Mexico history, see Iven Bennett's chapters in Jerry L. Williams, *New Mexico in Maps* (Albuquerque: University of New Mexico Press, 1986): 32-54.

[2]    *Albuquerque Journal,* July 3, 1936; *Gila Monster*, June 1936; *Yucca*, June 1938; *Animas Announcer*, February 20, 1936.

[3]    Hernandez interview; Casaus interview; H. Baca interview; Partridge interview, OHPB; *Ghost Talks*, January 1937 and February 1937.

[4]    Gallegos, Lucero, and Quintana interviews, OHPB; *Wasp*, January 1937; Camp Inspection Report, Conchas Dam, July 24, 1941, and Camp Inspection Report, Mountainair, October 8, 1935, CCC, NA.

[5]    *El Conejo*, December 1936; *Lonely Pennsylvanian,* April 1940.

[6]    Matthew J. Bower to Charles H. Kenlan, Roswell, January 31, 1940, and Camp Inspection Report, Mountainair, October 8, 1935, and Camp Inspection Report, High Rolls, February 8, 1935, and Camp Inspection Report, Sandia Peak, September 13, 1940, and Camp Inspection Report, Redrock, October 1, 1935, CCC, NA; Beck interview; Henington interview; *Black Ranger*, February 12, 1936.

[7]    *Follies of 1830*, August 1935 and October 1935; *New York Times*, November 2, 1937; Gibson interview.

[8]    Matthew J. Bowen to Charles H. Kenlan, Conchas Dam, August 10, 1940, and Camp Inspection Report, Jemez, October 1, 1935, and Camp Inspection Report, Silver City, October 16, 1935, CCC, NA; *Kangarowl*, February 1, 1936; *CCC Annual, 1936, Albuquerque District*, 29; *Lonely Pennsylvanian*, May-June 1940; Johnson interview; Westwood interview.

[9]    Sanders Memoirs, 114; Partridge interview, OHPB; *Glenwood News*, February 1937 and June 1937. APC pills consisted of aspirin, phenacetin, and caffeine. Phenacetin was later discovered to cause damage to livers.

[10]    Gorham, "Ambiguous Practices," 241; *Wasp*, November 1937; *Silver City Daily Press,* December 14, 1939.

[11]    Camp Inspection Report, Jemez, October 1, 1935, and Camp Inspection Report, Redrock, October 18, 1935, and Camp Inspection Report, Mountainair, October 8, 1935, and unsigned complaint by sixty enrollees, Columbus, n.d., CCC, NA; Westwood interview.

[12]    Porter Memoirs, 10; Maestas interview; Perea interview; Samuel L. Reed entry in Nolte, *We Remember*, 175; Camp Inspection Report,

Redrock, October 6, 1937, and Camp Inspection Report, Conchas Dam, July 24, 1941, CCC, NA; *La Piedra Lumbre*, October 1936; *Fresnal Ranger*, March 8, 1935, and March 22, 1935.

[13] Harrison *et al., Bandelier*, 17; *Happy Days*, May 19, 1934; Camp Inspection Report, Mayhill, December 13, 1938, and Camp Inspection Report, Conchas Dam, July 24, 1941, and Special Investigative Report, Columbus, May 20, 1941, CCC, NA.

[14] Leo Murphy to Mary Murphy, Conchas Dam, July 22, 1940, CCC, NA; *Yucca*, June 1938.

[15] William S. Stevens entry in Nolte, *We Remember*, 197; Low, *Diary*, 153; *Ghost Talks*, January 1937.

[16] Merrill, *Roosevelt's Forest Army*, 154; Otis *et al., Forest Service and the CCC*, 29.

[17] *Clovis Evening News-Journal*, May 24, 1933; *Carson Pine Cone*, June 8, 1933; *Fresnal Ranger*, April 29, 1935; *Kangarowl*, February 25, 1936; *Dark Canyon Avalanche*, July 23, 1936, and February 15, 1937; *Stanton Static*, January 1937; *Mirager*, April 1937; Partridge and Roybal interviews, OHPB; Camp Inspection Report, Jemez, June 30, 1934, CCC, NA.

[18] Camp Inspection Report, Santa Fe, March 21, 1934, and Camp Inspection Report, Ruidoso, August 28, 1940, CCC, NA; Huffman interview; Sanders Memoirs, 110; Partridge interview, OHPB; *Pink Pebble Periodical*, May 7, 1935, and January 15, 1937; *Black Ranger*, October 15, 1935, and November 1, 1935; *Mirager,* April 1936.

[19] Reid A. Holland, "The Civilian Conservation Corps in Oklahoma, 1933-42" (Unpublished M.A. thesis, Oklahoma State University, 1969): 73; *Pink Pebble Periodical*, November 15, 1936; *Gila Monster*, March 15, 1937.

[20] Kemp interview; Senator Elmer Thomas to Robert W. Fechner, Washington, D.C., May 13, 1936, CCC, NA. For examples of Oklahoma enrollees who enjoyed their service in New Mexico, see Shirley and Williams interviews.

[21] Judge William Jones, Jr., to J.J. McEntee, McAlester, Oklahoma, May 2, 1936, and David Breede to Ray Breede, Santa Fe, June 23, 1936, CCC, NA; *Albuquerque Journal*, July 3, 1936.

[22] Camp Inspection Report, Roswell, December 15, 1938, and Camp Inspection Report, Roswell, January 31, 1940, CCC, NA.

[23] Camp Inspection Report, Roswell, January 31, 1941, and Leon Boyd to Congressman Clyde L. Garrett, January 8, 1940, and Senator Elmer Thomas to Robert W. Fechner, Washington, D.C., May 13, 1936, CCC, NA. Differences between New Mexico and Texas and Oklahoma

enrollees were discussed in Guy Neal, Report of CCC Field Visit: New Mexico, December 4, 1937, CCC Papers, NMSRCA.

[24] *Tumbleweed*, January 1939 and June 1939; Emerson, *Braun*, 153-4; *Albuquerque Journal*, July 8, 1938; Thomas H. Coode and John F. Bauman, *People, Poverty, and Politics: Pennsylvanians during the Great Depression* (Lewisburg: Bucknell University Press, 1981): 15; Richard M. Ketchum, *The Borrowed Years, 1938-41* (New York: Random House, 1989): 618. Emphasis in the original.

[25] Philip M. Conti, *The Civilian Conservation Corps: Salvaging Boys and Other Treasures* (n.p.: privately published, [1998]): 3-5; Ketchum, *Borrowed Years*, 618; Charles Clugston interview, May 14, 1998.

[26] Steve Bubernak interview, May 15, 1996; Shish interview; Clugston interview; Edward Busch to the author, East Dublin, Georgia, April 25,1980; Reed entry in Nolte, *We Remember*, 175; Mooney interview; *NACCCA Journal*, 21 (December 1998): 5.

[27] *Lonely Pennsylvanian*, May-June 1940; Bubernak interview.

[28] Sherraden, "Effectiveness of the Camps," 139-40.

[29] Camp Inspection Report, Las Cruces, December 1, 1938, CCC, NA; Poorbaugh interview.

[30] *Woodpecker* referred to in the *Socorro Chieftain*, July 15, 1933; *Kangarowl*, February 1, 1936; *Gila Monster*, September 28, 1934.

[31] *Truchas Echo*, February 22, 1939; *Wasp*, September 1937; Camp Inspection Report, Glenwood, September 16, 1936, and Charles Watkins to Matthew J. Bowen, Roswell, CCC, NA; Kemp interview; Sanchez interview.

[32] M.L. Grant to Robert W. Fechner, Socorro, March 27, 1934, CCC, NA. Special Investigator Grant reported on conditions at F-31-N as a result of Mrs. L.A. Doty's letter to Eleanor Roosevelt from the Doty home in Aztec, New Mexico.

[33] Charles Romero to Dennis Chavez, Mountainair, October 28, 1938, and Judge William Jones, Jr., to J.J. McEntee, McAlester, Oklahoma, May 2, 1936, and Senator Elmer Thomas to Robert W. Fechner, Washington, D.C., May 13, 1936, CCC, NA.

[34] M.J. Bowen to Charles H. Kenlan, Roswell, January 31, 1940, and M.J. Bowen to Charles H. Kenlan, Carlsbad, February 5, 1940, and J.J. McEntee to Dennis Chavez, Washington, D.C., December 14, 1938, CCC, NA. R.R. Greiner was the commanding officer in both Roswell and Mountainair at the time of these complaints.

[35] *Lonely Pennsylvanian*, May-June 1940.

[36] Lacy, *Soil Soldiers*, 207-8; Paige, *CCC and the Park Service*, 93; Dawson interview; Johnson, "Army," 199, 222-3.

[37] Sherraden, "Effectiveness of the Camps," 123; Major General H.J. Brees to Adjutant General, Ft. Sam Houston, March 1, 1939, CCC, NA; Serna interview.

[38] Salazar interview, OHPB.

[39] *Pink Pebble Periodical*, April 16, 1935, *El Gallo de Pelea*, February 24, 1936; *Kangarowl*, May 30, 1935.

[40] Serna interview; Thomas interview; Jennie M. Kirby to W. Frank Persons, Santa Fe, November 8, 1941, Governor Miles Papers, NMSRCA.

[41] *Dark Canyon Avalanche*, April 30, 1938; *Peñasco Pennant*, February 28, 1936.

[42] Lee H. Kostora to M.J. Bowen, Conchas Dam, August 9, 1940, and Camp Inspection Report, Glenwood, September 16, 1936, and Camp Inspection Report, Carlsbad, February 12, 1942, and Camp Inspection Report, Roswell, February 13, 1942, and Camp Inspection Report, Ruidoso, February 26, 1942, CCC, NA.

[43] Paige, *CCC and the Park Service,* 88-9. Desertion rates in New Mexico calculated from a sample of CCC Enrollment Cards, CCC Papers, NMSRCA.

[44] Serna interview.

[45] Chacon interview; Thomas interview; Arellanes interview; Roybal interview, OHPB; Jim Craig interview, April 1, 1994.

[46] Jack O. Perry to the author, n.p., May 25, 1991; Reta interview; Gibson interview; H. Baca interview; Serna interview; Shish interview.

[47] *Mayhill Lookout*, June 1937; Thomas interview; Henington interview; Sanders Memoirs, 111; Dawson interview; Barela interview; Lopez interview; Hendrickson, "CCC in the Southwest," 20; Serna interview; Guy Neal, Report of CCC Field Visit: New Mexico, December 4, 1937, CCC Papers, NMSRCA. Charles S. Pearce also wrote of a CCC fight ending in death. The accused enrollee was brought through the Los Alamos Ranch School on his way to jail. Charles S. Pearce, *Los Alamos Before the Bomb* (New York: Vantage Press, 1990): 32-4.

[48] Camp Inspection Report, Santa Fe, November 10, 1938, CCC, NA; Pearce, *Before the Bomb*, 62-3.

[49] Draves, *Builder*, 91; Booth, "CCC in Arizona," 68, 204; Patrick Clancy, "Conserving the Youth: The Civilian Conservation Corps Experience in the Shenadoah National Park," *Virginia Magazine of History and Biography*, 105 (Autumn 1997): 463-7; Paige, *CCC and the Park Service*, 93; Baldridge, "Nine Years," 299, 306; Perea interview.

[50] Parham, "CCC in Colorado," 146-8; Chavez interview; Vega interview; Lujan and Martinez interviews, OHPB.

[51] Salmond, *CCC*, 88.

[52] *Ibid.*, 91; Otis *et al.*, *Forest Service and the CCC*, 7; Cole, *African-American Experience*, 13-16.

[53] Calculated from a random survey of 9,685 CCC enrollment cards, 1936-42, CCC Papers, NMSRCA; Barela interview.

[54] *CCC Annual, 1936, Ft. Bliss District*, 70; Cole, *African-American Experience*, 26, 34, 38. Nationally, there were 152 segregated black camps, with fifty-five percent in Southern states. Another seventy-one camps had a small number of black enrollees; nine of these camps were located in New Mexico. Holland and Hill, *Youth*, 111.

[55] Vega interview; Chavez interview.

[56] Calvin W. Gower, "The Struggle of Blacks for Leadership Positions in the CCC, 1933-42," *Journal of Negro History*, 61 (August 1976): 123-35; Arthur P. Hayes to Franklin D. Roosevelt, New York, April 15, 1935, CCC File, FDRL.

[57] Casaus interview; Station List and Roster, February 14, 1941, CCC Papers, NMSRCA.

[58] Barela interview; Perea interview; Lopez interview; Sanders Memoirs, 110; *Fresnal Ranger*, February 1, 1935; *Kangarowl*, July 12, 1935; *Gila Monster*, April 1936; *La Poliza*, December 1936; *El Chicito*, December 1937.

[59] Salazar interview, OHPB; Barela interview; Camp Inspection Report, Silver City, September 10, 1936, CCC, NA.

[60] *Fresnal Ranger*, February 22, 1935; *Mirager*, September 1936 and April 1937, *Lonely Pennsylvanian*, October 1939; Cole, *African-American Experience*, 19, 67.

[61] Garcia interview; Arnellas interview.

[62] *La Piedra Lumbre*, October 1936; Oliver C. Payne, Camp Report, Bosque del Apache, December 1939 and January 1940, BANWR; Bryant, "Education," 121; Forrest, *Preservation*, 180; *Carson Pine Cone*, May 5, 1939. In contrast to New Mexicans, enrollees uprooted from their home states were in danger of losing much of their native cultures. When youths from Kentucky were sent to CCC camps out West, their culture reportedly "broke down" during their months far from home. August C. Bolino, *From Depression to War: American Society in Transition, 1939* (Westport, Connecticut: Praeger, 1998): 55-6.

[63] Booth, "CCC in Arizona," 204-5, 218; Logan, "Golden Memory," 8; Parham, "CCC in Colorado," 138-42; Beckinridge, "Nine Years," 338; Manuel Fraijo entry in Nolte, *We Remember*, 98. On Hispanic New Mexican enrollee complaints in camps in Arizona see Willie B. Baca to Clyde Tingley, Safford, Arizona, June 10, 1936, and J.J. McEntee to Clyde Tingley, Washington, D.C., July 24, 1936, Governor Tingley Papers, NMSRCA.

# CONCLUSION

# Last Call & Legacy

The Civilian Conservation Corps had been created in response to a national economic crisis that took a terrible toll on every age group in the United States, but especially the young. After many years and great efforts, the nation's economy had largely recovered by the early 1940s. But now the United States faced a new and, in many ways, more terrifying crisis: Fascist powers in Europe and Asia threatened peace and the future of democratic freedoms around the world. The CCC and thousands of its enrollees sought to help the nation fight its Fascist enemies with all the resources and determination it had used to help fight its earlier economic foe. The question was whether the CCC could play a worthwhile role in war preparedness or if it had become an anachronism, appropriate for combat in the domestic struggle of the 1930s, but not for the foreign combat that lay ahead in the 1940s.

The CCC attempted to prove its usefulness in the new crisis by adjusting its focus to include war-related labor and training. A new emphasis was placed on vocational training that could prove useful in war industries or in the military itself. Educational advisors now offered additional classes in mechanics, automotive maintenance, and welding. In one of the most ambitious efforts of this kind, camp SCS-27-N in Albuquerque planned to send fifteen to twenty enrollees to the new Albuquerque air base to learn gas and electric welding. A dozen others served as apprentices to learn heavy equipment servicing. Eight to twelve learned machine tool operation; an undisclosed number became efficient in radio communications. By mid-1941, 625 enrollees were taking twenty-eight national defense training classes throughout New Mexico. Meeting in June 1941, educational advisors in New Mexico and west Texas set a goal to have no less than half of all enrollees participating in national defense classes of one kind or another. As Captain Arthur Marshall of camp SCS-17-N reported in a radio interview broadcast in Santa Fe and Albuquerque, the plan was to have "practically all work [and training] done in the camps ... contribute directly toward national defense."[1]

Much of what enrollees accomplished on a daily basis contributed to their preparedness and value in the war to come. Carpenters who had built CCC barracks and facilities in the wilderness were well prepared to build barracks and facilities at military bases in the United States and overseas. Supply clerks in the CCC could likewise use their knowledge of Army procedures and procurement during the war. CCC cooks, numbering 22,000 nationwide since 1933, were ready to become mess sergeants after years of cooking Army recipes for hundreds of hungry young men at a time. Heavy equipment operators in the CCC were similarly prepared to operate heavy equipment in the military; those who had driven transport trucks in the CCC were just as ready to drive troop trucks in the coming war. Enrollees trained to operate field radios during forest fires could use their skills in the signal corps on a new front line. Enrollees who had spent hundreds of man-hours building roads and small bridges in forests could now construct roads and bridges in combat zones. First aid, taught to all enrollees, would be especially valuable in the military. The list went on and on. According to the CCC's new national director, James J. McEntee, "If war comes, the men of the CCC will be specialists in a dozen [non-combat] fields ... as vital to the carrying on of conflict as firing a rifle or machine-gun."[2]

Ironically, many of the military-like practices of CCC life previously suppressed for fear of criticism in peacetime were now stressed and admired on the eve of combat. In fact, without a devious master plan in mind, the CCC had done what its pacifist critics had always suspected: it had groomed thousands of young men for eventual service as American soldiers. Surviving far from home, living in barracks, passing inspections, eating in mess halls, following orders, and responding to bugles (or at least whistles)— in these and countless other ways enrollees were well prepared for their transition to military life. Army training officers soon concluded that six months of service in the CCC was worth a year of conventional military training. Nationally, an estimated fifty to eighty percent of the three million men who had served in the CCC faced this rather easy transition as volunteers or draftees in the terrible war to come.[3]

For enrollees like Alex Salazar, Benito Montoya, and Sam Chavez, Army training "was nothing" after months of similar duty in the CCC. CCC training was so thorough and effective that when Felix Vega reported for duty in the Army at Ft. Bliss, his sergeant asked who among the new recruits had served in the CCC. Once Vega identified himself as a former enrollee, the sergeant asked him to demonstrate several basic procedures to his fellow soldiers. Vega did so proudly.[4]

With a leg up in experience, enrollee Leaders were specifically sought by military recruiters who were now allowed to visit camps and speak to enrollees about enlisting in the armed forces. One former Leader wrote to his CCC camp foreman to report that he was a first class private and an expert rifle shot in the Army by late 1941; he acknowledged that the CCC was "doing very good work ... in putting some character into so many kids," including himself. Camp officers were also respected for their experience in leading young civilians in the CCC. Based on their CCC experience, many reserve officers were well prepared to serve as regular Army officers in command of novice young soldiers in World War II. Even CCC chaplains were better qualified for what lay ahead, having dealt with enrollee spiritual needs and problems for years. A rare few, including Father Braun, had served in both World War I and the CCC already.[5]

Of course many aspects of military training, including drills, marching, and rifle practice, had long been taboo in the CCC. They remained off limits, despite urgent requests for such training by groups like the Veterans of Foreign Wars and the American Legion. In Congress, as many as nine bills to allow military training in CCC camps were introduced and defeated over the years. Eager enrollees and their commanding officers nevertheless clamored for such training as the likelihood of war increased. By 1940, a former educational advisor in New Mexico predicted that the country's "imminent need" would soon bring "the rhythm of drilling feet" to CCC camps everywhere. But official policy never changed: to their final days CCC camps were never converted into Army boot camps or para-military installations.[6]

Unofficially, some drilling, marching, and even weapons instruction had taken place on an irregular, make-shift basis. In 1935, for example, camp SCS-2-N at Redrock offered weekly lectures on marksmanship conducted by camp commander Lt. Basil Baila. Redrock's camp newspaper reported about thirty enrollees in attendance. That same year the educational advisor at Glenwood organized a class on the use of the Army's .45 caliber pistol. A rifle team took target practice at the Rodeo camp in 1941, although it is unlikely that they used live ammunition. As the war drew near, more and more officers led marching drills, albeit with broom sticks rather than rifles. Camp officers like Fred Poorbaugh could do little more, given continued civilian opposition. When Lt. Poorbaugh began leading marching drills in his southern New Mexico camp, an enrollee's mother protested to district headquarters. Poorbaugh was ordered to write to the concerned mother to alleviate her fears. Instead, Poorbaugh simply returned his orders to headquarters with a note that he must have been confused with some other commander. Determined to prepare his enrollees for what lay ahead, Poorbaugh resumed his drills without further interference.[7]

✗ Taking national defense classes, learning non-combat skills, and receiving unofficial military training helped make former enrollees better soldiers, if called to duty, and better industrial workers, if employed in essential war industries. But the CCC's greatest contribution in preparing young males for wartime service was far less tangible. At every stage of a youth's experience in the CCC, from his first days in camp to his last hours prior to discharge, most enrollees learned values, shouldered responsibilities, and acquired the self-confidence essential for their transition to manhood. They had, in short, experienced important rites of passage and come of age in the CCC at a time in American history when few other institutions offered similar opportunities for the young. Such a transition could not be measured with traditional yard sticks, but it was readily apparent to employers, friends, and relatives back home. Describing a former enrollee named Tito from her small community in Albuquerque, Irene Fisher wrote of her neighbor's triumphant return from a CCC camp. It was Tito, wrote Fisher, but it was "a different Tito. He seemed to have grown several inches, but perhaps this was due to the fact [that now] he stood straighter and looked directly at you." Tito had grown to be a man. His grandfather was also impressed by what had become of Tito and his friend, Frank. In his grandfather's admiring words, "the gov'ment had made men out of these boys. *Por Dios* (for heaven's sake), they went away *no bueno por nada* (good for nothing) and they came back big and strong."[8]

But the free enterprise economy had recovered and offered opportunities for individual growth and success outside the CCC by the early 1940s. The CCC had done its job in hard economic times and in the shift to a wartime economy, but it had clearly outlived its purpose by mid-1941 and early 1942. Enrollees who had remained in camp now departed in droves. Many enrollees were drafted straight from their camps. Many others volunteered. Roy Huffman received his discharge from the CCC at 10:00 a.m. on June 3, 1941; by 1:00 p.m. he was sworn into the Army Air Corps in Santa Fe. He reported to boot camp in California five days later. Others volunteered in groups: three friends left their CCC camp near Albuquerque, enlisted in the Marines, and reported for training in San Diego by July 1941. Larger numbers followed suit, especially following Japan's surprise attack on Pearl Harbor on December 7, 1941. Many became war heroes, including Alejandro Ruiz who won the Medal of Honor for his great bravery at Okinawa in April 1945. Several suffered the misery and torture of the Bataan Death March. Some, including Jeremias G. Martinez, Frank Madrid, and Father Braun, became prisoners of war. Tony Sanchez, John Mooney, Earl Shirley, Julian Shish, and others remained in the military after the war, making the service their life-long careers.[9]

As more youths left the CCC, the number of camps needed in New Mexico declined as well. While forty-one camps remained open in February of 1941, only twenty-eight were still operative in November of that year. The number of U.S. Forest Service camps in New Mexico dropped to only two by March 1942. For enrollees still on duty, CCC work focused on packing up supplies and dismantling camps. Becoming a specialist in closing camps (just as other officers had earlier been specialists in opening them), Fred Poorbaugh closed five New Mexico camps in the waning months of the CCC. Understandably, enrollee morale suffered and productivity declined. At the Bosque del Apache camp, superintendent Phillip A. Campredon reported that camp morale was so low in mid-1942 that "no work was derived from the boys." The few remaining enrollees at Bosque del Apache were discharged when their camp was disbanded on July 22, 1942.[10]

But the CCC in New Mexico did not succumb without resistance. Comparing enrollment based on state population quotas, New Mexico still led all forty-eight states in enrollment levels in the last six months of 1941. As late as November 1941 Governor John E. Miles had requested an increase in the number of camps and enrollees in New Mexico, citing the need to assist in flood-damaged areas and complete unfinished conservation projects. The governor's pleas fell on deaf ears in Washington, D.C. Not deterred, Miles urged New Mexico's two senators and single congressman to support a scheme to convert abandoned CCC camps into "health centers where youths rejected in the draft could build themselves up for [eventual] military service." Miles argued that these centers would be of "great benefit" to "the government, the state, and the young men" involved. Although favored by the *Albuquerque Journal* and others in the state, nothing came of the governor's proposal. Finally, as the end drew near, congressional hearings on the CCC's fate were held in 1942. Senator Dennis Chavez was among the few who testified in defense of the program, as if to honor a fallen patriot who had served his country well, but now faced his final hours.[11]

Newspaper editorials and public opinion polls showed that while most Americans appreciated the CCC's original role as a relief agency, they could no longer support its wartime funding. Not even the program's founder and greatest admirer could save it now. President Roosevelt had hoped that the CCC might still benefit boys under draft age and perform "essential war work" such as fighting forest fires set by the enemy if the Japanese attacked the West Coast. But such a threat never materialized and every federal dollar was needed to help fight the war. The CCC's fate was sealed. Congress delivered the coup de grâce on June 30, 1942. Within hours, CCC director McEntee ordered the "immediate cessation" of new enrollments in camps across the nation, including New Mexico.[12]

Even in passing, the CCC remained intent on serving the nation in its newest crisis. Prefab buildings, once moved from camp to camp in the wilderness, were now transported to new or enlarged military bases as needed. In New Mexico, the Army moved CCC structures to newly established air bases near Roswell, Alamogordo, and Albuquerque. Other buildings didn't need to be moved to be of service to the military. Reserve troops used a former CCC camp on the mesa east of Albuquerque when they conducted maneuvers in January 1942. Over two hundred naval trainees were housed at Las Cruces's two abandoned CCC camps while receiving training at New Mexico A&M in the summer of

*above*:  The CCC's pre-fab buildings were transported to various sites for war-related functions during World War II.  *Courtesy:  Photo Archives, College of Agriculture, New Mexico State University.*    *below:* Seven plaques were placed at CCC sites in New Mexico. This one is at Bandelier National Monument.  *Courtesy:  The Author.*

1942. NP-1-N near Carlsbad was converted into a recreation camp for military personnel in 1943. CCC equipment and supplies were similarly salvaged for wartime use. Everything, from cots and blankets to bulldozers and trucks, were shipped to military installations, including Ft. Bliss, Texas, and the air base in Albuquerque. A list of the last fifteen camps in New Mexico, Arizona, and Texas identified nearby freight railheads from which CCC equipment and supplies could be shipped to wherever they were needed most. The CCC "thus ended its life providing badly needed war material for [the same] hard-pressed Army" that had helped it mobilize so quickly in 1933. The Army's earlier assistance to the CCC was now "rewarded in full measure."[13]

As the war raged on, former CCC camps were also converted to serve as detainment facilities in New Mexico and other states. Over four hundred German merchant marines were held at a camp constructed with materials from the CCC camp at Ft. Stanton; enrollees encircled the new camp with three thousand feet of fencing, topped with barbed wire, as one of their last tasks in 1942. One hundred and sixty-five Italian prisoners of war were held at a former CCC camp near Tingley Beach in Albuquerque. Other Italian soldiers were detained at one of Las Cruces's abandoned CCC camps when it was no longer needed for naval trainees. In the largest camp of its kind in New Mexico, thousands of German POWs were imprisoned at a former CCC camp outside Roswell from July 1943 to June 1945. With a capacity of 4,800 prisoners, this isolated facility became one of the ten largest POW camps in the United States.[14]

Not to be confused with POW camps, Japanese-American internment camps were created at three sites in New Mexico during World War II. Two of the three sites, at Ft. Stanton and near Santa Fe, were converted CCC camps. Thirty-two Japanese-American railroad workers and their family members from Clovis, New Mexico, were relocated to what remained of the CCC camp near Ft. Stanton from January to December 1942. Unlike other, more assimilated and accepted Japanese in communities like Gallup, Grants, and Belen, those in Clovis were so menaced by the local population that they were held at Ft. Stanton in a form of protective custody. Six additional CCC camps were "speedily prepared for occupancy" in early 1942, with rumors that they were to be used for Japanese-Americans following their forced evacuation from the West Coast. Scattered protests were heard regarding this possible use of the abandoned camps. The *Albuquerque Journal* insisted that any Japanese interned in New Mexico should be "forced to do some work for their upkeep," suggesting that perhaps they could continue the good work begun by the CCC.[15]

But of the six abandoned camps considered for this purpose, only the former camp west of Santa Fe was converted into an internment camp during World War II. In all, 4,555 Japanese-American males, judged to be among the most dangerous of all Japanese-Americans in the United States, were imprisoned near Santa Fe from March 1942 to April 1946. Unfairly identified with the nation's Asian enemy, those interned at the former CCC camp were seldom allowed to work in the surrounding community, no less continue the work of the CCC, as the *Journal* had urged.[16]

Former CCC structures even played a part in the testing of the atomic bomb that finally ended World War II. CCC buildings from an Albuquerque camp were dismantled, trucked 115 miles south to Trinity Site southeast of Socorro, and reconstructed at the Army's base camp established for some two hundred Manhattan Project personnel. These buildings were located within eleven miles of ground zero and the atomic blast (equivalent to 21,000 tons of TNT) that rocked south central New Mexico on July 16, 1945.[17]

Abandoned CCC camps played more benign roles as well. As early as 1936, the remains of a camp near Socorro were used as a hospital for transients in need of government health care while passing through New Mexico. Old CCC buildings also served educational purposes. Just prior to World War II, twenty-seven students and three professors from Iowa A&M College used an empty CCC camp in the Sacramento Mountains for living quarters and teaching facilities during a 1941 summer course on forestry. At war's end, when thousands of veterans arrived on college campuses to make use of the G.I. Bill, colleges often transported old CCC barracks for emergency student housing. In the midst of "near-panic preparations," New Mexico A&M resorted to such housing in the fall of 1946. It was fitting that the same structures that had housed a generation of youths as they weathered the economic storm of the 1930s served that same generation as military installations during the early 1940s and as postwar quarters while many completed their education in the late 1940s.[18]

But the CCC's impact on the Southwest extended far beyond World War II and the structures left behind for emergency use. Over half a century later, it is almost impossible to travel through New Mexico without finding evidence of CCC labor in every corner of the state. From Carlsbad Caverns in the south to Bandelier in the north, from the Bosque del Apache wildlife reserve in the Rio Grande Valley to the Kiwanis Cabin atop the Sandias, CCC projects dot the public landscape as monuments to the proud, hard work of thousands of youths. As early as 1939, on the CCC's sixth anniversary, a U.S. Forest Service publication declared that the CCC in the Southwest had accomplished so much

> that the statistics [could] ... daze a sensible man, enrapture a mathematician or choke a horse ... . Truly, the woodsman's mythological Paul Bunyan has had a son ... and his footprints in the forests of the Southwest will be visible for decades to come.

The CCC can be measured a success because its projects have impressed so many, have served so many, and have lasted so long.[19]

But while most CCC projects received well-deserved praise in New Mexico and across the United States, some observers found fault with the program's conservation methods and results, either in the 1930s or since. Aldo Leopold, the most respected ecologist of the twentieth century, spent the summer of 1933 supervising CCC erosion control projects in New Mexico and Arizona.

Leopold found that crews of enrollees often worked at cross-purposes. In one instance he noticed a tree planting crew "setting pines all over the only open clover-patch available to the deer and partridges." On another occasion, Leopold discovered a "road-side-cleanup crew burning all the down oak fuel wood available to the fireplaces built by the recreation-ground crew." But Leopold did not blame CCC crews for this confusion; they were simply following the directions of their supervisors from uncoordinated state and federal agencies. Moreover, Leopold's observations were made in the CCC's first summer of work. Efforts usually improved with time.[20]

Other conservationists reportedly "viewed the Corps's arrival in the nation's woods as a farmer might welcome a herd of elephants to a lettuce field." To purist conservationists, the CCC was a "noxious harbinger of civilization." One such purist, Ernest M. Dickerman, declared that

> The C.C.C. was one of the best things any government ever did anywhere but they overdid it ... . They built endless numbers of fire roads up every [mountain] hollow, and damn many automobile camps ... . Guys like me considered them another form of devastation.

Critics of the road into Frijoles Canyon had similar misgivings about too much human access to natural settings and ancient ruins in 1933. The *Santa Fe New Mexican* went so far as to print a political cartoon anticipating a commercial invasion of Bandelier, including a hot dog stand and gasoline pumps among the treasured Indian ruins. But much of this criticism dissipated when work at Bandelier and elsewhere was completed and, eventually, admired. A later edition of the *New Mexican* apologized for its earlier protest and lauded the National Park Service for its sensitive work and accomplishments at Bandelier in conjunction with the CCC.[21]

Despite such praise, much of what was accomplished by the CCC has perished for lack of funding and maintenance over the years. This was especially true of CCC projects involving soil conservation and forest preservation. Lamenting this loss, conservationists remember the 1930s as a golden age of conservation, if only because the CCC could provide so much labor in emergencies and in long-overdue projects throughout the state and nation. In appreciation, plaques or inscriptions have been placed at the sites of seven major CCC projects in New Mexico. An eighth, dedicated to the CCC in general, is one of only three plaques that adorn the walls of the Capitol Rotunda in Santa Fe.[22]

The approval of modern conservationists is well deserved and much appreciated by the thousands of enrollees and supervisors who served in the CCC. The CCC helped save New Mexico's endangered environment at a critical moment. But the Corps was also meant to conserve the endangered youth of the 1930s. How did these youths evaluate the CCC in the final analysis?

Some enrollees offered their opinions of the CCC as they left the Corps and reentered "civilian" life. Interviewed as they departed in 1937, a typical group of out-of-state enrollees found good things to say about the CCC and usually about New Mexico. Cecil Sharbutt of Levelland, Texas, gave his opinion that "the CCC has brought about more results than any other [program] made by our great President. It is the conservation and preservation of men and soil. I have enjoyed my stay in the CCC." In 1941 a former enrollee wrote his Forest Service foreman that he considered his single year of experience in the CCC to be as valuable as three years of schooling. The out-of-state youth closed his letter with the declaration that "I'll never forget my days in New Mexico."[23]

New Mexicans were just as enthusiastic in their evaluation of the CCC. When Tito returned to Irene Fisher's neighborhood of Los Griegos, Fisher and Tito's relatives knew that he had become a man, but it was even more important that Tito clearly saw a change in himself and his perception of his future. After months in the CCC, Tito proudly flexed his muscles, told of the new road he'd helped build, spoke of returning to school, and

Former enrollee Charles Clugston of Monroeville, Pennsylvania, revisits the Tucumcari municipal pool site he helped build. Clugston is one of thousands of former enrollees who are convinced that the CCC made a significant contribution in their coming of age in the 1930s. *Courtesy: Clarles Clugston.*

gladly helped with the chores on his family's farm. As a dramatically changed Tito told his mother, "it is good to get home, but I like[d] to go for the experience at the CCC camp."[24]

Most former enrollees agreed with Tito's assessment of the CCC's impact on their transition from adolescence to manhood. Most had achieved the rites of passage that had formerly eluded them during the Great Depression: they had left home, had learned a work ethic, had acquired more education and training, had gotten their first jobs, and had contributed to a larger community in which they felt a valued part. In the process, most had also matured into the independent adults, ideal workers, and loyal citizens the CCC had intended to create. Having worked so hard to conserve natural resources, many became strong advocates of conservation for the rest of their lives; some, in fact, worked for the National Park Service or the U.S. Forest Service for their entire careers. New Mexicans took additional pride in the work they had done to conserve their history and culture in the CCC. As a bonus to the nation that provided them with so many personal opportunities, the fine young men shaped by the CCC were ready and able to serve as fine young soldiers, airmen, sailors, and defense workers when their country needed them most in the Second World War. Their slogan "we can take it" in the CCC became "we can do it" in World War II.[25]

From the perspective of six decades or more, former enrollees attest that their CCC experience was not only the key to their coming of age, but also the turning point in their entire lives. As a final testimony of their enduring respect for the CCC, most veterans of the program contend that a new CCC would help solve the serious problems of the current generation. This solution is debatable: given the unique characteristics of each generation, solutions that work in one age do not always work well for others. But the veterans' intent is genuine and their admiration for the CCC is sincere. Having had their individual lives profoundly altered in the depths of the Great Depression, the proud, aging veterans of New Mexico's CCC camps simply wish the same positive transformation for their grandsons, their state, and the nation today. The Civilian Conservation Corps is long gone, but its proud legacy endures.[26]


## Endnotes - Conclusion

[1]    *Ft. Sumner Bugler*, April 1941; *Albuquerque Journal*, June 15 and 16, 1941; *Albuquerque Tribune*, July 17, 1941; Gibson interview; Dautin W. Rockey to District Educational Advisor, Albuquerque, January 3, 1941, CCC, NA; Bryant, "Education," 71; *Santa Fe New Mexican*, June 23, 1940.

[2]    Newspaper clipping, October 10, 1940, CCC, NA; *Albuquerque Journal*, March 31, 1941; McEntee, *Final Report*, 63. McEntee became director of the CCC when Robert Fechner died following a heart attack in December 1939. Salmond, *CCC*, 176.

[3]    Salmond, *CCC*, 195; Garraty, "New Deal," 911; Shish interview. Approximately 300,000 enrollees left their CCC camps for military service or defense jobs from July 1940 to June 1941 alone. Dixon Wecter, *The Age of the Great Depression, 1929-41* (New York: Viewpoints, 1975): 186n.

[4]    Salazar and B. Montoya interviews, OHPB; Chavez interview; Vega interview.

[5]    *Forest Pioneer,* 4th quarter, 1941; McEntee, *Final Report*, 48, 80-1; Conti, *Salvaging Boys*, vii. Father Braun, who served as an Army chaplain in World War I, received orders to report to Ft. Sam Houston in San Antonio, Texas, on November 1, 1940. Tragically, he was present at the fall of Bataan and was held as a prisoner of war for forty months, until August 1945. Emerson, *Braun*, 55-71, 161-97.

[6]    *Albuquerque Journal*, July 21, 1936, Rawick, "New Deal and Youth," 114-5; Bryant, "Education," 129.

[7]    *Pink Pebble Periodical*, March 12, 1935; *Kangarowl,* May 30, 1935; Camp Inspection Report, Ft. Sumner, February 17, 1942, CCC, NA; *Memories of the CCC: SCS-26-N, Rodeo, New Mexico, 1941* (Little Rock, Arkansas: Service Publications, 1941); H. Baca interview; L. Baca interview; Poorbaugh interview.

[8]    Fisher, *Bathtub*, 148-9. K. Edd Teston's parents were equally proud of their maturing son, as described in Teston, "Shanty on the Claim," 58.

[9]    *Forest Pioneer,* 4th quarter, 1941; Smith, "Role of the Army," 8; Kemp interview; Huffman interview; *Albuquerque Journal*, June 28,

1941; Angie S. Lopez, *Blessed Are the Soldiers* (Albuquerque: Sandia, 1990): 70, 138-41, 150, 174; Dorothy Cave, *Four Trails to Valor* (Las Cruces: Yucca Tree Press, 1998): 134; Emerson, *Braun*, 174-98; Sanchez interview; Mooney interview; Shirley interview; W.C. Rogers to the author, Sonora, California, April 9, 1980. Julian Shish served in World War II, Korea, and Vietnam during his twenty-six years in the Navy. Shish interview.

  [10] Station List and Roster, 1941, and News Release, November 6, 1941, Governor Miles Papers, NMSRCA; *Albuquerque Journal*, March 12, 1942; Dawson interview; Poorbaugh interview; Phillip A. Campredon, Camp Report, Bosque del Apache, April-May-June 1942, and A.D. Campbell, Fish and Wildlife Report, May 1-August 31, 1942, BANWR.

  [11] John E. Miles to Claude R. Wickard, Santa Fe, February 18, 1941, and John E. Miles to Paul V. McNutt, Santa Fe, November 6, 1941, and Charles H. Taylor to John E. Miles, Washington, D.C., November 7, 1941, and Paul V. McNutt, Washington, D.C., November 13, 1941, Governor Miles Papers, NMSRCA; *Albuquerque Journal,* January 23 and February 12, 1942; Salmond, *CCC*, 215; Hearings on S.2295: The Termination of the CCC and NYA Before the Committee on Education and Labor, U.S. Senate, 77th Congress, 2nd Session, March 23-April 17, 1942 (Washington, D.C.: Government Printing Office, 1942). Senator Chavez served as a member of the Senate Committee on Education and Labor.

  [12] John Morton Blum, *V Was For Victory* (San Diego: Harcourt Brace Jovanovich, 1976): 235; Nixon, *Roosevelt and Conservation,* 547-8; Salmond, *CCC*, 212, 217; J.J. McEntee to Jennie M. Kirby, Washington, D.C., July 2, 1942, Governor Miles Papers, NMSRCA.

  [13] Dawson interview; Don E. Alberts, *Balloons to Bombers: Aviation in Albuquerque, 1882-1945* (Albuquerque: Albuquerque Museum, 1987): 76; *Albuquerque Journal*, January 20 and March 1, 1942; Kropp, *All May Learn*, 277; Sellars, *Preserving Nature*, 151; *Carlsbad Current-Argus*, October 9, 1987; Barela interview; Station List and Roster, May 28, 1942, CCC Papers, NMSRCA; Smith, "Role of the Army," 8.

  [14] *Albuquerque Journal*, January 16 and 21 and March 14 and 18, 1941, and February 24, 1942, and October 9, 1943; John J. Culley, "A Troublesome Presence: The World War II Internment of German Sailors in New Mexico," *Prologue*, 28 (Winter 1996): 279-95; Susan Badger Doyle, "German and Italian Prisoners of War in Albuquerque, 1943-46," *New Mexico Historical Review*, 66 (July 1991): 328, 330, 332; Kropp, *All May Learn*, 283-4; Jake W. Spidle, "Axis Invasion of

the American West: POW's in New Mexico, 1942-46," *New Mexico Historical Review*, 49 (April 1974): 93-122.

[15] *Albuquerque Journal*, February 26 and March 1 and 8, 1942. The third internment camp, at Lordsburg, had not been a CCC camp. The Board of Regents at the New Mexico Military Institute was among those who protested, arguing that the former CCC camp (by then NMMI property) was too close to campus and would adversely alarm students and staff. William E. Gibbs and Eugene T. Jackman, *New Mexico Military Institute: A Centennial History* (Roswell: Centennial Commission, 1991): 151.

[16] Richard Melzer, "Casualties of Caution and Fear: Life in Santa Fe's Japanese Internment Camp, 1942-46" in Judith Boyce DeMark, *Essays in Twentieth Century New Mexico History* (Albuquerque: University of New Mexico Press, 1994): 213-40.

[17] Lansing Lamont, *Day of Trinity* (New York: Atheneum, 1985): 94-5.

[18] *Health City Sun*, September 25, 1936; *Albuquerque Journal*, June 26, 1941; Kropp, *All May Learn*, 298. A former CCC camp in McKinley County was even used to house overflow guests at a convention held in Gallup in the summer of 1941. *Albuquerque Journal*, July 21 and 22, 1941.

[19] *Forest Pioneer*, 2nd quarter, 1939. For the CCC's contributions to the nation as a whole, see T.B. Plair, "How the CCC Has Paid Off," *American Forests*, 60 (February 1954): 28-30, 44-5.

[20] Sellars, *Preserving Nature*, 100-1 and 129-31; Curti Meine, *Aldo Leopold: His Life and Work* (Madison: University of Wisconsin, 1988): 302, 306.

[21] Cutler, *Public Landscape*, 95; New York Times, August 5, 1998; Harrison, *et. al.*, *Bandelier*, 21. For criticism of CCC fire fighting methods in the U.S., see W.B. Sheppard to the Editor, *New York Times,* November 18, 1934; Low, *Dust Bowl Diary*, 128, 152. Also see Otis *et al.*, *Forest Service and the CCC*, 10; Booth, "CCC in Arizona," 25, 34, 228-9. Recent critics have suggested that the CCC fought forest fires to a fault, not allowing for periodic prescribed burns. On the value of prescribed burns, see *Prescribed Fire* (Albuquerque: Cibola National Forest, 1992): 1-7; *Albuquerque Journal,* April 4, 1999.

[22] Sellars, *Preserving Nature*, 173; Edwin A. Tucker, "The Forest Service in the Southwest," Unpublished ms., U.S. Forest Service Collection, CSWR, UNM; Gregory McNamee, *Gila: The Life and Death of an American River* (New York: Orion Books, 1994): 186-8. The seven CCC plaques or inscriptions are at Bandelier, Bosque del Apache,

Bottomless Lakes, Carlsbad, Elephant Butte, the Kiwanis Cabin, and the National Park Service building in Santa Fe.

²³ *Mirager*, September 1937; Forest Pioneer, 2nd quarter, 1941. For enrollee evaluations outside New Mexico see Holland and Hill, *Youth*, 237-40; Oliver and Dudley, *New America*, 65-110; Nolte, *We Remember*; Merrill, *Roosevelt's Forest Army*, 55-106 .

²⁴ Perea interview; Fisher, *Bathtub*, 148-9.

²⁵ Samuel P. Hays, *Explorations in Environmental History* Pittsburgh: University of Pittsburgh Press, 1998): 206; Todd, "Social Implications of the CCC," 154. Carl Walker, for example, served in the National Park Service for thirty-eight years, retiring in 1974. Walker interview.

²⁶ See, for example, Vega interview; H. Baca interview; L. Baca interview; Perea interview; Lopez interview; B. Montoya interview, OHPB; Guadalupe P. Flores to the author, Victoria, Texas, November 24, 1991; Jack O. Perry to the author, n.p., May 25, 1991. For other calls for a new CCC, see Stephen E. Ambrose, "Revive Roosevelt's C.C.C.," *New York Times,* November 28, 1992; David D. Draves to the Editor, *New York Times*, December 19, 1992; monthly editions of the *NACCC Journal*. In 1982, a Senate bill to create a contemporary version of the CCC was introduced without success. Otis *et al.*, *Forest Service and the CCC*, 12. In 1984, a bill to create an American Conservation Corps for unemployed men and women was vetoed by President Ronald Reagan. Cole, *African-American Experience*, 96n. William Stauss and Neil Howe point out that the "G.I. Generation," born between 1901 and 1924, was characterized by a strong faith in collective behavior, civic virtue, and government action to solve social ills. The current generation has other virtues, but few of these, making its members less-than-ideal candidates for CCC-like programs. William Strauss and Neil Howe, *Generations: The History of America's Future, 1584-2069* (New York: William Morrow and Company, 1991): 261-78, 317-34. New Mexico is one of only a handful of states that have a CCC-like program of its own. Created through legislation written by Vicente T. Ximenes and sponsored by Chapter #141 of the National Association of CCC Alumni, the New Mexico Youth Conservation Corps has employed 2,446 young men and women in conservation projects in all but two counties of the state since it began in 1992. *New Mexico Youth Conservation Corps Annual Report, 1999*. California, Ohio, and Wisconsin are among the few other states with similar programs. Cole, *African-American Experience*, 73; *NACCCA Journal,* 22 (July 1999): 8-9. The Peace Corps and Americorps also trace their roots to the CCC.

# APPENDIX A

104 Identified Civilian Conservation Corps Camps
in New Mexico*

**National Agricultural Research Center (A)**
A-4-T          Berino (Black enrollees)

**Bureau of Reclamation (BR)**
BR-1-N     Roswell
BR-2-N     Carlsbad
BR-3-N     Carlsbad (World War I veterans)
BR-8-N     Elephant Butte
BR-9-N     Elephant Butte
BR-39-N    Las Cruces
BR-54-N    Elephant Butte
BR-82-N    Carlsbad

**Biological Survey (BS)**
BS-1-N     Roswell (Bitter Lake)
BS-2-N     San Antonio (Bosque del Apache)
BS-3-N     Roswell

**Division of Forestry (DF)**
DF-2-N     Tularosa
DF-17-N    Capitan

**Division of Grazing (DG)**
DG-3-N     Carlsbad
DG-36-N    Mirage
DG-37-N    Cuchillo
DG-38-N    Radium Springs
DG-39-N    Tularosa
DG-40-N    Carrizozo
DG-41-N    Lake Arthur
DG-42-N    Magdalena
DG-43-N    Animas
DG-69-N    Alamogordo

*CCC camps in New Mexico were sometimes transfered to other locations in the state. F-7-N, for example, was transfered from its Mt. Sedgwick location west of Grants to the Jornada Range near Las Cruces in November 1933. Each camp's most frequent location is noted here.

## Division of Grazing Public Land (DPG)

DPG-1-N     Silver City

## U.S. National Forest Service (F)

| | |
|---|---|
| F-1-N | El Rito |
| F-2-N | Apache Creek |
| F-3-N | Vallecitos |
| F-4-N | Tres Piedras |
| F-5-N | Mountainair |
| F-6-N | Tres Ritos |
| F-7-N | Mt. Sedgewick |
| F-8-N | Sulpher Canyon |
| F-9-N | Magdelena |
| F-10-N | Grants |
| F-11-N | Mimbres |
| F-12-N | Redstone |
| F-13-N | La Madera |
| F-14-N | Beaverhead |
| F-15-N | Little Walnut |
| F-16-N | Sacramento Valley |
| F-17-N | Ft. Stanton |
| F-18-N | Cloudcroft |
| F-19-N | Los Alamos |
| F-20-N | Rowe |
| F-21-N | Rio Gallinas |
| F-22-N | La Cueva |
| F-23-N | Tesuque |
| F-24-N | High Rolls |
| F-25-N | Glenwood |
| F-26-N | Juan Tabo |
| F-27-N | Stuart Well (Jornada Experimental Range) |
| F-29-N | Santa Fe |
| F-30-N | Wooften Ranch |
| F-31-N | Polica Canyon |
| F-32-N | Peñasco |
| F-33-N | Peña Blanca |
| F-34-N | Mayhill |
| F-35-N | Manzano |
| F-36-N | El Rito |
| F-37-N | Carlsbad |
| F-38-N | Espanola |
| F-39-N | Jornada Experimental Range |
| F-41-N | Corona |
| F-43-N | La Madera |
| F-51-N | Monticello |

| F-52-N | Glenwood |
| F-53-N | Glorieta |
| F-54-N | Ruidoso |
| F-55-N | Vallecitos |
| F-56-N | Coyote |
| F-57-N | Magdelena |

## Fish & Wildlife Service (FWS)

| FWS-2-N | San Antonio |
| FWS-3-N | Roswell |

## Grazing Service (G)

| G-33-N | Melrose |
| G-36-N | Deming |
| G-37-N | Cuchillo |
| G-38-N | Radium Springs |
| G-39-N | Tularosa |
| G-40-N | Carrizozo |
| G-41-N | Lake Arthur |
| G-42-N | Magdalena |
| G-43-N | Animas |
| G-69-N | Orogrande |
| G-101-N | Bloomfield |
| G-103-N | Quemado |
| G-123-N | Quemado |
| G-147-N | San Antonio |
| G-148-N | Carlsbad |
| G-149-N | Roswell |
| G-150-N | Columbus |
| G-174-N | Cambray |
| G-178-N | Las Cruces |

## National Monuments (NM)

| NM-1-N | Bandelier |

## National Park Service (NP)

| NP-1-N | Carlsbad |
| NP-2-N | Chaco Canyon |
| NP-3-N | Bandelier |
| NP-4-N | Bandelier |
| NP(D)-1-N | Tularosa |
| NP(D)-2-N | San Antonio |

## Private Land Erosion (PE)

| PE-201-N | Santa Fe |
| PE-202-N | Silver City |

## Soil Conservation Service (SCS)

| | |
|---|---|
| SCS-1-N | Albuquerque |
| SCS-2-N | Redrock |
| SCS-3-N | Abiquiu |
| SCS-4-N | El Rito |
| SCS-5-N | Velarde |
| SCS-6-N | Ft. Stanton |
| SCS-7-N | San Ysidro |
| SCS-8-N | San Ysidro |
| SCS-9-N | Albuquerque |
| SCS-10-N | San Mateo Springs |
| SCS-14-N | Silver City |
| SCS-15-N | Whitewater |
| SCS-16-N | Las Cruces |
| SCS-17-N | Santa Fe |
| SCS-18-N | Buckhorn |
| SCS-19-N | Hidalgo County |
| SCS-20-N | Silver City |
| SCS-21-N | Mountainair |
| SCS-22-N | Kingston |
| SCS-23-N | Ft. Sumner |
| SCS-24-N | Hatch |
| SCS-25-N | Magdelena |
| SCS-26-N | Rodeo |
| SCS-27-N | Albuquerque |
| SCS-28-N | La Cueva |
| SCS-29-N | High Rolls |
| SCS-30-N | Tualrosa |
| SCS-31-N | Lincoln |
| SCS-32-N | Hondo |
| SCS-33-N | Melrose |

## State Parks (SP)

| | |
|---|---|
| SP-1-N | Santa Fe (Hyde State Park) |
| SP-2-N | La Joya (Game Preserve) |
| SP-3-N | Roswell (Bottomless Lakes State Park) |
| SP-4-N | Santa Fe (Hyde State Park) |
| SP-5-N | Portales (Eastern New Mexico State Park) |
| SP-6-N | Carlsbad (Metropolitan Park) |
| SP-7-N | Tucumcari (Metropolitan Park) |
| SP-8-N | Conchas Dam State Park |

# APPENDIX B

Number of Civilian Conservation Corps Camps
in New Mexico 1933-1942

| YEAR | CAMPS |
|------|-------|
| 1933 | 16 |
| 1934 | 38 |
| 1935 | * |
| 1936 | 40 |
| 1937 | 36 |
| 1938 | 37 |
| 1939 | * |
| 1940 | 42 |
| 1941 | 28 |
| 1942 | 0** |
| Average, 1933-42 | 32 |

\* Insufficient data
\** All camps had closed by June 30, 1942.

Sources:  Civilian Conservation Corps Camp Inspection
Reports, Record Group 35, National Archives,
Washington, D.C.; James J. McEntee, *Final Re
port of the Director of the Civilian Conservation
Corps, April 1933 to June 30, 1942* (Washington,
D.C.: Federal Security Agency, 1942): 110-11.

# APPENDIX C

Identified Civilian Conservation Corps
Projects in New Mexico

**Animal Preservation Projects**
Bosque del Apache National Wildlife Refuge
Cattleguards
Corrals
Fencing & Walls (2,177 miles)
Fish Hatcheries
La Joya State Game Preserve
Quail Plots
Stock Drive to Magdalena*
Stock Tanks

**Archaeological & Historical Sites**
Abo Spanish Mission*
Jemez Spanish Mission
Lincoln County Courthouse*
Quarai Spanish Mission*
Roadside Historical Markers

**Emergency Operations**
Fire Fighting
Flood Control
Search & Rescue

**Infrastructure Construction Projects**
The Catwalk, Gila National Forest
Foot & Vehicle Trails & Roads (4,996 miles)
Horse Trails
Map Making
Parking Areas
Rural Telephone Lines (2,081 miles)
Sign Construction
Surveying
Wilderness Bridges (1,158)

**Insect & Rodent Control Projects**
Grasshopper Wars
Rodent Control (10,091,544 acres)

## Lookout Towers (471), Cabins, & Observatory
Bandelier Fire Lookout Tower, Canon de los Frijoles
Cedro Peak Fire Lookout, Cibola National Forest
Grassy Mountain Lookout Cabin, Cibola National Forest
Kiwanis Cabin, Cibola National Forest
Monjeau Fire Lookout, Lincoln National Forest*
Mt. Withington Observatory, Cibola National Forest

## National Forest Ranger Stations
Beaverhead Ranger Station, Gila National Forest
Canjilon Ranger Station, Carson National Forest
Jaral Ranger Station, Cibola National Forest
Mayhill Ranger Station, Lincoln National Forest
Mimbres Ranger Station, Gila National Forest
Mountainair Ranger Station, Cibola National Forest

## Projects at National Parks & Monuments
Bandelier National Monument*
Carlsbad Caverns National Park*
Chaco Canyon National Monument*
National Park Service Southwest Regional Headquarters, Santa Fe*
White Sands National Monument*

## Projects at New Mexico State Parks
Bottomless Lakes State Park
Eastern New Mexico State Park
Hyde Memorial State Park
Santa Fe River State Pa

## Recreational Facilities
Bear Trap Canyon Campground
Capillo Peak Recreational Area, Cibola National Forest
Carlsbad Metropolitan Park
Conchas Dam Recreational Area
Elephant Butte Reservoir*
El Rito Ski Run
Fourth of July Recreational Area, Cibola National Forest
Hyde Memorial State Park Ski Run
Juan Tabo Picnic Area, Cibola National Forest
La Cueva Picnic Area, Cibola National Forest
La Junta Campground, Jemez

La Luz Plaza*
La Madera Ski Run, Cibola National Forest
Leasburg Dam Recreational Area
Ponderosa Campground, Santa Fe National Forest
Red Canyon Recreational Area, Cibola National Forest
Sandia Mountain Ski Run, Cibola National Forest
Sitting Bull Falls Recreational Area, Lincoln National Forest*
Tajique Recreational Area, Cibola National Forest
Tucumcari Metropolitan Park & Swimming Pool*

**Soil, Water, & Forest Conservation Projects**
Dams, including Apache Dam & Spring Canyon Dam
Dike Construction & Drainage
Ditch Clearing
Diversion Dams (606)
Erosion Check Dams (799,646)
Jornada Experimental Range
Range Revegetation
Reforestation (5,968,200 trees planted)
Stream & Lake Bank Protection
Tree & Plant Disease Control

* Listed on the National Register of Historic Places and the New Mexico State Register of Cultural Properties

Sources:  "A Brief Survey of Certain Phases of the C.C.C. Program in New Mexico, April 1933-September 30, 1941," Governor John E. Miles Papers, New Mexico State Records Center and Archives, Santa Fe, New Mexico; Judith G. Propper, "A Job at Honest Pay: The Legacy of the Civilian Conservation Corps," *U.S. Forest Service Southwestern Region News* (December 1998): 36; "CCC Projects on the State Register of Cultural Properties and the National Register of Historic Places," New Mexico State Office of Cultural Affairs, Historic Preservation Division, Santa Fe, New Mexico.

# SOURCES

## ARCHIVES & SPECIAL COLLECTIONS

Bancroft Library, University of California, Berkeley
    Oral History Collection
Bosque del Apache National Wildlife Refuge, San Antonio, New Mexico
    Civilian Conservation Corps Camp Reports
Center for Research Libraries, Chicago, Illinois
    Civilian Conservation Corps Camp Newspapers
Center for Southwest Research, Zimmerman Library, University of New
    Mexico, Albuquerque, New Mexico
        Ross Calvin Papers
        Dennis Chavez Papers
        Erna Fergusson Papers
        U.S. Forest Service Papers
        U.S. Soil Conservation Service Papers
Civilian Conservation Corps Museum, Jefferson Barracks, St. Louis,
    Missouri
Franklin D. Roosevelt Library, Hyde Park, New York
    Civilian Conservation Corps File
National Archives, Washington, D.C.
    Civilian Conservation Corps Camp Inspection Reports, Record
    Group 35
National Park Service, Southwest Regional Headquarters,
    Santa Fe, New Mexico
    Civilian Conservation Corps Files
New Mexico State Records Center and Archives, Santa Fe, New Mexico
    Alfred M. Bergere Papers
    Civilian Conservation Corps Papers
    Governor Andrew Hockenhull Papers
    F.A. Koch Papers
    Governor John E. Miles Papers
    Governor Arthur Seligman Papers
    Governor Clyde Tingley Papers
Rio Grande Historical Collection, New Mexico State University Li-
    brary, Las Cruces, New Mexico
    Civilian Conservation Corps Collection
    Stewart Henry Robeson Collection
U.S. Forest Service, Cibola National Forest Headquarters, Albuquer-
    que, New Mexico
    Civilian Conservation Corps Files
U.S. Forest Service, Southwest Region Headquarters, Albuquerque, New
    Mexico
    Civilian Conservation Corps Files

## ORAL HISTORIES

**Interviews by the author:**
Henry Arellanes, March 23, 1996
Hilario Baca, June 5, 1993
Levi Baca, July 22, 1993
A.B. Barela, March 12, 1991
Fred Beck, May 29, 1991
Delores Bogart, February 14, 1992
Steve Bubernak, May 15, 1996
Felix Cabrera, July 24, 1993
Bennie Casaus, April 19, 1991
Jose Chacon, July 25, 1984
Sam Chavez, May 20, 1993
Charles Clugston, May 14, 1998
R.L. Coker, April 12, 1994
Roy Colbert, February 22, 1980
Jim Craig, April 1, 1994
Harold Davis, June 9, 1996
Ray Dawson, May 14, 1991
E. Ricardo Garcia, July 12, 1996
Ed Geiger, October 23, 1996
Noah Gibson, September 7, 1990
David Gonzalez, May 23, 1996
George 'Midge' Green, March 25, 1997
Doug Hall, May 15, 1991
Graham Henington, July 3, 1991
Andres Hernandez, January 4, 1996; February 10, 1996
Ray Hetzel, March 8, 1996
Roy Huffman, May 25, 1992
Sherman Ingram, August 3, 1992
Jim Johnson, October 31, 1992
Lee Roy Jones, May 14, 1991
Harry Kemp, March 13, 1991
Roy Lemons, September 1, 1990
Rupert Lopez, July 6, 1999
Salo Maestas, June 7, 1991
Jefferson Maner, June 9, 1996
Tony Marinada, May, 9, 1996
Tom Montoya, March 12, 1991
John Mooney, February 5, 1994
Theodore V. Nelson, October 16, 1992
Harry Newbury, May 28, 1996
Demicio Perea, August 20, 1998
Fred Poorbaugh, June 21, 1991
Fernando Reta, October 18, 1991
James Rivers, October 31, 1992

Tony Sanchez, March 11, 1991
Martin Serna, March 12, 1991
Earl Shirley, June 9, 1996
Julian Shish, July 2, 1999
Emery Smith, October 18, 1991
Robert Thomas, May 17, 1991
Herman Trujillo, August 3, 1992
Leon Ullrich, July 25, 1984
Felix Vega, October 16, 1992
Carl O. Walker, January 25, 1997
W.W. Westwood, May 28, 1996
Galen Chester Williams, May 21, 1998

**Interviews by others:**
Ele Baker by Cheryl Foote, August 30, 1988
Leon Blake by Cheryl Foote, September 29, 1988
George L. Collins by Ann Lage, 1978-79, Oral History Collection,
    Bancroft Library, University of California, Berkeley
Oral History Collection of Bandelier National Monument by María
    Montoya for the National Park Service, 1988
Nabor Rael by Corine Romero, May 9, 1999
Gregorio Villasenor by Dorothy Cave, August 7, 1985

## CORRESPONDENCE

Mildred Blanche to the author, Aurora, Colorado, May 25, 1991
Edward Busch to the author, East Dublin, Georgia, April 25, 1980
James T. Duffy to the author, Philadelphia, Pennsylvania, October 3, 1991
Charles Clugston to the author, Monroeville, Pennsylvania, July 21, 1998
Guadalupe P. Flores to the author, Victoria, Texas, November 24, 1991
Van Dorn Hooker to the author, Alameda, New Mexico, September 1, 1998
Paul Manderscheid to the author, Okemos, Missouri, February 1999
Eva Jane Matson to the author, Las Cruces, New Mexico, August 5,1998
Jack O. Perry to the author, n.p., May 25, 1991
Leonard W. Porter to the author, Belen, New Mexico, October 1, 1991
James E. Reynolds to the author, Wheat Ridge, California, June 12, 1991
W.C. Rogers to the author, Sonora, California, April 9, 1980
Clay W. Smith to the author, San Antonio, Texas, April 19, 1980
Robert H. True to the author, n.p., June 13, 1991

## UNPUBLISHED MEMOIRS

Leonard 'Si' Porter Memoirs
Lee F. Sanders Memoirs

## NEWSPAPERS

*Alamogordo News*
*Albuquerque Journal*
*Albuquerque Tribune*
*Artesia Advocate*
*Belen News*
*Carlsbad Current-Argus*
*Clovis Evening News-Journal*
*Deming Headlight*
*El Paso Times*
*Farmington Times-Hustler*
*Forest Pioneer*
*Gallup Independent*
*Grant County Bulletin*
*Grant Review*
*Happy Days*
*Health City Sun*
*Las Cruces Daily News*
*Los Alamos Monitor*
*New Mexico Daily Examiner*
*New York Times*
*Raton Range*
*Roswell Daily Record*
*Santa Fe New Mexican*
*Silver City Enterprise*
*Socorro Chieftain*
*Taos Valley Review*

## CCC Camp Newspapers:
*Animas Announcer* (Animas)
*Bi-Weekly Blast* (Mountainair)
*Black Ranger* (Hillsboro)
*Blue Buffalo* (Silver City)
*Buckhorn Buzzer* (Buckhorn)
*Cactus Courier* (Carlsbad)
*Camp Cactus Carrier* (Carlsbad)
*Camp Chatter* (Carlsbad)
*Camp News* (Cloudcroft)
*Dark Canyon Avalanche* (Carlsbad)
*Dope Sheet* (Carlsbad)
*El Campo* (Española)
*El Conejo* (Grants)
*El Gallo de Pelea* (Corona)
*Follies of 1830* (Carlsbad)
*Ft. Sumner Bugler* (Ft. Sumner)
*Fresnal Ranger* (High Rolls)

*Ghost Talks* (Española)
*Gila Monster* (Gila)
*Glenwood News* (Glenwood)
*Goldbricker* (Glenwood)
*Greasewood Gossip* (Cuchillo)
*Hoot Owl* (Silver City)
*Kangarowl* (El Rito)
*La Piedra Lumbre* (Abiquiu)
*La Poliza* (Jemez)
*Lincoln Lookout* (Corona)
*Lonely Pennsylvanian* (Ft. Stanton)
*Los Frijoles* (Española)
*Mal Pais* (Carrizozo)
*Mayhill Lookout* (Mayhill)
*Mirager* (Deming)
*Organ Echoes* (Las Cruces)
*Organ View Optic* (Radium Springs)
*Peñasco Pennant* (Mayhill)
*Pink Pebble Periodical* (Redrock)
*Rio Chicito* (Jemez)
*Ripple* (Albuquerque)
*Save Our Soil* (Whitewater)
*The Spinner* (Santa Fe)
*Staton Static* (Ft. Stanton)
*3830 News* (Elephant Butte)
*Tip Topper* (Mountainair)
*Truchas Echo* (Truchas)
*Tumbleweed* (Tucumcari)
*Un-Conchas* (Conchas Dam)
*Yucca* (Whitewater)
*Velarde Views* (Española)
*Wahoo* (Cuchillo)
*Wasp* (Española)
*Whirlwind* (Animas)
*Winds* (Elephant Butte)
*Woodpecker* (Socorro)

## U.S. Forest Service Newsletters:
*Carson Pine Cone* (Taos)
*El Cibollero* (Albuquerque)
*Forest Pioneer* (Albuquerque)

## Civilian Conservation Corps Yearbooks & Journal

*Civilian Conservation Corps: Official Annual, 1936, Albuquerque District, 8th Corps Area.* n.p.: Direct Advertising Company, 1936.

*Civilian Conservation Corps: Official Annual, 1936, Fort Bliss District, 8th Corps Area.* n.p.: Direct Advertising Company, 1936.

*Memories of the CCC: Camp SCS-26-N, Rodeo, New Mexico, 1941.* Little Rock, Arkansas: Service Publications, 1941.

*National Association of Civilian Corps Alumni Journal*, 1990-99.


## FEDERAL AND STATE GOVERNMENT REPORTS & PUBLICATIONS

Avery, James E. *In the Midst of Loneliness: The Architectural History of the Salinas Missions.* Santa Fe: Southwest Cultural Resources Center, 1988.

Cassady, John T. and George E. Glendening. *Revegetating semi desert Range Lands in the Southwest.* Washington, D.C.: U.S. Government Printing Office, 1940.

Churches, John. "History of the CCC, Cibola New Mexico, 1933-42." Unpublished U.S. Forest Service report, n.d.

Harrison, Laura Soulliere, Randall Copeland, and Roger Buck. *Historic Structure Report: CCC Buildings at Bandelier National Monument, New Mexico.* Denver: National Park Service, 1988.

Kammer, David. *The Historic and Architectural Resources of the New Deal in New Mexico.* Santa Fe: New Mexico Historic Preservation Division of the Office of Cultural Affairs, 1994.

Kylie, H.R. and G.H. Hieronymus, and A.G. Hall. *CCC Forestry.* Washington, D.C.: U.S. Government Printing Office, 1937.

McEntee, James J. *Final Report of the Director of the Civilian Conservation Corps, April 1933 to June 30, 1942.* Washington, D.C.: Federal Security Agency, 1942.

Otis, Alison T., W.D. Honey, T.C. Hogg, and K.K. Lakin. *The Forest Service and the Civilian Conservation Corps, 1933-1942.* n.p.: U.S. Forest Service, 1986.

Paige, John C. *The Civilian Conservation Corps and the National Park Service, 1933-42.* Washington, D.C.: National Park Service, 1985.

Scurlock, Dan. *From the Rio to the Sierra: An Environmental History of the Middle Rio Grande Basin.* Ft. Collins: U.S. Department of Agriculture, 1998.

Tucker, Edwin A. and George Fitzpatrick. *Men Who Matched the Mountains: The Forest Service in the Southwest.* Washington, D.C.: U.S. Department of Agriculture, 1972.


## VIDEO DOCUMENTARY

Uys, Michael and Lexy Lovell. *Riding the Rails.* Boston: WGBH Video Production for the American Experience, 1997.

# SELECTED BOOKS & ARTICLES

Ares, Fred N. T*he Jornada Experimental Range: An Epoch in the Era of Southwestern Range Management*. Denver: Society for Range Management, 1974.

Bernstein, Irving. *A Caring Society: the New Deal, The Worker, and the Great Depression*. Boston: Houghton, Mifflin, 1985.

Berton, Pierre. *The Great Depression, 1929-39*. Toronto: McClelland and Stewart, 1990.

Biebel, Charles D. *Making the Most Of It: Public Works in Albuquerque during the Great Depression, 1929-42*. Albuquerque: Albuquerque Museum, 1986.

Bremer, William W. "Along the 'American Way': The New Deal's Work Relief Programs for the Unemployed." *Journal of American History*, 62 (December 1975): 636-52.

Brown, Tomás Wesley. *Heritage of the New Mexico Frontier*. New York: Vantage Press, 1995.

Captain X. "A Civilian Army in the Woods." *Harper's Monthly*, 168 (March 1934): 487-97.

Christopher, Nancy Geyer. *Right of Passage: The Heroic Journey to Adulthood*. Washington, D.C.: Cornell Press, 1996.

Clepper, Henry. "The Birth of the CCC." *American Forests*, 79 (March 1973): 8-11.

Cohen, Stan. *The Tree Army*. Missoula, Montana: Pictoral Histories Publishing Company, 1980.

Cole, Olen, Jr. *The African-American Experience in the Civilian Conservation Corps*. Gainesville: University Press of Florida, 1999.

Conti, Philip M. *The Civilian Conservation Corps: Salvaging Boys and Other Treasures*. n.p.: privately published, [1998].

Cox, Thomas R. *et al. This Well-Wooded Land: Americans and Their Forests from Colonial Times to the Present*. Lincoln: University of Nebraska Press, 1985.

Cross, Whitney R. "Ideas in Politics: the Conservation Policies of the Two Roosevelts." *Journal of the History of Ideas*, 14 (June 1953): 421-38.

Cutler, Phoebe. *The Public Landscape of the New Deal*. New Haven: Yale University Press, 1985.

Dearborn, Ned H. *Once In a Lifetime: A Guide to the CCC Camp*. New York: Charles E. Merrill, 1936.

Donovan, Leo. "The Establishment of the First Civilian Conservation Corps Camp." *Infantry Journal*, 40 (July-August 1933): 245-9.

Draves, David D. *Builder of Men: Life in C.C.C. Camps of New Hampshire*. Portsmouth, N.H.: Peter E. Randall, 1992.

Eberly, Donald and Michael Sherraden, editors. *The Moral Equivalent of War? A Study of Non-Military Service in Nine Nations*. New York: Greenwood Press, 1990.

Emerson, Dorothy. *Among the Mescalero Apaches: The Story of Father Albert Braun, OFM*. Tucson: University of Arizona, 1973.

Ermentrout, Robert Allen. *Forgotten Men: The CCC*. Smithtown, New York: Exposition Press, 1982.

Fay, H. Burton. "Erosion Control at La Cueva C.C.C. Camp." *New Mexico Magazine*, 12 (June 1934): 24-5, 38.

Flynn, Kathryn A., editor. *Treasures on New Mexican Trails: Discover New Deal Art and Architecture*. Santa Fe: Sunstone Press, 1995.

Folsom, Franklin. *Impatient Armies of the Poor: The Story of Collective Action of the Unemployed, 1808-1942*. Boulder: University Press of Colorado, 1991.

Forrest, Suzanne. *The Preservation of the Village: New Mexico's Hispanics and the New Deal*. Albuquerque: University of New Mexico Press, 1989.

Fuss, Henri. "Unemployment Among Young People." *International Labour Review*, 31 (May 1935).

Garraty, John A. "The New Deal, National Socialism, and the Great Depression." *American Historical Review*, 78 (October 1973): 907-44.

_____. *Unemployment in History: Economic Thought and Public Policy*. New York: Harper and Row, 1978.

Getz, Lynne Marie. *Schools of Their Own: The Education of Hispanos in NM, 1850-1940*. Albuquerque: University of New Mexico Press, 1997.

Gorham, Eric. "The Ambiguous Practices of the CCC." *Social History*, 17 (May 1972): 229-49.

Gower, Calvin W. "The CCC and American Education: Threat to Local Control?" *History of Education Quarterly*, 7 (Spring 1967): 58-70.

_____. "Conservatism, Censorship, and Controversy in the CCC, 1930s." *Journalism Quarterly*, 52 (Summer 1975): 277-84.

_____. "The Struggle of Blacks for Leadership Positions in the CCC, 1933-42." *Journal of Negro History*, 61 (April 1976): 123-35.

Graf, Enoch. "The Army's Greatest Peace-Time Achievement." *Quartermaster Review*, 15 (July-August 1935): 7-13.

Guthrie, John D. "The CCC and American Conservation." *Scientific Monthly*, 57 (November 1943): 401-12.

Hagerman, H.J. "How the Depression Is Affecting New Mexico." *New Mexico Tax Bulletin*, 10 (November-December 1931): 121-42.

Hendrickson, Kenneth E., Jr. "The Civilian Conservation Corps in the Southwestern States" in Donald W. Whisenhunt, ed., *The Depression in the Southwest*. Port Washington, New York: Kennikat Press, 1980.

Hill, Frank E. *The School in the Camps: The Educational Program of the Civilian Conservation Corps*. New York: American Association for Adult Education, 1935.

Holland, Kenneth, and Frank E. Hill. *Youth in the CCC*. Washington, D.C.: American Council on Education, 1942.

Hood, Margaret Page. "Conservationists Help the Cowman." *New Mexico Magazine*, 12 (June 1934): 19-20, 38.

James, William. *Essays on Faith and Morals*. Cleveland: World Publishing Company, 1962.

Johnson, Charles W. "The Army and the Civilian Conservation Corps, 1933-42." *Prologue*, 4 (February 1972): 139-56.

_____. "The Army, the Negro, and the CCC, 1933-42." *Military Affairs*, 36 (October 1972): 82-88.

Kauffman, Erle. "Heroes of the C.C.C." *American Forests*, 40 (July 1934): 303-4, 330-2.

Kennedy, Renwick C. "Military Interlude." *Christian Century*, 50 (September 13, 1933): 1144-5.

Ketchum, Richard M. *The Borrowed Years, 1938-41*. New York: Random House, 1989.

Kropp, Simon F. *That All May Learn: New Mexico State University, 1888-1964*. Las Cruces: New Mexico State University, 1972.

Lacy, Leslie A. *The Soil Soldiers: The CCC in the Great Depression*. Radnor, Pennsylvania: Chilton Book Company, 1976.

Leighton, George R. and Richard Hellman. "Half Slave, Half Free: Unemployment, the Depression, and American Young People." *Harper's Magazine*, 171 (August 1935): 342-53.

Leuchtenburg, William E. *The FDR Years: On Roosevelt and His Legacy*. New York: Columbia University Press, 1995.

Logan, Paul. "CCC: A Golden Memory." *Impact*, 6 (April 5, 1983): 4-8.

Lopez, Angie S. *Blessed Are the Soldiers*. Albuquerque: Sandia, 1990.

Lowitt, Richard. *The New Deal and the West*. Bloomington: Indiana University Press, 1984.

Macleod, David I. *Building Character in the American Boy: The Boy Scouts, YMCA and Their Forerunners, 1870-1920*. Madison: University of Wisconsin Press, 1983.

Macy, G.D. "State Park Conservation Camps." *New Mexico Magazine*, 11 (November 1933): 10-12.

McEntee, James J. *Now They Are Men: The Story of the CCC*. Washington, D.C.: National Home Library Foundation, 1940.

McNamee, Gregory. *Gila: The Life and Death of an American River*. New York: Orion Books, 1994.

Merrill, Perry H. *Roosevelt's Forest Army: A History of the Civilian Conservation Corps, 1933-1942*. Montpelier, Vermont: Perry H. Merrill, 1981.

Montoya, María E. "The Roots of Economic and Ethnic Divisions in Northern New Mexico: The Case of the CCC." *Western Historical Quarterly*, 26 (Spring 1995): 15-34.

Nash, Gerald D. *The American West in the Twentieth Century*. Albuquerque: University of New Mexico Press, 1977.

Nixon, Edgar B., editor. *Franklin D. Roosevelt and Conservation, 1911-45*. Hyde Park: Franklin D. Roosevelt Library, 1957.

Nolte, M. Chester, editor. *The Civilian Conservation Corps: The Way We Remember It, 1933-42*. Paducah, Kentucky: Turner Publishing Company, 1990.

Nostrand, Richard L. *The Hispano Homeland*. Norman: University of Oklahoma Press, 1992.

Ogburn, William F. *You and Machines*. Chicago: University of Chicago Press, 1934.

Oliver, Alfred C., Jr., and Harold M. Dudley. *This New America:The Spirit of the Civilian Conservation Corps*. London: Longmans, Green and Co., 1937.

Otero-Warren, Nina. *Old Spain in Our Southwest*. New York: Harcourt, Brace and Company, 1936.

Oxley, Howard W. "Colleges and CCC Camp Education." *School Life*, 21 (December 1936): 106, 120.

_____. "Enrollees Become Better Citizens." *School Life*, 22 (March 1937): 215-16.

Pandiani, John A. "The Crime Control Corps: An Invisible New Deal Program." *British Journal of Sociology,* 33 (September 1982): 348-58.

Parman, Donald L. "The Indian and the Civilian Conservation Corps." *Pacific Historical Review*, 40 (February 1971): 39-56.

Patton, Thomas W. "Forestry and Politics: Franklin D. Roosevelt as Governor of New York." *New York History*, 75 (October 1994): 397-418.

Petulla, Joseph M. *American Environmental History*. Columbus, Ohio: Merrill, 1988.

Plair, T.B. "How the CCC Has Paid Off." *American Forests*, 60 (February 1954): 28-30, 44-5.

Propper, Judith G. "A Job at Honest Pay: The Legacy of the Civilian Conservation Corps." *U.S. Forest Service Southwestern Region News* (December 1998): 34-7.

Pyne, Stephen J. *Fire in America: A Cultural History of Wildland and Rural Fire*. Princeton: Princeton University Press, 1982.

Raphael, Ray. *The Men From the Boys: Rites of Passage in Male America*. Lincoln: University of Nebraska, 1988.

Reiman, Richard A. *The New Deal and American Youth*. Athens: University of Georgia Press, 1992.

Richardson, Elmo R. "The CCC and the Origins of the New Mexico State Park System." *Natural Resources Journal,* 6 (April 1966): 248-67.

_____. "Was There Politics in the CCC?" *Forest History*, 16 (July 1972): 12-21.

Rothman, Hal K. *On Rims and Ridges: The Los Alamos Area Since 1880*. Lincoln: University of Nebraska Press, 1992.

Salmond, John A. *The Civilian Conservation Corps, 1933-42: A New Deal Case Study*. Durham: Duke University Press, 1967.

Sanchez, George I. *Forgotten People: A Study of New Mexicans*. Albuquerque: Calvin Horn, 1967.

Sellars, Richard West. *Preserving Nature in the National Parks: A History*. New Haven: Yale University Press, 1997.

Sherraden, Michael W. "Administrative Lessons from the CCC, 1933-42." *Administration in Social Work*, 9 (Summer 1985): 85-97.

Smith, Kathy Mays. "The Role of the Army in the CCC." *NACCCA Journal*, 21 (February 1998): 1, 5-8.

Steen, Harold K. *The U.S. Forest Service: A History*. Seattle: University of Washington Press, 1991.

Stewart, H.C. "The Soil Conservation Service in the Southwest." *New Mexico Business Review,* 7 (1938): 176-86.

Teston, K. Edd. "The Shanty on the Claim" in Ovid Butler, editor, *Youth Rebuilds: Stories from the C.C.C.* Washington, D.C.: American Forestry Association, 1934.

Todd, Arthur J. "Social Implications of the CCC." *The Clearing House*, 10 (November 1935): 152-8.

Utley, Dan K. and James W. Steely. *Guided With a Steady Hand.* Waco, Texas: Baylor University Press, 1998.

Vigil, Arnold. "Blood, Sweat and Mud." *New Mexico Magazine*, 67 (July, 1989): 81-2.

Watkins, T.H. *The Great Depression: America in the 1930s.* Boston: Little, Brown and Company, 1993.

Weigle, Marta. *Hispanic Villages of Northern New Mexico.* Santa Fe: Lightning Tree Press, 1975.

Whaley, Charlotte. *Nina Otero-Warren of Santa Fe.* Albuquerque: University of New Mexico Press, 1994.

Williams, Michael. *Americans and Their Forests: A Historical Geography.* Cambridge: Cambridge University Press, 1989.

Wohlforth, Robert. "Goose-Stepping the Jobless." *World Tomorrow,* 16 (February 15, 1933): 155-7.

Wolfskill, George and John A. Hudson. *All But the People: Franklin D. Roosevelt and His Critics, 1933-39.* London: Macmillan, 1969.

Young, John V. *The State Parks of New Mexico.* Albuquerque: University of New Mexico Press, 1984.


## DISSERTATIONS & THESES

Baldridge, Kenneth W. "Nine Years of Achievement: The Civilian Conservation Corps in Utah." Unpublished Ph.D. dissertation, University of Utah, 1971.

Bassett, Octavia R. "Health and Culture in the CCC Camps." Unpublished M.A. thesis, George Washington University, 1938.

Booth, Peter M. "The Civilian Conservation Corps in Arizona, 1933-42." Unpublished M.A. thesis, University of Arizona, 1991.

Bruce, Richard A. "School Enrollment in New Mexico." Unpublished M.A. thesis, UNM, 1935.

Bryant, M.P. "Education in the Civilian Conservation Corps Camps of New Mexico." Unpublished M.Ed. thesis, Texas Tech University, 1940.

Carter, Genevieve W. "Juvenile Delinquency in Bernalillo County." Unpublished M.A. thesis, University of New Mmexico, 1936.

Ely, Albert G. "The Excavation and Repair of the Quari Mission." Unpublished M.A. thesis, University of New Mexico, 1935.

Edmonson, Everett L. "Some Nation-Wide Educational Problems of the Civilian Conservation Corps." Unpublished Ph.D. dissertation, Northwestern University, 1940.

Holland, Reid A. "The Civilian Conservation Corps in Oklahoma, 1933-42." Unpublished M.A. thesis, Oklahoma State University, 1969.

Johnson, Charles W. "The Civilian Conservation Corps: The Role of the Army." Unpublished Ph.D. dissertation, University of Michigan, 1968.

Luhan, Roy. "Dennis Chavez and The Roosevelt Era, 1933-45." Unpublished Ph.D. dissertation, University of New Mexico, 1987.

Moody, F. Kennon. "F.D.R. and His Neighbors: A Study of the Relationship Between Franklin D. Roosevelt and the Residents of Dutchess County." Unpublished Ph.D. dissertation, State University of New York at Albany, 1981.

Parham, Robert B. "The Civilian Conservation Corps in Colorado, 1933-42." Unpublished M.A. thesis, University of Colorado, 1981.

Pickens, William L. "The New Deal in New Mexico." Unpublished M.A. thesis, University of New Mexico, 1971.

Rawick, George P. "The New Deal and Youth: The CCC, the NYA and the American Youth Congress." Unpublished Ph.D. dissertation, University of Wisconsin, 1957.

Riesch, Anna Lou. "Conservation Under Franklin D. Roosevelt." Unpublished Ph.D. dissertation, University of Wisconsin, 1952.

Sachs, Lucinda Lucero. "Cylde Tinley's Little New Deal for New Mexico, 1935-38. Unpublished M.A. thesis, University of New Mexico, 1989.

Severns, Mary I. "Tourism in New Mexico." Unpublished M.A. thesis, University of New Mexico, 1951.

Sherraden, Michael W. "The Civilian Conservation Corps:nn Effectiveness of the Camps." Unpublished Ph.D. dissertation, University of Michigan, 1979.

Sininger, Harlan. "New Mexico Reading Survey." Unpublished M.A. thesis, University of New Mexico, 1930.

Swayne, James B. "A Survey of the Economic, Political and Legal Aspects of the Labor Problem in New Mexico." Unpublished M.A. thesis, University of New Mexico, 1936.

# INDEX

308